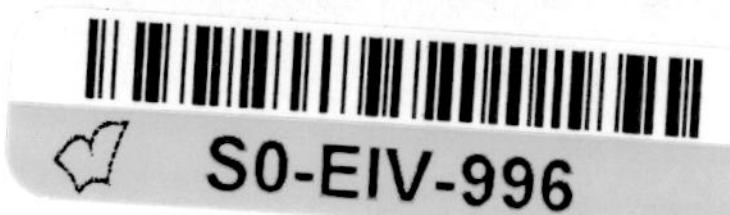
S0-EIV-996

DRAWN

Henry James

A Bibliography of Criticism, 1975-1981

Compiled by John Budd

GREENWOOD PRESS
Westport, Connecticut • London, England

Library of Congress Cataloging in Publication Data

Budd, John, 1953-
Henry James : a bibliography of criticism, 1975-1981.

Bibliography: p.
Includes index.
I. James, Henry, 1843-1916—Bibliography. I. Title
Z8447.B82 1983 [PS2123] 016.813'4 82-24163
ISBN 0-313-23515-5 (lib. bdg.)

Library of Congress Catalog Card Number: 82-24163
ISBN: 0-313-23515-5

First published in 1983

Greenwood Press
A division of Congressional Information Service, Inc.
88 Post Road West, Westport, Connecticut 06881

Printed in the United States of America

10 9 8 7 6 5 4 3 2 1

CONTENTS

ACKNOWLEDGMENTS

With any work of some magnitude, one must rely on the assistance and support of a number of individuals. Such is the case with this bibliography, and I would first like to acknowledge the encouragement (and occasional sympathy) offered by my friends. The task was made easier by their kindness. I would also like to thank the School of Library Science of the University of North Carolina at Chapel Hill for providing the facility used in the production of this work. I am very grateful to the institutional grants program of Southeastern Louisiana University, administered by Dr. Randy Webb, for providing funds to offset some of the expenses incurred in the course of the project. Special thanks go to Kathleen Sharp of the Sims Memorial Library of Southeastern Louisiana University, whose help was invaluable in obtaining numerous materials through interlibrary loans. I also thank my wife Sally for her constant support and for being more patient than I.

INTRODUCTION

When Henry James died in 1916, he left behind a wealth of novels, short fiction, plays, and criticism. The twenty-six volumes he selected for the New York Edition of his novels and tales (actually James selected twenty-four volumes; two were published posthumously) constitute only a portion of the James canon. Although his prolific output did not result in great financial gain during his lifetime, it did make him one of the major focuses of critical attention of this century. This bibliography is evidence of the magnitude of scholarship that has been produced (909 entries over a seven-year period). This interest has taken the form of theses and dissertations (the results of research conducted at universities in the United States and abroad), books and monographs, collections of essays, and articles in numerous scholarly journals.

Previous bibliographical studies of secondary materials conducted by Dorothy Scura (see entry 220), Kristin McColgin (see entry 207), and Beatrice Ricks (see entry 216) bring scholarship on James up to 1975. Since that time activity has proceeded at a furious pace. The reasons for the study of James are almost as varied as the number of scholars conducting research in the area, and this is reflected in recent criticism. Many different critical schools have turned their attention to the study of James as befitting their diverse literary and compositional theories. Although the New Critical approach is still adopted by many writers in the study of individual works, other theoretical techniques have been applied to James's oeuvre and to James himself.

Formalist criticism, for instance, has had some application in the study of James, as has Archetypal criticism. Structuralism has been applied to some of James's works, particularly (in recent years) *The Turn of the Screw*. Even that which has received the name Deconstructionism (which is not a school of criticism or theory at all), has been applied to James. This illustrates the considerable flexibility with which James endowed his works.

There is no absolute interpretation of his novels or tales; in fact, interpretation has been altered progressively as time has passed, and James's works have not only survived, they have thrived.

The reasons for the longevity of interest in James are many, varied, and complex. Not the least of which is the fact that James's writing constituted a departure from other nineteenth-century fiction. James read considerable amounts of French literature, notably Balzac and Flaubert, and he was a student of the writings of Turgenev. In addition, his Anglo-American literary background extended to Jane Austen, the Brontës, Walter Pater, Ralph Waldo Emerson, Nathaniel Hawthorne, and more. There is no doubt that each of these exerted some influence over James, but the influence provided a basis for Jamesian creativity which was different from anything existing in the literary world at that time. While his early writings most clearly reflect the influences of other figures, they anticipated the new literature James was to create.

With James, literature in English was altered and set on an entirely new course, and what has been termed modernism evolved. Although it is impossible and impractical to attribute absolutely the birth of modern literature to one person, James had a greater impact on the eventual history of Western literature than did any of his contemporaries. Just as it is impossible to worship one writer as the god of a new era in literary history, it is impossible to attribute James's unique position to a single aspect of his writing.

One of the things James did in his work was to add (to a greater degree than any writer of fiction preceding him) the psychological complexities of life and of the individual to fiction. There are reasons for the behavior of Jamesian characters, and while they are not always explicit, these reasons are usually implicit in the works themselves. These reasons for being and behaving are frequently linked to the characters' perception and consciousness. Perception, consciousness, and vision can have numerous layers and subtle shadings in an individual work, and the characters of the work are altered as these aspects of their beings change, develop, or regress. The result is a complexity of thought, motive, and sometimes action.

Perhaps the best illustration of this feature of James's work is *The Turn of the Screw.* The perception of the governess undergoes several metamorphoses in the course of the *nouvelle* as she attempts to come to grips with the evil she has become aware of, and in the flux of her relationship with the children. This is complicated by James's method of telling the tale. Rather than a strightforward narrative, the story is related through the writings of the governess after the fact. The reader of the tale (that is, the character who reads the governess's manuscript) also becomes a part of the tale as well as the subject of much speculation by critics. The role can never be absolutely deciphered, nor can the actual perception of the governess be completely understood. Do the ghosts actually exist, or are they hallucinatory images created by the governess? Does Miles embody evil, or is he an innocent victim? Does the reader of the manuscript have an intimate relationship with the governess? These questions not only present problems for the reader of *The Turn of the Screw,* they impose upon the reader an active role in the tale. The reader's perception becomes as important as that of the characters. Because of this process of reading, the tale is even more complex, and an absolute interpretation is even more illusory. James thus begins with a complex tale and a problematical text and incorporates the psychology of the characters and the psychology of the reader into the act of reading *The Turn of the Screw.*

As has been pointed out on many occasions (and as makes sense), James was influenced in this regard by his brother William. William James was an innovator in the world of psychological study, and Henry read his brother's writings carefully. It should also be noted that William read Henry's work and was, to a degree, influenced by him. Their relationship was a complex one that had intellectual as well as familial aspects. William, being older than Henry, was probably somewhat the more dominant in the relationship, but a strong mutual respect accentuated both of their lives.

Another important feature of James's fiction is the relationship of the moral and the aesthetic, not only in art, but in life as well. James believed very strongly that art should have a moral purpose, and this concern was a governing force in his composition. Morality should coexist with aesthetics, which James saw as having a moral goodness when well executed. *The Golden Bowl* is an example of this admixture, with the golden bowl itself as perhaps the premier symbol of the union of these qualities. The bowl is a thing of beauty at first glance, but upon some examination one sees that it is flawed, as is the marriage of Amerigo and Maggie. A coat of gold cannot repair the crack in the crystal, nor can a gloss of civility hide the strains within the marriage.

In this regard James was influenced somewhat by his father's thought. The moral sense of the elder Henry James had its roots in Swedenborg and Emerson. The juxtaposition of morality and aesthetics was thus introduced to his son at an early age. In all likelihood this sense was heightened by the James family's extensive travel in Europe in Henry's youth. The contrast between America and Europe became obvious to him, but it presented some difficulties for him also. The traditional American view, which, to a great extent, echoed the puritan base of New England behavior and thought, emphasized the moral, frequently at the expense of the aesthetic. What James saw in Europe was often the reverse. The aesthetic frequently held a much more important place. This dichotomy was deeply felt by James and was reflected in many of his works, such as *The Ambassadors.* Lambert Strether is awakened to the possibility of the union of the moral and the aesthetic, but he remains faithful to his ambassadorial duty.

Another aspect of James's writing that set him apart from the rest of the literature of the Victorian period was his style and the reflection of that style in his language. This was not an overnight phenomenon; actually it took most of his writing career to develop the style of his later period, his "major phase," as F. O. Matthiessen termed it. This is not to say that he does not exhibit a unique style in ealier writings. *The Portrait of a Lady* prefaced his later period and was different from anything that then existed in the literary world. He had felt so strongly that the style he had developed was so superior to his previous writing that he chose to revise many of his works for the New York Edition of his novels and tales. Some of this revision substantially altered the content of the works, as in the case of *The American.* The result was sometimes nearly a separate work rather than a revision.

The process of revision itself is a fascinating one that, of course, has implications for textual study but also can affect critical assessment of a work. *The Spoils of Poynton* is one novel that James revised for the New York Edition. The novel appeared in 1897 in serialized form in *The Atlantic* and exhibited some flaws inherent in the process of composition for serialization. Many of the errors in *The Atlantic* version were corrected for the first English and American editions, but the work was further revised for the New York Edition. Taken as a whole the revised work implies interpretations that are somewhat different from the earlier versions as far as personalities, relationships, and the conflict over the spoils are concerned. In the case of *The Spoils of Poynton,* at any rate, argument could well be made for the superiority of the later text over the earlier ones.

The above discussion illustrates the complexity of James's life and work and, in part at least, attempts to offer some rationale for the extensive interest in James today. James broke thematic and stylistic ground for writers who were to follow. As a result, Virginia Woolf, James Joyce, D. H. Lawrence, and even a number of contemporary writers owe a debt to James for introducing many modern features into literature. Of course, this realization serves to broaden the range of James studies even beyond the large body of his own work.

Further evidence of the extensive interest in James that has been increasing in recent years is the birth of a new journal devoted to James studies. In 1979 the first issue of *The Henry James Review* appeared. This publication is edited by Daniel Mark Fogel at Louisiana State University and includes on its editorial board many notable scholars who have devoted considerable time and attention to James. In the course of the first three volumes of the journal (in which there are three issues per volume), a number of articles have been published on a variety of subjects related to James scholarship.

At this time special mention should be made of the foremost James scholar of the century, Leon Edel. While Professor Edel maintains many diverse interests, a considerable portion of his career has been spent in the study of James. Edel wrote the masterful five-volume biography of James which, appropriately enough, incorporates a sort of psychohistory of the life and work of the subject. Edel has also been editing a large selection of James's letters, of which there are three volumes now in print: the first, covering 1843-1875 and published in 1974; the second, covering 1875-1883 and published in 1978; and the third, covering 1883-1895 and published in 1980. Each of these volumes was published by Harvard University Press. A fourth and concluding volume of selected letters is to be published soon. In the very near future a third edition of *A Bibliography of Henry James,* compiled by Edel along with Dan H. Laurence and James Rambeau, is to be published. Leon Edel is the focus of an issue of *The Henry James Review* (vol. 3, no. 3, Spring, 1982). Included in the issue is a bibliography of Edel's writings on James up to the time of publication. The bibliography numbers 193 items. Professor Edel has been responsible for making James much more accessible to students of American literature, and scholars are thus deeply indebted to him.

This bibliography consists of criticism and other secondary works written on Henry James from 1975 through 1981. The 909 items included in the work consist of theses and dissertations, books (along with reviews of the books whenever possible), chapters and materials in books, and articles. There are some exceptions: some materials dated prior to 1975 are listed in this bibliography because they were not included in previous bibliographical works on James, and some articles published in 1982 are also included. These articles were published in *The Henry James Review* and are listed here because they constitute volume three of the journal, of which the first issue appeared in mid-1981. I felt that efficiency would be served if the entire volume were included.

The vast majority of the items in this bibliography are annotated, and the annotations were made after an examination of the individual work itself whenever possible. Those items not annotated were published in a language other than English or could not be obtained for examination. The annotations are descriptive in nature, rather than evaluative. Although opinion is split on the desirability of one type of annotation over another, I made the decision to attempt to describe the content of the work briefly, allowing anyone consulting this work to judge the appropriateness of each item to his or her purpose based on the content. I have tried to incorporate the major thrust and particular features of the item into the annotation. In so doing I hope that students and scholars will find this bibliography useful to their study.

The sources consulted in the compilation of this work are too numerous to list fully. Major sources included the *MLA Bibliographies, Humanities Index, Arts & Humanities Citation Index, Current Contents: Arts & Humanities, Essay and General Literature Index,* and *Cumulative Book Index.* Numerous other bibliographical tools were also useful. In addition to the use of these works, several items were found through serendipity, a process too valuable to discount.

Since the entries are listed alphabetically by author in each section, some additional forms of access had to be devised to assist individuals in the use of the works. The general subject index that follows the bibliography anticipates this need. Effort was made to include those subjects that identify the author's central thesis in each work. Hence, the index includes what might be considered pure subject terms such as "love," "art," "manners," and "renunciation." Since James's writing is frequently seen in conjunction or comparison with that of other writers, and since individuals feature prominently in some of the entries, names such as William Dean Howells, Walter Pater, and William James are included in this index. In addition to the above, works by James that constitute focal points of the individual critical writings are also listed as points of access.

Immediately following this introduction is a list of the principal works by James, along with the date of first (book) publication. For assistance in the preparation of this list I am indebted to *A Bibliography of Henry James,* second edition, compiled by Leon Edel and Dan H. Laurence (London: Rupert Hart-Davis, 1961).

PRINCIPAL WORKS BY HENRY JAMES

The Ambassadors, 1903.

The American, 1877.

The American: A Comedy in Four Acts, 1891.

The Aspern Papers, 1888.
Contents: V. I. The Aspern Papers
V. II. "Louisa Pallant"
"The Modern Warning"

The Author of Beltraffio, 1885.
Contents: "The Author of Beltraffio"
"Pandora"
"Georgina's Reasons"
"The Path of Duty"
"Four Meetings"

The Awkward Age, 1899.

The Better Sort, 1903.
Contents: "Broken Wings"
"The Beldonald Holbein"
"The Two Faces"
"The Tone of Time"
"The Special Type"
"Mrs. Medwin"
"Flickerbridge"
"The Story in It"
"The Beast in the Jungle"
"The Birthplace"
"The Papers"

The Bostonians, 1886.

A Bundle of Letters, 1880.

Confidence, 1879.

Daisy Miller, 1878.

Daisy Miller: A Comedy, 1882.

Embarrassments, 1896.
Contents: "The Figure in the Carpet"
"Glasses"
"The Next Time"
"The Way It Came"

English Hours, 1905.

Essays in London and Elsewhere, 1893.

The Europeans, 1878.

The Finer Grain, 1910.
Contents: "The Velvet Glove"
"Mora Montravers"
"A Round of Visits"
"Crapy Cornelia"
"The Bench of Desolation"

French Poets and Novelists, 1878.

The Golden Bowl, 1904.

Guy Domville, 1894.

Hawthorne, 1879.

In the Cage, 1898.

An International Episode, 1879.

Italian Hours, 1909.

The Ivory Tower, 1917.
Added to the New York Edition as Vol. XXV in 1918.

Julia Bride, 1909.

The Lesson of the Master, 1892.
Contents: "The Lesson of the Master"
"The Marriages"
"The Pupil"
"Brooksmith"
"The Solution"
"Sir Edmund Orme"

A Little Tour of France, 1884.

A London Life, 1889.
Contents: V. I. A London Life
V. II. "The Patagonia"
"The Liar"
"Mrs. Temperly"

The Madonna of the Future and Other Tales, 1879.
Contents: V. I. "The Madonna of the Future"
"Longstaff's Marriage"
"Madame de Mauves"
V. II. "Eugene Pickering"
"The Diary of a Man at Fifty"
"Benvolio"

The Middle Years, 1917.

Notes of a Son and Brother, 1914.

Notes on Novelists, 1914.

The Novels and Tales of Henry James (New York Edition), 1907-1909.
Contents: V. I. Roderick Hudson
V. II. The American
V. III. The Portrait of a Lady (vol. 1)
V. IV. The Portrait of a Lady (vol. 2)
V. V. The Princess Casamassima (vol. 1)
V. VI. The Princess Casamassima (vol. 2)
V. VII. The Tragic Muse (vol. 1)
V. VIII. The Tragic Muse (vol. 2)
V. IX. The Awkward Age
V. X. The Spoils of Poynton, "A London Life," "The Chaperon"
V. XI. What Maisie Knew, In the Cage, "The Pupil"
V. XII. The Aspern Papers, The Turn of the Screw, "The Liar," "The Two Faces"
V. XIII. The Reverberator, "Madame de Mauves," "A Passionate Pilgrim," "The Madonna of the Future," "Louisa Pallant"
V. XIV. "Lady Barberina," "The Siege of London," "An International Episode," "The Pension Beaurepas," "A Bundle of Letters," "The Point of View"
V. XV. "The Lesson of the Master," "The Death of the Lion," "The Next Time," "The Figure in the Carpet," "The Coxon Fund"
V. XVI. "The Author of Beltraffio," "The Middle Years," "Greville Fane," "Broken Wings," "The Tree of Knowledge," "The Abasement of the Northmores," "The Great Good Place"
V. XVII. "The Altar of the Dead," "The Beast in the Jungle," "The Birthplace," "The Private Life," "Owen Wingrave," "The Friends of the Friends," "Sir Edmund Orme," "The Real Right Thing," "The Jolly Corner," Julia Bride

V. XVIII. Daisy Miller, "Pandora," "The Patagonia," "The Marriages," "The Real Thing," "Brooksmith," "The Beldonald Holbein," "The Story in It," "Flickerbridge," "Mrs. Medwin"
V. XIX. The Wings of the Dove (vol. 1)
V. XX. The Wings of the Dove (vol. 2)
V. XXI. The Ambassadors (vol. 1)
V. XXII. The Ambassadors (vol. 2)
V. XXIII. The Golden Bowl (vol. 1)
V. XXIV. The Golden Bowl (vol. 2)

The Other House, 1896.

The Outcry, 1911.

Partial Portraits, 1888.

A Passionate Pilgrim and Other Tales, 1875.
Contents: "A Passionate Pilgrim"
"The Last of the Valerii"
"Eugene Pickering"
"The Madonna of the Future"
"The Romance of Certain Old Clothes"
"Madame de Mauves"

Picture and Text, 1893.

The Portrait of a Lady, 1881.

Portraits of Places, 1883.

The Princess Cassamassima, 1886.

The Private Life, 1893.
Contents: "The Private Life"
"The Wheel of Time"
"Lord Beaupré"
"The Visits"
"Collaboration"
"Owen Wingrave"

The Real Thing and Other Tales, 1893.
Contents: "The Real Thing"
"Sir Dominick Ferrand"
"Nora Vincent"
"The Chaperon"
"Greville Fane"

The Reverberator, 1888.

<u>Roderick Hudson</u>, 1875.

<u>The Sacred Fount</u>, 1901.

<u>The Sense of the Past</u>, 1917.
Added to the New York Edition as Vol. XXVI in 1918.

<u>The Siege of London</u>, 1883.
Contents: "The Siege of London"
"The Pension Beaurepas"
"The Point of View"

<u>A Small Boy and Others</u>, 1913.

<u>The Soft Side</u>, 1900.
Contents: "The Great Good Place"
"Europe"
"Paste"
"The Real Right Thing"
"The Great Condition"
"The Tree of Knowledge"
"The Abasement of the Northmores"
"The Given Case"
"John Delavoy"
"The Third Person"
"Maud-Evelyn"
"Miss Gunton of Poughkeepsie"

<u>The Spoils of Poynton</u>, 1897.

<u>Stories Revived</u>, 1885.
Contents: V. I. "The Author of Beltraffio"
"Pandora"
"The Path of Duty"
"A Light Man"
"A Day of Days"
V. II. "Georgina's Reasons"
"A Passionate Pilgrim"
"A Landscape Painter"
"Rose-Agathe"
V. III. "Poor Richard"
"The Last of the Valerii"
"Master Eustace"
"The Romance of Certain Old Clothes"
"A Most Extraordinary Case"

<u>Tales of Three Cities</u>, 1884.
Contents: "The Impressions of a Cousin"
"Lady Barberina"
"A New England Winter"

Terminations, 1895.
Contents: "The Death of the Lion"
"The Coxon Fund"
"The Middle Years"
"The Altar of the Dead"

Theatricals, 1894.
Contents: *Tenants*
Disengaged

Theatricals: Second Series, 1894.
Contents: *The Album*
The Reprobate

The Tragic Muse, 1890.

Transatlantic Sketches, 1875.

Washington Square, 1880.

Watch and Ward, 1878.

What Maisie Knew, 1897.

William Wetmore Story and His Friends, 1903.

The Wings of the Dove, 1902.

THE BIBLIOGRAPHY

DISSERTATIONS AND THESES

1. Albers, Christina. "Henry James's Watch and Ward: Prelude to the Later Novels." Mater's Thesis. University of North Carolina, Chapel Hill, 1981.

   Albers contends that Watch and Ward, frequently ignored by critics, provided groundwork for many themes and concerns to recur in James's works. She notes particular parallel with The Portrait of a Lady and observes the issues of the conflict of the natural and the artificial, class conflict, and the complexities of characters' relationships.

2. Allen, Jeanne Thomas. "Aspects of Narration in The Turn of the Screw and The Innocents." Diss. University of Iowa, 1975.

   Allen explores the effects of James's narrative and compares them to the effects achieved in the film adaptation. Her study begins with a close reading of the novella, examining narration, dramatic structure, rhetoric, and descriptive detail. She then repeats this analysis with The Innocents. Finally, there is an attempt to evaluate the film's ability to create an experience comparable to the novella.

3. Armstrong, Paul Bradford. "Henry James: Impressionism and Phenomenology." Diss. Stanford University, 1976.

   Armstrong contends that James's affinity for phenomenological theory is strong and that it anticipates later existential theory. Moreover, there is a link between Henry and the philosophy of his brother William. Through a reading of several texts Armstrong investigates the meaning of "impression" to James and various aspects of phenomenology. Armstrong states that he uses James in his study also as a means of providing an introduction to phenomenology.

4. Auchard, John Francis. "Silence in Henry James." Diss. University of North Carolina, Chapel Hill, 1980.

Auchard examines silence as communication and as metaphor. There is an apparent rich, full, active world that lies beneath a quiet surface. James uses silence as a dramatic device and, sometimes, to communicate a philosophical idea. Some characters are able to use silence to increase their power over others and to exert psychological pressure. Auchard sees silence as providing the structural code for the energies of the characters and their imaginative inspiration.

5. Babiiha, Thaddeo Kitasimbwa. "A Review of Research and Criticism on the James-Hawthorne Relation, 1918-1973." Diss. Brown University, 1976.

Babiiha begins with an analysis of James's writings on Hawthorne. Next Babiiha examines, chronologically, works in English that deal with the general relationship between the two writers. He then pays special attention to the role of the artist in society and the heroines of the works of the two writers. The influence of Hawthorne's work on James is examined to determine similarities of techniques, themes, and position in the development of American literature.

6. Bailie, R. H. "The Creative Evolution of the Fiction of Henry James: A Study of Artistic Development." Diss. Queen's University of Belfast, 1976.

7. Barr, David Brewster. "Characterization in Henry James: Statement and Narrative Situation in Four Novels." Diss. University of North Carolina, Chapel Hill, 1977.

Barr examines Jame's use of different kinds of fictional statement (the verbal presentation of information attributable to the author or to another source within the novel) with regard to characterizations. He focuses on the narrative situations in which the statements occur. In The Bostonians characterizations are dominated by expository statements. In The Awkward Age figural statements with behavioral references are predominant. The Ambassadors contains primarily a combination of the above. The Portrait of a Lady uses all of the kinds of statements variously incorporated by James in his works.

8. Beauchamp, Andrea Louise Roberts. "The Heroine of Our Common Scene: Potrayals of American Women in Four Novels by Edith Wharton and Henry James." Diss. University of Michigan, 1976.

Beauchamp compares Isabel Archer of The Portrait of a Lady with Lily Bart of The House of Mirth and Maggie Verver of The Golden Bowl with Ellen Olenska of The Age of Innocence. She notes that James portrays these women as active, responsible for their desinies. Wharton's heroines are more victims of circumstance. Beauchamp believes that these portrayals mark basic differences in the philosophies of the two writers.

9. Benert, Annette Larson. "Passion and Perception: A Jungian Reading of Henry James." Diss. Lehigh University, 1975
Benert applies Jung's theories of personality structure and development to the fiction of James. She studies James's fiction chronologically to determine what his contributions were to the development of the novel and to the understanding of self. Through the study of James's development with regard to characters' perception and interpersonal relationships this is evident.

10. Bennett, Maurice Johnnance. "The Consciousness of the Artist: Charles Brockton Brown, Nathaniel Hawthorne, and Henry James." Diss. Harvard University, 1979.

11. Bent, Nancy Pettengill. "Romance and Irony in Henry James's View of Women." Diss. Syracuse University, 1980.
Bent states that one of the indications that James is indeed a modern writer is the fact that he does not reduce his women characters to formerly-held stereotypes. Within his writing, James uses both irony and romance (and sometimes a combination) in his depiction of women. One traditional characteristic of the romance that James departs from is the male hero. In fact, in some novels and tales it is a child whose consciousness is predominant.

12. Berkson, Dorothy Warren. "The Ordeal of the American Girl: Female Initiation in Henry James's Fiction." Diss. University of Illinois at Urbana-Champaign, 1978.
Berkson maintains that the American girl is the key to James's moral and social ethic. His treatment is not traditional since it deals with female initiation and sees women as victims of a patriarchal society. In his earlier fiction James used social realism to expose the societal ills that entrap women. Later in his writing he mythologized the female role which, according to Berkson, was not as convincing.

13. Blasing, Mutlu Konuk. "In Colossal Cipher: Thoreau, Whitman, James, and Adams." Diss. Brown University, 1974.
Blasing examines some autobiographical writings, writings which effectively convert form into history. In the course of the dissertation Blasing studies James's Prefaces which shed light on his narrative structures and illustrate the development of his self-consciousness that is evident in his fiction.

14. Bogardus, Ralph Frank. "Pictures and Texts: The Collaboration Between Henry James and Alvin Langdon Coburn." Diss. University of New Mexico, 1974.

    Bogardus studies the collaboration of the writer and the photographer, specifically with regard to the production of the plates which serve as frontispieces for the New York Edition. Coburn's aesthetics seem to be very close to those of James and he was able to demonstrate to James a different quality of photographic art.

15. Boren, Lynda Sue. "A Study of the Relationship of the Philosophical Ideas of Henry James, Senior, and William James to the Later Fiction of Henry James." Diss. Tulane University, 1979.

    Boren begins the study by looking at Henry James, Senior's religious and philosophical writings and also those by William James. These ideas influenced Henry James and became most evident in his late work. At that stage of his life and work he incorporated many of his father's and brother's ideas of self and society and attempted to illustrate these by fictionally depicting the process of discovery.

16. Bose, Mita. "Fictional Conventions in the Novels of Henry James and Edith Wharton." Diss. Kent State University, 1980.

    Bose examines the differences in the fictional methods of James and Wharton by looking at the personal relationships between the two writers. James emphasizes the consciousness and perception of the protagonist while Wharton stresses societal influence. Bose defines these as two forms of realistic fiction--"poetic realism" in the case James and "prosaic or literal realism" in the case of Wharton.

17. Bowen, Elsie Van Buren. "The Gardens of Henry James." Diss. Tufts University, 1979.

    Bowen examines James's use of the garden in scenes of particular significance. There is reference to the Garden of Eden, with its connotations of revelation and moving from innocence to experience. The garden is sometimes used as a means of allowing comment on character or theme without authorial intrusion. The garden is also present in James's Prefaces and other criticism and develops throughout the entirety of his work.

18. Bradbury, N. A. L. "The Process and the Effect: A Study of the Development of the Novel Form in the Later Work of Henry James." D. Phil. Thesis. University of Oxford, 1977.

19. Brina, Robert Richard. "The Larger Ether: A Study of Henry James's Romantic Fiction." Diss. University of California, Berkeley, 1980.

Brina uses James's definitions of "romance" and the "romantic" as stated in his Preface to The American as the basis of his study. James's early works rely upon other writers such as Hawthorne and even uses similar imagery in novels and tales. The rewards of the romance as written by James are not material; rather, they represent an expanded vision and a heightened awareness on the parts of the characters and the reader.

20. Burlui, Irina. "Short Fiction in the Work of Henry James." Diss. Bucharest University, 1978.

21. Burns, Marylyn Elixson. "The Significance of the Architectural Motif in Selected Novels by Henry James." Master's Thesis. Pan American University, 1977.

Burns focuses attention on The American, Daisy Miller, The Portrait of a Lady, The Aspern Papers, and The Golden Bowl in her study. These five novels share an American abroad theme. Burns examines the architectural and landscape imagery and the relation with character development in the novels. The characters are analyzed in relation to places, such as ruins, cathedrals, Roman and Florentine villas, etc., and in relation to things, such as fireplaces, windows, facades. and stairways.

22. Burt, Della Ann. "The Widening Arc and the Closed Circle: A Study of Problematic Endings." Diss. Indiana University, 1979.

Burt studies the structure of novels that have problematic endings. With James, she examines the "open" ending of The Portrait of a Lady. The novel uses a balanced two-part structure to prepare for the unfinality of the ending.

23. Byers, Pamela McLucas. "Realism and Convention in Thomas Middleton's City Comedies. The Responsible Narrator: Authorial Presence in Henry James's Late Novels. Bonnie Prince Charles and the Myth of the Highlands: Literature's Remaking of History." Diss. Rutgers University, 1975.

James's presence is evident in the narrators of The Ambassadors and The Golden Bowl, according to Byers. This is in some opposition to the widely held view that James consistently operated through a restricted viewpoint in his later fiction. His presence emphasizes the relativity of vision in the novel. The narrator helps to separate points of view and helps to direct reader responses since an accurate vision is an important moral and aesthetic value.

24. Caldwell, Rachel Monk. "Liberation for Women in the Fiction of Henry James." Diss. Kansas State University, 1976.

Caldwell studies the feminist issue of liberation as it relates to some of James's women characters. One issue dealt with is the economic dependence of some of the women and the limitations inherent in such dependence. Another factor limiting liberation is the restricted perception of some characters. Caldwell maintains that the capacity for liberation (from the standpoint of economics and perception) is greatest in Maggie Verver.

25. Calvert, Steven Lamont. "Christian Redemption from Chaos: The Religious Henry James in The Princess Casamassima." Diss. Rutgers University, 1975.

Chaos for James was represented by the instability of the multitude of human relations which comprise society, particularly the many "varieties of human experience." Calvert then interprets Hyacinth Robinson's suicide which is seen to be as much formal as physical. Robinson is unable to choose between Paul Muniment and the Princess because of his religion of Friendship. Because of this Robinson creates his own chaos and is destroyed by it.

26. Carr, Barbara Catherine L. "Variations on the Anarchist: Politics Reflected in Fiction." Diss. Indiana University, 1976.

Carr examines the political fact that goes into making the political fiction. She tries to seek out historical models, ideologies of successive generations, and the independence of the fictional characters. James incorporates the revolutionary as the force of the action in The Princess Casamassima. Though James and the other novelists studied are not anarchists, there is some identification in selected novels with the anarchist "hero."

27. Chamberlain, V. C. "Techniques and Effects of Realism in the Late Novels of Henry James." Diss. University of Oxford, 1975.

28. Chapin, Helen Geracimos. "Mythology and American Realism: Studies in Fiction by Henry Adams, Henry James and Kate Chopin." Diss. Ohio State University, 1975.

Within realism and realistic writing there is also an element of mythology. Mythology was a part of the nonrational that was usually relegated to romance but which was present in realist writing particularly in the form of the goddess archetype. This form developed from a sense of the disintegration of the patriarchal culture. The origin of the archetypal woman in the lives of the writers is also examined. The conclusion is that realism, naturalism, and mythology can form an artistic unity.

29. Chase, Jeanne Lowey. "Confined Spaces: Limits, 'Fidgets and Starts': The World of James's Late Short Stories." Diss. Brandeis University, 1976.

Chase examines James's late stories in regard to his earlier work. She also attaches importance to those tales and how they illuminate James's consciousness with regard to the practical aspects of survival. She finds a fear in the work for the fate of the "common man." The changes in the world are seen as eliminating possibilities for growth and limiting the imagination. She claims this is akin to the view of many absurdist writers.

30. Church, Micheal Torrence. "The Celibate Ideal: Transformation and the Process of Identity in Henry James's The Ambassadors." Diss. University of Kentucky, 1976.

Church recognizes that James and most critics focus their attention on the scene in The Ambassadors in which Strether exhorts Bilham to live. He sees this as adding to the renunciation theme in James and focuses rather on what he calls the "celibate ideal" in the persons of Chad Newsome and Jeanne de Vionnet. Church further claims that James plots Strether's release from all the women and that in giving up Maria Strether did not relinquish anything he really desired.

31. Cody, Susan Milner. "Henry James and James Joyce: A Study in the Continuity of the Modern Novel." Diss. University of Toronto, 1981.

Cody examines James's fictional method, particularly of his later fiction, to illustrate James's influence on Joyce's experimentation. Cody studies James's views on psychology and their influence on point of view in The Ambassadors, his use of successive centers in The Wings of the Dove, and the influence of James's allusive method on that of Joyce.

32. Cohen, Paula Marantz. "Heroinism: The Woman as the Vehicle for Values in the Nineteenth-Century English Novel from Jane Austen to Henry James." Diss. Columbia University, 1981.

It is Cohen's contention that, prior to James, the heroine was plagued by tension and ambivalence because of her role. James does not artificially impose the self-effacing role upon her; he rewrites the former social relationships. Cohen further contends that the woman (heroine) embodies certain values which novelists were not able to express except through the woman.

33. Collins, Angus Paul. "Three Apocalyptic Novels: Our Mutual Friend, The Princess Casamassima, Tender Is the Night." Diss. Indiana University, 1976.

Collins attempts to examine the apocalyptic vision of the writers in the form of the interaction of aspects of social change and the susceptibilities of the writers at particular points in their careers. With The Princess Casamassima there is the conflict of aesthetic and moral allegiance. Collins notes that at that time James was trying to convince his audience, through his fiction and his criticism, of the moral integrity of minority art.

34. Corse, Sandra Bailey. "The Image of the Novelist in the Critical Works of Henry James." Diss. Georgia State University, 1978.

The examination of James's Criticism of other novelists helps to determine his criteria for judgment. James maintained that environment strongly influences writers and that a writer's nationality can determine perception of the world. James found characteristic problems or attitudes in writers from each country. In his later criticism James saw the novel as moral and psychological and found most satisfying those novelists who are able to recognize and incorporate those elements.

35. Costanzo, William Vincent. "Entangling Metaphors: A Study of Figurative Language in James and Conrad." Diss. Columbia University, 1978.

Costanzo maintains that in both Conrad and James metaphor can have the effect of muddying distinctions between literal and figurative language. James tended to use language to conceal and to manipulate. Costanzo studies a number of works of each author to show how dependent the representation of relity is upon imagination, an aspect of writing that prefigured the works of later authors.

36. Cousineau, Diane Levine. "Henry James and Virginia Woolf: A Comparative Study." Diss. University of California, Davis, 1975.

Cousineau looks at the imaginative visions of the two writers, particularly the difference between the apprehension of space in the visual and the auditory modes of perception. Cousineau then seeks to examine the implications of the differences of the fictional worlds of James and Woolf. Her discussion is influenced by several French phenomenological critics and focuses on The Wings of the Dove and The Golden Bowl.

37. Cowdery, Lauren Tozek. "The Nouvelle of Henry James in Theory and Practice." Diss. Cornell University, 1980.

Cowdery seeks to find James's definition of *nouvelle* as he applied it to his works by outlining the tradition of the *nouvelle* and by examining its theoretical basis. James incorporated the form of the *nouvelle* as a technical exercise to apply the rules to practice and to test his own skill. James also defined the *nouvelle* to be economic treatment of a romantic subject, that which consists of an unknown dimension of life, accessible only through imagination.

38. Crosby, Patricia Lauer. "Growth to Fulfillment: A Psychological Analysis of Six Heroines of Henry James." Diss. Miami University, 1975.

Crosby examines some of James's female characters and how they fit into two general psychological types. Isabel Archer is seen to be morally masochistic, concerned primarily with ethical standards. Fleda Vetch and Milly Theale resemble her in that they are neurotic heroines limited, for the most part, to passivity. Maisie Farange, Nanda Brookenham, and Maggie Verver exhibit "healthy narcissism," in their independence and the resolution of their conflicts.

39. Cross, Mary. "Henry James: Fiction as Style." Diss. Rutgers University, 1980.

Cross maintains that James's novels are verbal creations and that reading them is a verbal experience. The sentence structure lends a drama to his fiction by its syntactic density. This dimension serves to transform style into substance by the extensive use of modifiers and intricacies of syntax to define gradations of meaning. The two works examined in particular, *The Portrait of a Lady* and *The Ambassadors*, demonstrate most completely James's refinement of his style.

40. Crowley, Frank Edward. "Identity Themes and Double Consciousness in Henry James, James Joyce and John Fowles: The Myth in Metaphor." Diss. State University of New York at Buffalo, 1980.

According to Crowley, Henry James and James Joyce signify the birth of modern literature and particularly embody the themes of the artist in society and the significance of human consciousness. This depiction of inner states of consciousness marks a growth in fictional art. James effectively broke ground for later writers with his creations of many perceptual points of view. With James began the fictional examination of the two worlds, rational and emotional, of perception.

41. Cull, Francis Cyril Duncan. "Love and Marriage in the Works of Henry James." Diss. University of South Africa, 1979.
Cull examines several works which display various treatments of love and marriage by James. For example, he observes the failure of Isabel Archer's relationship with Lord Warburton, Caspar Goodwood, and Gilbert Osmond, and her return to Osmond. Cull notes traits of certain characters that lead to success in marriage. He maintains that those who have respect for others and allow for their development and expression are those likely to create successful relationships.

42. Davis, Sara de Saussaure. "The Female Prtagonist in Henry James's Fiction, 1870-1890." Diss. Tulane University, 1974.
Davis examines feminism in the nineteenth century and James's response to the women's movement. Many of James's heroines embody the feminist ideals of freedom and equality. The worth of the Jamesian woman is usually measured in moral and intellectual terms and her freedom is not limited to sexual liberty.

43. Demille, Barbara Munn. "The Imperatives of the Imagination: Dickens, James, Conrad, and Wallace Stevens." Diss. State University of New York at Buffalo, 1978.
Demille defines imperatives as "the demands made by the imagination upon both continual perception and consequent evaluation of external experience, as well as the imperative of its exercise, in an Existentialist sense, as a definition of us as human beings." James stresses the exercise of the imagination and his works illustrate the possibilities of both success and unsuccessful perceptions.

44. Diorio, Mary Ann Lucia Genova. "'Vessels of Experience': A Comparative Study of Women in Selected Novels of Gustave Flaubert and Henry James." Diss. University of Kansas, 1977.
Diorio uses psychoanalytic techniques, particularly those propounded by Jung, as the bases of her study of women in the novels of Flaubert and James. She examines the sensibilities of some women characters and finds that they share that element of the psyche identified with the feminine, the anima. She further states that Flaubert and James, in their probing of the subconscious and their approach to art, exhibit essentially feminine sensibilities.

45. Dooling, John Joseph. "The Late Victorian Novel of Culture: Walter Pater, Henry James, E. M. Forster." Diss. University of Pennsylvania, 1976.

Dooling states that much fiction of the late Victorian and early Edwardian periods continue, to a degree, the culture debate of earlier years. He examines James's reaction to Pater's literary career and James's continuation of the debate. He concludes with the recognition that James, like Pater, saw the need for a resolution of the conflict between aestheticism and life and morality.

46. Doria, Patricia Jamison. "Narrative Persona in George Eliot and Henry James." Diss. University of Texas at Austin, 1975.

Doria gives a close reading of The Portrait of a Lady and Middlemarch. In both there are tensions of narrative attitudes which reveal the authors' awareness of the limitations of individual human understanding. James uses images to comment on characters. These images may affect the characters' thought processes and their conscious decisions are used by James to probe the imagination.

47. Duhling, Sallie Ruth. "Women in the Tales of Henry James: A Study of His Changing Attitudes toward Europe and America." Diss. University of Georgia, 1976.

By a chronological examination of his tales, Duhling studies James's portrayal of women, particularly the differences between American and European women. Early in his career James characterized American women as innocent and European women as sophisticated but sinister. Later, the European woman was more frequently found in the role of heroine. The lack of manners of the American women was eventually shown to be rather deleterious to their characters.

48. Dunkle, John Jacob. "Henry James's The Aspern Papers: A Comprehensive Critique." Diss. St. John's University, 1977.

Dunkle claims that The Aspern Papers is a misunderstood book, owing primarily to James's misleading Preface. He surveys the criticism of the novella and focuses his attention on character, the awareness of the immediate past, and the metaphor of sexual conquest. He also examines the revisions James made for the New York Edition. Dunkle concludes with a look at how The Aspern Papers fits into the genre and into James's oeuvre.

49. Eckstein, Barbara Jo. "Conventions of Irony in Some American Novels." Diss. University of Cincinnati, 1980.

Eckstein maintains that James, a practioner of irony, experiments with the conventions of ironic narrative voice which leads to a self-reflective art that comments on its own aesthetics. With The Aspern Papers the gap between the nineteenth century and the twentieth century is crossed by use of conventional and ironic narration. Other works of James involve the change from conventions of irony to conventions of art about art.

50. Edwards, Mary Emily Parsons. "I. Henry James and the Woman Novelist: The Double Standard in the Tales and Essays. II. Collaborative Learning: Small, Student-centered Discussion Groups in the English Classroom." Diss. Univer- of Virginia, 1978.

This dissertation attempts to discern James's attitude towards women novelists by studying his interaction with some of his female counterparts. Early in his writing career James was apt to categorize books by women according to popular and preconceived notions. Edwards examines those tales by James in which there are women writers and James's essays on some of his contemporaries. He eventually recognized that many women were struggling to dispel traditional ideas about their work and to emerge as serious writers.

51. Eisenstadt, Beverly D. "The Changing Reader: A Study of Three Novels by Henry James." Diss. Columbia University, 1981.

Eisenstadt studies The Tragic Muse, The Awkward Age, and The Wings of the Dove, three novels from the period 1890-1902. These three novels represent widely divergent forms and narrative techniques. The Tragic Muse is closer to the traditions and conventions of some Victorian novelists. The Awkward Age relies heavily on dialogue, an influence of James's dramatic efforts. The Wings of the Dove presents a more conventional narrative, but with the syntactic intricacy of the later works. This variety makes definite and strenuous demands on the reader, which Eisenstadt sees as a step towards modernism.

52. Elder, Harris James. "From Literature to Cinema: The American Short Story Series." Diss. Oklahoma State University, 1979.

Elder examines the problem of adapting a literary work to the cinema. "The Jolly Corner" presents the difficulty of interpreting an interior world evident in the story to the screen.

53. Elion, Sally Lloyd. "'The Anguish of Exasperated Taste': Problems of Jamesian Refinement." Diss. Tufts University, 1976.

Refinement and vulgarity are sometimes in obvious opposition in James's works. Other approaches to James's refinement include his moral censure and aesthetic delight in the worldly woman (which can include the question of speaking or remaining silent). Elion also examines the psychological sources of James's refinement. This refinement affects James's realism and also complicates his writing because of the fear of the vulgar.

54. Euart, Patricia Mary. "The Theme of Betrayal in the Fiction of Henry James." Diss. Brown University, 1975.

Euart analyzes the experience of betrayal in James's fiction and posits that it is the essence of structural significance before it was, for James, the essence of human experience. Euart maintains that the theme of betrayal was present in James's fiction from 1864 to 1910 because it was present in his life and, in fact, was the source of his creative energy. James transformed his experience into art.

55. Finn, Helena Kane. "Design of Despair: The Tragic Heroine and the Imagery of Artifice in Novels by Hawthorne, James, and Wharton." Diss. St. John's University, 1976.

The three writers used various nuances to portray the metamorphoses of their women characters. All three use images of Christianity, classical Greece and Rome, and awareness of self in portraying women and in elucidating action. Finn states that there is a move form the natural to the artificial, the created. These writers portayed this move and its effect on women and used images to express the effects of the move on the characters.

56. Fogel, Daniel Mark. "Extremes and Moderations: The Dialectic of Consciousness in the Later Novels of Henry James." Diss. Cornell University, 1976.

Fogel maintains that James's novels are essentially bipolar in that inexperience becomes experience, innocence becomes knowledge, and incomprehension becomes insight. In the quest for experience the jamesian protagonist attempts to resolve the polarities. The journey is usually a spiral from a point of origin through its antithesis and back, but on a higher plane.

57. Ford, Jane M. "The Father/Daughter/Suitor Triangle in Shakespeare, Dickens, James, Conrad, and Joyce." Diss. State University of New York at Buffalo, 1975.

Ford accepts Freud's Oedipal theory as fact and examines the relationship between the incest theme and the artistic process. In _Watch and Ward_ the father-surrogate triumphs over two suitors and retains his ward. Ford sees the impossibility of a union between Isabel Archer and Gilbert Osmond as being due to Osmond's abnormal attachment to his daughter. She then posits that the separation at the end of _The Golden Bowl_ and Maggie's sense of guilt as being due to her pregnancy by her father.

58. Fowler, Virginia Carol. "The Renunciatory Heroine in Henry James." Diss. University of Pittsburgh, 1976.
Fowler observes that James concerns himself with renunciation itself as a response to experience and as a peculiarly American response. She also notes that renunciation in James's works is valueless and meaningless, engendered by the heroine's fear of reality. James attempts to show the harm goodness and innocence do in the name of renunciation. Fowler says the biographical roots of James imagination lie in his cousin Minny Temple and his sister Alice.

59. Frank, Ellen Eve. "Promises in Stone: The Architectural Analogy in Walter Pater, Gerard Manley Hopkins, Marcel Proust, Henry James." Diss. Stanford University, 1975.
Architecture can be used as an image of the mind and as an artistic analogue for literature. Frank examines the houses present in James's Prefaces as well as in his fiction. James uses the metaphor of architecture for mind and he "furnishes" the mind abundantly with thoughts and ideas. Frank includes some of the frontispieces from the New York Edition.

60. Frickey, Pierrette M. "The Reception of Henry James in France." Diss. University of South Carolina, 1974.
Though James was very fond of French art and culture, his reception by French literary critics was reserved. A recurring criticism was that James's fiction was lifeless. Later critics to some degree recognized the experimental nature of James's novels, particularly with point of view and the complexities of consciousness, but such criticism is not common. Frickey further states that, although most of the translations are very good, James never achieved wide popularity in France.

61. Funk, Ruth Christy. "Order and Chaos: A Study of Cultural Dialectic in Adams, James, Cather, Glasgow, Warren, and Fitzgerald." Diss. Syracuse University, 1979.
Funk uses Henry Adams' symbols, the Virgin and the Dynamo, to study order and chaos in selected novels. In The American, The Princess Casamassima, and The Ambassadors Funk. maintains that James achieves stasis in which the order of the past and the chaos of the present coexist. These and the other novels discussed confirm the American cultural dialectic.

62. Fussell, Mary Burton. "Last Testaments: Writers in Extremis." Diss. University of California, San Diego, 1976.
Fussell studies three novels as statements of the authors' artistic beliefs, though none of the works is a complete statement. The Sense of the Past is an intensely

personal work and, since it was written at the end of James's life, it can be seen as a "last word" of his artistic beliefs. Fussell studied the preliminary drafts of the novel in order to speculate on the place of the novel within James's oeuvre. Also studied are F. Scott Fitzgerald and Herman Melville.

63. Galenbeck, Susan Lynn Carlson. "Women, Manners, and Morals: Henry James's Plays and the Comedy of Manners on the Turn-of-the-Century British Stage." Diss. University of Oregon, 1980.

Galenbeck begins with an overview of the comedy-of-manners tradition from Congreve to Maugham. She also examines the tradition as reflected by some of James's contemporaries. The women characters in James's plays have a great deal of importance. In his earlier plays, James was influenced by French theater and protrayed strong women. The later plays depict some women as social artists and saviors of the mannered life. James's plays capture the social comfort of the upper classes of the period and so are not strained by class battles or social change.

64. Galloway, I. L. "Toward Aesthetic Synthesis: The Fusion of Form and Meaning in the Late Style of Henry James." Master's Thesis. University of Manchester, 1975.

65. Garner, Frances Adrien. "Henry James's Use of Architecture." Diss. University of Tennessee, 1974.

James's use of architecture is frequently significant and can tell much about character and theme. There is often a connection between the architectural structure and the quality of life of its inhabitants. There can be a link between an event and the place in which it occurs. Also, the structures can be used as metaphors for human capability.

66. Gervais, D. C. "Gustave Flaubert and Henry James: A Study in Contrasts." Diss. University of Edinburgh, 1975.

67. Getz, Thomas Theodore. "Henry James: The Novel as an Act of Self-Consciousness and Conscience." Diss. University of Iowa, 1976.

Getz sees James's novels as acts of shaping feeling into the elements of fiction: character, action, setting, and language. The Portrait of a Lady is seen as the act of drawing the portrait. Getz believes What Maisie Knew fails because the elements of the novel are not the articulation of the feeling. James is closest to his main character in The Sacred Fount. James's conscience embodies Maggie Verver and so causes a negative evaluation of Maggie through the recognition of self-depletion.

68. Gibson, Mary Virginia. "Event and Consciousness in Certain Novels of Henry James and Virginia Woolf." Diss. University of Chicago, 1976.

69. Gilchrist, Andrea Lynn. "Melancholy and Mirth: Realistic and Self-Conscious Modes in Thackeray, Trollope, and James." Diss. Ohio State University, 1978.

Gilchrist defines realism as a literary convention through which the author and the reader agree to accept the illusion of verisimilitude produced by the work. Self-consciousness is a similarly produced agreement to recognize literary artifice. James, in The Princess Casamassima, combines both modes by use of some narrative devices. Such a combination was and is used by a number of writers who are frequently studied.

70. Gladding, Martha W. "A Pattern of Distancing in Three Stories by Henry James." Master's Thesis Florida Atlantic University, 1978.

Gladding maintains that James's structuring of time and space is related to the development of characters' consciousness in three stories. Caroline Spencer ("Four Meetings"), Paul Overt ("The Lesson of the Master"), and John Marcher ("The Beast in the Jungle") are faced with knowledge beyond their recognition. Through personal loss and failure and distancing in time and space, they come to perceive certain truths. The author notes the impact of distancing on emotional and intellectual development in James's early fiction and its progress in later works.

71. Goetz, William Robertson. "The Apology for Narrative in Balzac, Henry James, and Proust." Diss. Yale University, 1976.

The novelists studied attempt to validate and affirm their narrative by noting that its origins are other modes of existence, according to Goetz. In vindication there is a reduction of narrative which is opposed by figurative aspects of language. Goetz focuses on James's Prefaces which discuss narrative and also constitute a narrative. He notes the conflict between theoretical claims and rhetorical procedures and examines "The Figure in the Carpet" to illustrate the conflict.

72. Gohrbandt, G. "Aspekte der Heldenfunktion in den Romanen von George Eliot, Henry James und Virginia Woolf." Diss. Universität des Saarlandes, 1975.

73. Goldberg, Raquel Prado-Totaro. "The Artist Fiction of James, Wharton, and Cather." Diss. Northwestern University, 1975

Goldberg examines the artist in the fiction of the three writers--the nature of the artist, the relationship between the artist and his work, and the relationship between the artist and life. Goldberg finds numerous differences in the portrayal of the artist among the three writers and concludes that all three derive ideas from the portrait-of-the-artist tradition rather than Cather and Wharton being imitators James.

74. Gottfried, Marianne Hirsch. "Confrontation of Cultures: Perception and Communication in the Novels of Henry James, Uwe Johnson and Michel Butor." Diss. Brown University, 1975.

The international theme is the subject of Gottfried's dissertation, specifically the fictional portrayal of a foreign country as an effort to transcend self. She maintains Lambert Strether manages to succeed in imposing a personal vision on the foreign environment. _The Golden Bowl_ illustrates the cultural divisions that exist and the attempts at resolution.

75. Grabler, Stuart Mark. "Symmetry and Ideology: Studies of _The American_, _The Tragic Muse_, and _The Golden Bowl_." Diss. State University of New York at Stony Brook, 1979.

Grabler studies symmetry as a literary device used by James in the three novels, which are are somewhat representative of the early, middle, and late periods of his career. Grabler then uses symmetry to examine the ideologies through which James worked in the course of his writing. The purpose of the study is to find the relationship between form and ideology.

76. Greenstein, Susan Mitchell. "The Negative Principle and the Virtuous Character Undercutting in the Work of Richardson, Austen, and James." Diss. Indiana University, 1974.

Greestein states that these writers often undercut slightly the virtues of their "good" characters in order to avoid reader antagonism. In the case of James the undercutting may be due to the fact that some characters are partial portraits of himself. At other times, as in _The Ambassadors_, virtue is seen in aesthetic rather than moral terms. Realization of this helps to explain the character of Strether.

77. Greenwald, Elissa Ann. "The Hawthorne Aspect: Henry James and American Romance." Diss. Yale University, 1981.

Greenwald studies the influence of Hawthorne on James and each writer's theory of romance. In considering romance as narrative she focuses on _The Scarlet Letter_ and _The Portrait of a Lady_. She also looks at the conflict between sense and spirit in _The Bostonians_. Finally, Greenwald sees _The Wings of the Dove_ as the fusion of romance and realism.

78. Greenwald, Fay T. "The Young Girls in the Novels of W. D. Howells and Henry James." Diss. New York University, 1974.

Greenwald sees a relationship between the moral stance of America and the moral responsibility of the young girls in the fiction of James and Howells. Greenwald notes that the families from which some of the girls come are not normal due to absent or ineffectual mothers and close relationships with fathers. Heroines are often complicated characters with strong wills. Sexual aberration in some novels is also studied.

79. Gregory, Robert Douglas. "Reading as Narcissism: Freud, Twain, James, and Hawthorne." Diss. University of California, Irvine, 1981.

Gregory states that Freud's theory of reading and writing emphasized several desires, among which is a desire for a self (narcissism). He further examines Freudian theory and then applies it to some novelists, stating that the theory stresses a "negative metapoetics," for instance, anxiety of influence in James.

80. Gustafson, Judith Alma. "Strategies of Deception: Hawthorne and James and Their Readers." Diss. Wayne State University, 1978.

Gustafson states that Hawthorne and James confirm the expectations of the Victórian reader while at the same time undermining them through deception. James's source for comedy in his trickery is the same as his source for evrything--the bewildered consciousness. The unreliability of the perspective of the narrator or narrators is frequently used by James to deceive his audience.

81. Haggerty, George. "Gothic Fiction from Walpole to James: A Study of Formal Development." Diss. University of California, Berkeley, 1977.

Haggerty studies the history of Gothic fiction, tracing it from Walpole's attempts to write a new kind of fiction. He carries his study of the development of Gothic fiction through Poe and then through to Hawthorne and James, who bring once again the seriousness of literary convention to the Gothic novel.

82. Hall, Marlene LaVerne. "Consciousness and the Unconsciousness: Henry James and Jungian Psychology." Diss. University of New Mexico, 1974.

Hall maintains that James displays an interest in what has come to be referred to as Jungian archetypes. In particular the anima, the shadow, and the mask are evident in James's major phase. Hall traces the development of an ego throughout the periods of Jmaes's life and finds that there are marked stages of development from The Awkward Age to The Golden Bowl.

83. Hallisey, Jereliah Joseph. "Provincials in a Wider World: The National Novels of Twain, Adams, Howells, and James." Diss. Stanford University, 1978.

Hallisey examines changes in America as a nation, increased wealth and urbanization among other changes, by studying novels about the experiences of regional figures in the context of the changes. Hallisey maintains that in The Bostonians James depicts a New England in decline due to public and private corruptions (as well as a provincial view of the South) set against the cosmopolitan world of New York.

84. Hanson, Kathryn Schefter. "A Comparative Study of Matthew Arnold and Henry James." Diss. University of Chicago, 1976.

85. Hardin, James Budd. "Henry James and Idealistic Self-Interest." Diss. Syracuse University, 1976.

Hardin contends that James wanted to represent love of life that endured through intelligence and moral courage. These aspects set some characters above others and displayed James's idealism in the face of cynicism. Often Jamesian characters struggle with conscience which can result in expanded perception and perhaps sacrifice which leads to a new understanding of life. Harding states that James's idealism is understood in the characters' conflict with a corrupt and selfish society.

86. Hardwig, Marilyn Ross. "Henry James's American Males in Europe: Roderick Hudson, The American, The Ambassadors, and The Golden Bowl." Diss. University of Tennessee, 1978.

Hardwig studies the novels as two pairs representing two stages of James's life and career. They are taken to reflect James's identity, particularly with regard to the interdependence of intellect and material wealth in the develpment of the American culture. One of each pair, Roderick Hudson and The Ambassadors reflect the American's attempt to comprehend European complexity. The others, The American and The Golden Bowl, focus on Americans of wealth with time for intellectual endeavors.

87. Hatch, Eric Kent. "Henry James and the Aesthetic Movement." Diss. University of Virginia, 1974.

Aestheticism is taken to be recognition of the primacy of art and the application of the principles of art to individuals' lives. James's views are shown in relation to John Ruskin, Edward Burne-Jones, and Walter Pater. Study of three of James's novels focuses on his view of social aestheticism, the moral possibilities of the relationship of aestheticism and truth (verisimilitude), and aestheticism without verisimilitude.

88. Hayes, Dennis James. "Reliability in James's Fiction of the Dramatic Period." Diss. Auburn University, 1975.
The issue of reliability first comes under scrutiny with The Turn of the Screw and The Sacred Fount, where first-person narrators offer reports of supernatural occurrences. In these works reliability is questioned. Third-person narratives written by James at this time, however, offer no questions of reliability. James apparently intended for his heroines in these works to be admired.

89. Hendricks, Vicki Due. "Polarities of Age in the Fiction of Henry James." Master's Thesis. Florida Atlantic University, 1979.
The study of "age" in James's fiction necessitates consideration of psychological or emotional age as well as chronological age. Hendricks chooses to study the significance of age with regard to ambiguity (in The Awkward Age, "The Middle Years," and "The Jolly Corner"), transformation (in "The Last of the Valerii," The Aspern Papers, The Golden Bowl, and The Ambassadors), and paradox (in Daisy Miller, "The Pupil," The Ambassadors, and The Golden Bowl). The author connects polarity in James's fiction to William James's pragmatism.

90. Holloway, Anna Rebecca. "Henry James and the Intellectuals: Relativism and Form in G. Eliot, R. Browning, W. Pater, and H. James." Diss. Kent State University, 1981.
Holloway focuses her attention on The Portrait of a Lady, The Wings of the Dove, and The Ambassadors and looks at James's works in relation to George Eliot, Robert Browning, and Walter Pater. James's novels differ from the works of the other writers in that they avoid absolutist and non-relativis standards. James, while applying the relativism of psychological development, also demostrates the complexities of individuals' consciousnesses and of social relations.

91. Holly, Carol Thayer. "Portraits of the Self in Henry James's Autobiography and Vladimir Nabokov's Speak, Memory." Diss. Brown University, 1976.
Holly compares the theories of fiction of James and Nabokov as expressed in their autobiographical writings. Topics discussed include consciousness, imagination, memory, and the shaping of the material of fiction. The pasts of each writer also has an effect on the writing. Holly notes that James's autobiographical writing is in confessional tradition of Rousseau because of certain social and family pressures.

92. Holmberg, Lawrence Oscar, Jr. "Autobiography and Art: Aesthetic Uses of the Creative Process in the Autobiographies of Henry Adams, Mark Twain, and Henry James." Diss. University of New Mexico, 1977.

Holmberg studies the autobiographical writings of the three authors as their struggles to find forms for their ideas. James is directed by the theme of consciousness as the critical standard and aesthetic principle. Holmberg maintains that there is a fundamentally interrogative nature in the autobiographies. He sees then as processes of discovering the modes of expression.

93. Hughes, Catherine Boulton. "The Detective Form: A Study of Its Sources and Meaning in Late Nineteenth Century Popular Fiction and Works of James and Conrad." Diss. Brandeis University, 1981.

The dissertation begins with an analysis of the components of detective fiction in the late nineteenth and early twentieth centuries, also acknowledging detective fiction's debt to Poe. Hughes then examines What Maisie Knew as embodying some of the concerns of popular detective fiction. She also looks at The Ambassadors as having some basis in the detective genre.

94. Jablow, Betsy Lynn. "Illustrted Texts from Dickens to James." Diss. Stanford University, 1978.

An "illustrated text" usually implies some mutual enhancement. Jablow contends that the product of the collaboration of James and Alvin Langdon Coburn, the frontispieces for the New York Edition, can serve as a model for what the illustrated text can aspire to. Coburn used "symbolized or generalized" images, rather than specific elements of the texts to not only enhance the works but to "optically echo" the words.

95. Jackson, Katherine Rothschild. "The Larger Adventure: The Realm of Consciousness in the Fiction of Henry James." Diss. Harvard University, 1977.

96. Jacobson, Judith Irvin. "The Nature and Placement of Metaphorical Language in Henry James's The Wings of the Dove." Diss. University of Florida, 1976.

Jacobson studies the matephoric elements of selected passages of The Wings of the Dove to attempt to determine general characteristics of the grammatical nature, context, distribution, and function of all instances of figurative language. Jacobson pays special attention to simple noun and verb metaphors which appear more frequently than the more complex structures noted by a number of critics.

97. Johannsen, Robert Ray. "Romantic Imagery and Realistic Implications in Henry James's Early Novels." Diss. Arizona State University, 1976.

Johannsen, in studying James's first six novels, finds that, while they are initially romantic, they ultimately become more realistic. The figurative images of the novels supply a sense of romanticism which relies on emotion rather than action. Realistic considerations eventually deny romantic possibilities, however. He also finds that James's figurative patterns actually destroy stereotypes and de-romanticize life.

98. Johnson, Jo Lynn. "Imagery and Idea of Scale in Three Stories by Henry James." Master's Thesis. Florida Atlantic University, 1976.

Johnson states that some themes central to James's fiction are expressed by means of the placement of values on a vertical scale. The construction of such a scale and the fixation of values on it indicates the difficulty of permanence in a world of change. The author focuses on "The Lesson of the Master," "The Real Thing," and "The Birthplace" to illustrate respectively perfection on the scale, a paradoxical perpendicular scale, and an ironical version using non-fixed values.

99. Johnson, Julie McMaster. "Death in the Fiction of Henry James: A Formal and Thematic Study." Diss. Georgia State University, 1979.

Johnson maintains that most of the deaths that occur in James's work serve thematic purposes. As a formal device, James occasionally employs death as a mechanism to eliminate unnecessary or awkward characters. Johnson also treats widows and orphans and the effect of death on the family structure and suicide or murder in response to passivity. She also examines James's attitudes towards death and the memorialization of the dead and his application of his attitudes in specific works.

100. Johnson, Stuart Hicks. "The Stroke of Loss: Writing as Activity and as Metaphor in Henry James." Diss. Boston University, 1980.

Johnson intends his study as an exploration into James's theory of artistic creation and also into his thoughts on human experience. James's idea of the writer's relation to his subject is examined in two ghost stories. Allegories of writing are also studied in <u>The Sense of the Past</u> and "The Jolly Corner." The remainder of the study focuses on James's metaphors of writing and on experience and its relation to the subject of writing.

101. Kaston, Carren Osna. "Fictions of Life in the Novels of Henry James." Diss. Rutgers University, 1976.

James's protagonists often forsake material profit for less tangible gains such as consciousness, vision, and memory. Some renunciations come, however, not from an inner sense of freedom or fulfillment, but from the designs of others. For instance, Strether returns to Mrs. Newsome out of his sense of his ambassadorial role. Kaston maintains that only Maggie and Maisie use attained consciousnesses as instruments for possessing their own feelings.

102. Kerr, Susan Jean Anderson. "Self-Interpretations: The Uses of the Past in Autobiography." Diss. University of Texas at Austin, 1975.

Kerr examines James's use of reflection as autobiography. Time is not linear; there is no clear progression evident in his reflection. Rather, time is associational; moments intersect in an atmosphere of the flux. Through this reflection James responds to the past.

103. Kirkpatrick, Judith Ann. "The Artistic Expression of the Psychological Theories of William James in the Writings of Henry James." Diss. University of Delaware, 1975.

Kirkpatrick examines the psychological principles of William James that can be found in the writings of Henry. She concentrates on Henry James's theory of perception as evident in his non-fiction (which are consonent with his brother's) and goes on to illustrate the thought processes of his fictional perceivers. The finding is that Henry James conveys his moral system in his fiction through analysis of perceptual changes.

104. Kirschke, James Joseph. "Henry James and Impressionism." Diss. Temple University, 1977.

Kirschke attempts to place James in the tradition of impressionism in literature and the visual arts. Sources for James's impressionistic tendencies, including Continental, English, and American sources, are also identified. A theoretical approach to James's fictional technique places him in the impressionistic tradition. Kirschke looks to James's non-fiction (_Notebooks_, Prefaces, and letters), as well as his fiction, in order to trace impressionism in his writing.

105. Krawitz, Henry. "Writers on Painting: A Study of the Theory and Criticism of the Visual Arts in Zola, Wilde, James, and Proust and Its Relevance to Their Fiction." Diss. City University of New York, 1976.

This dissertation examines the contact these writers had with the visual arts and their favorites with regard to schools and individual painters. Krawitz finds that the art criticism of the writers is most perceptive when it is free of jargon and relies on intuitive evaluation. Their views of art can be used as a tool to illuminate the theoretical bases of their writings. The works by James discussed are The Sacred Fount and The Wings of the Dove.

106. Lay, Mary M. "The Sibling-Protector in Henry James." Diss. University of New Mexico, 1975.

The character typeof the sibling-protector, as used by James, usually assumes the role of elder brother or sister and may live vicariously through his or her charge. Lay traces the development of the sibling-protector from "Gabrille de Bergerac" to The Ambassadors. She also speculates on the effects of James's own sibling relationships on his literary work. Lay considers Henry William's charge and Alice Henry's charge.

107. Leitch, Thomas Michael. "The James Tradition: An Investigation in Literary History." Diss. Yale University, 1976.

There is a pluralism in contemporary and recent literary criticism. The causes are close attention to irony and indirection and a reluctance to accept direct assertions of meaning. This critical technique is applied particularly to problematical texts. One source of the critical attitude is Henry James. In his fiction and criticism he stresses relations and states of consciousness rather than more concrete reality. Thus, the reader is encouraged to develop a moral consciousness.

108. Lescinski, Joan M. "An Examination of Marriage in Six Novels by Jane Austen and Henry James." Diss. Brown University, 1981.

Lescinski posits that Jane Austen and Henry James exhibit similar approaches to marriage. Particularly, she notes that they both believe that a successful marriage is based on mutual respect, the ability to learn and change, and a degree of intellectual equality. Lescinski focuses on marriage in The American, The Portrait of a Lady, and The Golden Bowl.

109. Liberman, Terri Rae. "The Open Ending in the Later Novels of Henry James." Diss. Case Western Reserve University, 1976.

The lack of complete thematic endings in James's fiction is indicative of the ambiguous and complex worlds he creates. Liberman contends that it also symbolizes the lack of coherent structure and the breakdown of moral values. The characters usually attain vision, but vision which is constrictive in that insight carries loss with it. Ultimately, protagonists turn to renunciation rather than action.

110. Ling, Amy. "The Painter in the Lives and Works of Thackeray, Zola, and James." Diss. New York University, 1979.
This study examines the prominence that the painter has in the works and the lives of the three writers: the painting they did; the painters they knew; the art criticism thye wrote; and the place of painting and the painter in the fiction of all three. Ling maintains that there is an equation of the attitude toward the painter and towards each writer's perception of his art.

111. Loeb, Helen Marie. "Cinderella Displaced and Replaced: Mythic Displacement in 'Tristan and Iseult,' Jane Eyre, Tess of the D'Urbervilles, and Turn of the Screw." Diss. University of Wisconsin, Madison, 1979.
Loeb examines the literary use of two archetypal female figures: the seductive Eve and the virtuous Virgin Mother. In looking at The Turn of the Screw Loeb finds that the governess embodies characteristics of both. The governess vacillates between the two, which has a deleterious effect on the children, and, as a result of her confusion, there is no resolution to the tale.

112. McColgan, Kristin Pruitt. "The World's Slow Stain: The Theme of Initiation in Selected American Novels." Diss. University of North Carolina, Chapel Hill, 1974.
In studying the initiation theme in American fiction McColgan examines international aspects of The Portrait of a Lady. In it there are a number of New World responses to the Old World. Through her experiences, Isabel Archer moves from her rather primitive view of life to a refined consciousness, deepened moral awareness, and elevated sense of values.

113. McGinty, Susan Linda. "The Development of the American Heroine in the Short Fiction of Henry James." Diss. University of Denver, 1977.
McGinty traces the development of the heroine in James's short fiction. She states that he began by describing American women who did not conform to conventional types but were his own version of a type of American woman. Later in his career he ceased to create types and concentrated on women as characters. The descriptions of the heroines became increasingly compressed as James more frequently portrayed them as sensitive women with highly developed consciousnesses.

114. McIntire, Mary Beth. "The Buried Life: A Study of The Blithedale Romance, The Confidence Man, and The Sacred Fount." Diss. Rice University, 1975.
McIntire likens American fiction, and particularly these three novels, to Romantic poetry in its use of

the divided self and the unconscious. She finds the narrator of The Sacred Fount to be self-deceiving and reader-deceiving and a kind of self-parody by James of his idealistic inclinations. The reader is urged to accept the veracity of the narrator, but truth is fragmented and possibly unknowable.

115. McKenzie, Lee Smith. "Jane Austen, Henry James, and the Family Romance." Diss. University of Oklahoma, 1980.
McKenzie studies the similarities of the works of Austen and James, particularly in the depiction of the social structure of the nineteenth century. The fragmentation of society is due primarily to advanced industrialization and urbanization and innocence is glorified. McKenzie compares Pride and Prejudice and "An International Episode" and finds likenesses in form, manners, and ironic voice. He sees the woman as symbol of the individual and marriage as microcosm of society. Variant themes are evident in Mansfield Park and The Spoils of Poynton.

116. McMurray, David Allen. "The Populist Romance: A Study of Michelet's Le Peuple and Selected Novels of Hugo, Zola, James, and Glados." Diss. University of Texas at Austin, 1980.
This dissertation examines the romantic view of the common people. Jamesian elements of this theme are evident in The Princess Casamassima. The large theme is viewed in historical, psychological, and sociological terms.

117. McNamara, Peggy Anne. "The Language of Money in the Fiction of Henry James." Diss. Rice University, 1977.
McNamara claims that certain Jamesian characters misuse economic language in two ways: some reify economic language, others attempt to literalize metaphors, particularly when trying to materialistically evaluate human relationships, often with sexual connotations. As a result a kind of exchange system develops, which McNamara traces throughout several of James's novels.

118. Mack, Stanley Thomas. "Portraits and Portraitists in Hawthorne and James." Diss. Lehigh University, 1976.
Mack focuses on the writers' treatment of portraits and portraitists, noting James's affinity for John Singer Sargent. Art is viewed differently in different works: it can bless, it can be subverted, it can be a kind of religion. Portraits have special significance. The past and the present can be brought into conflict by it. It can also represent the psychic double of a character. Portraits help explain the psychological complexities in the writings of both Hawthorne and James.

119. Manthey, Ethel Vern. "The Sentimentally Educated Hero: A Comparison of Some Aspects of the Hero of Gustave Flaubert with Two Leading Characters of Henry James." Diss. Case Western Reserve University, 1976.

Manthey compares James's fictional accounts of some heroes' educational processes from the standpoint of their surroundings with Flaubert's "sentimentally educated hero." As with Frédéric in l'Education sentimentale, James's heroes in The Princess Casamassima and The Ambassadors have idealistic views of women and are subsequently betrayed. The education of James's heroes is in the form of expanded consciousness and perception.

120. Margalioth, Daniel Zvi. "Taste and Morality: A Study of the Works of Henry James." Diss. Columbia University, 1974.

Margalioth studies the interaction between aesthetics and morality in the three stages of James's life. In his early period James fights against repressive judgments. During the middle period James becomes more conservative but, in perceiving moral flaws in society, he is at variance with society. In the final phase James sees aesthetics and morality as mutually redeeming.

121. Margolis, Anne Throne. "An International Act: Henry James and the Problem of Audience." Diss. Yale University, 1981.

Margolis maintains that James perceived an "audience" for his work rather than a "readership." She seeks to establish that, during James's middle years his audience was split. She then states that James recognized the split in the reviews and in the dichotomy of the poor sales and the ardent admirers. Next, she posits that James's fiction attempts to heal the split by trying to enhance the imagination of those not in his camp.

122. Margulies, Jay Warren. "The Marriage Market: A Study of the Variations of the Marriage Plot Convention in Novels by Austen, Thackeray, Eliot, James, and Hardy." Diss. University of California, Berkeley, 1974.

123. Marks, Margaret Louise. "Flannery O'Connor's American Models: Her Work in Relation to That of Hawthorne, James, Faulkner, and West." Diss. Duke University, 1977.

O'Connor admired James for his depictions of manners, especially manners in change or conflict. She felt the need to convey what she called "mystery" to the secular reader and that mystery is best shown through manners (something she learned from James).

124. Miller, Vivienne Ester. "The Relation of Art and the Artist to Life and Morality in Selected Works of Henry James." Master's Thesis. University of the Witwatersrand, 1977.

125. Montgomery, Stephen Edward. "The Rhetoric of Pathology: Paradoxical Communication in Henry James's Fiction." Diss. University of California, San Diego, 1977.

There is considerable pathological behavior in James's fiction and so considerable psychological criticism has been written. Montgomery looks at this behavior as a product of disorders of communication. In particular he examines paradoxical patterns of language that can enclose characters in a desperate trap of confusion. James's characters are then compelled to pathological attempts at escape.

126. Moon, Heath. "Henry James and the English Cult of Nostaligia: The Past Recaptured in the Fiction and Autobiography of Elizabeth Bowen, Sir Osbert Sitwell and L. P. Hartley." Diss. University of California, Salta Barbara, 1977.

James, in his late fiction, explored themes of the Oedipal character of nostalgia and the fondness for a ruling class combined with the knowledge that such a class was ultimately moribund. Reaction against a modern world is evident in The Awkward Age, which contrasts old and new. The Sacred Fount, on the other hand, presents a depiction of the decay of the upper class. James's use of these themes strongly influenced Elizabeth Bowen and L. P. Hartley, according to Moon.

127. Norrman, R. G. "Techniques of Ambiguity in the Fiction of Henry James, with Special Reference to 'In the Cage' and 'The Turn of the Screw'." Diss. University of Oxford, 1976.

128. Nowick, Nacy Ann. "Melodrama in the Late Novels of Henry James." Diss. Ohio State University, 1976.

Nowick points out that the elements of melodrama were still a part of James's fiction even in his later works. The background and education of James shaped his moral and aesthetic vision and so the influence of melodrama through books and theater was definitely felt. Nowick focuses the study of melodrama on The Sacred Fount, The Ambassadors, The Wings of the Dove, and The Golden Bowl.

129. O'Connor, Dennis Lawrence. "Henry James and the Language World of Renunciation." Diss. Cornell University, 1975.

Linguistic analysis is used to determine from James's language the motives and compensations behind renunciation. O'Connor sees renunciation as commonly the responses of "poor gentleman" heroes and "exquisite" heroines who give up certain advantages for marriage or career. He then examines the effect of renunciation on the relationship of world, self, and other, a reciprocal relationship through which the self attains its existence.

130. Oelschlegel, Lawrence Edward. "Rhythmic Elements in Three Novels from the Post-Dramatic Period of Henry James: What Maisie Knew, The Awkward Age, and The Spoils of Poynton." Diss. University of Maryland, 1980.
Oelschlegel discusses first the theory of narrative rhythm and James's use of rhythm as a function of his work. Oelschlegel focuses on What Maisie Knew (rhythmic structure and the coupling of rhythms of balance to unify the novel), The Awkward Age (a single rythm and the characters' perspective), and The Spoils of Poynton (the rhythm of Fleda's dramatic imagination). The Study demostrates the relation of rhythm to form in the narrative.

131. Ohi, Dee Hansen. "The Limits of Revision: Henry James's Rewriting of Daisy Miller: A Study." Diss. University of Denver, 1981.
Ohi begins her study with an extensive survey of the critical literature devoted to James's revisions. Focusing on Daisy Miller, she finds that the early version displays the lessons James learned from the French and that it reflects James's early use of point of view. The later version has Winterbourne as central consciousness, so his character had to be revised so that the reader could see more through his consciousness.

132. Pancost, David William. "Washington Irving's 'Sketch Book' and American Literature to the Rise of Realism: Framed Narrative, the Pictorial Mode, and Irony in the Fiction of Irving, Longfellow, Kennedy, Poe, Hawthorne, Melville, Howells, Twain, James, and Others." Diss. Duke University, 1977.
Irving established the framed narrative, used in his Sketch Book, as a literary convention that transcended romanticism. As an example, James used the framed narrative device (though adapted to other literary values) in A Passionate Pilgrim and Other Tales, a work of realism.

133. Panetta, Eileen Harriet. "The Anti-Heroine in the Fiction of Henry James." Diss. University of Notre Dame, 1980.
Anti-heroines are distinguished from cruel, selfish women by the ambivalent nature of their willfulness, according to Panetta. There is something of the victim in the anti-heroine. She typically has some admirable

attributes, but is self-destructive in her single-mindedness. These women are doomed not to have what they want, but to remain in some degree admirable in their dishonor.

134. Passow, Emilie Scherz. "Orphans and Aliens: Changing Images of Childhood in Works of Four Voctorian Novelists." Diss. Columbia University, 1979.

Childhood and children can be used to symbolize estrangement and the movement from innocence to experience. Passow looks at three works by James which study the child's response to neglect. The child is brought into the mainstream of fiction and the sorrows and uncertainties of the human condition take their toll on children just as they do on other characters.

135. Patterson, Richard Alvin. "Henry James's Fiction on the Twentieth-Century Stage: A Study of Problems in Adaptation and a History of the Critical Response to Dramatizations Produced in London and New York Theatres since 1916." Diss. New York University, 1979.

The plays adapted from the novels and tales of James form the basis of this study. Many of the adaptations enjoyed critical and popular success, even though James was considered a failure as a playwright. Patterson reexamines James's own career as a dramatist and the differences between his work and adaptations and the difficulties he had in adapting his own works for the stage. The operas based on James's fiction are also examined, as well as some radio, television, and motion picture adaptations.

136. Petrick, Joanne Luckino. "Nathaniel Hawthorne, Henry James, and 'The Deeper Psychology'." Diss. Ohio State University, 1979.

Petrick discusses similarities between James and Hawthorne in the ideas of human psychology and its influences on their moral concerns, and the techniques by which they incorporate this into their works. Petrick examines evil, young heroines, dreams, narrative techniques, and the role of the artist as depicted by each and finds likenesses between the writers' handling of of each of these.

137. Philbin, Alice Irene. "The Literary Femme Fatale--A Social Fiction: The Willful Female in the Deterministic Vision of Thomas Hardy and in the Psychological Vision of Henry James." Diss. Southern Illinois University, Carbondale, 1977.

Philbin maintains that both writers study the _femme fatale_ as an emerging woman. Both also portray some of their femme fatales as heroines. With James's early writings the woman is frequently presented stereotypically. Later in his career he added more complex analysis and complicated symbolism. As a result of the disappearance of the stereotypical and traditional view, the analysis of the femme fatale becomes more sympathetic than condemning.

138. Phillips, Kathy Janette. "Self-Conscious Narration in the Works of Henry James, Marcel Proust, Gertrude Stein, and Alain Robbe-Grillet." Diss. Brown University, 1977.

Phillips identifies as some devices of self-consciousness reticence, plot-repitition, and a type of internal gloss. James leaves some ambiguities in his works purposely. He also uses internal commentary from time to time. Also, his characters often seek to transform stories into life, to escape the confines of their enclosed world.

139. Posnock, Ross. "Henry James and the Problem of Robert Browning." Diss. Johns Hopkins University, 1980.

James's apparent interest in Browning the man and Browning the poet is the subject of this study. The duplicity of Browning's public and private lives prompted James to fictionalize his impression in "The Private Life." Posnock studies several Browning poems as inspiration for fictional works by Jamesand the problem Browning presented for James. The solution to the problem, in creative terms, was James's writing of two late novels, The Wings of the Dove, and The Golden Bowl which involve the use of introspective consciousness.

140. Probert, Kenneth Gordon. "Romance by Intent: A Study of Generic Procedure in The Blithedale Romance, Moby-Dick, The American, and The Great Gatsby." Diss. York University (Canada), 1979.

Probert asserts that there are many kinds and types of traditional romances and that focus on a singular view or definition hinders a study of the genre. The American, he maintains, is an artful manipulation of chivalric and gothic romance. This work and the others he examines use the romance tradition particularly to reflect the form and fate of contemporary American idealism.

141. Przybylowicz, Donna. "The Deconstruction of Time and the Displacement of Desire: The Phenomenological World of the Late Works of Henry James." Diss. Brandeis University, 1978.

Przybylowicz examines the importance of time and the

past in James's later writings. She also says that his preoccupation with this is reflected in the text in the form of more distorted narrative structures and rhythms, longer and more abstruse sentence, and the mirroring of the internal vision by the temporal world. Thus, there is a removal of the self from society, from the material world, to the inner world of the mind.

142. Rimmon, S. "'Mutual Incompatibility': The Concept of Ambiguity Illustrated from Some Novels and Stories of Henry James." Diss. University of London, 1975.

143. Rivkin, Julia Helen. "Perspectivism in the Late Novels of Henry James." Diss. Yale University, 1980.

Rivkin notes the relationship between the Jamesian idea of "centre of consciousness" and "perspectivism," defined by Nietzche as the philosophical notion of the world existing only as perceived by a particular point of view. Conflicting points of view are evident in The Ambassadors, which threaten Strether's center of vision. The effects of the conflict on James's form are examined in a reading of The Wings of the Dove. The Questions raised by this examination are further studied in The Golden Bowl.

144. Ron, Moshe. "The Subject and the Matter: Interpretations of Henry James and Narrative Theory." Diss. Yale University, 1975.

Ron first offers an interpretation of "The Real Thing," examining the relationship between meaning and structure in the tale. Next he focuses on the structure of mimesis. He uses several texts to look at ambivalent representational and personal relations. Ron also includes a detailed examination of narrative theory in general, particularly the Formalist-Structuralist tradition.

145. Roth, Ellen Shamis. "The Rhetoric of First Person Point of View in the Novel and Film Forms: A Study of Anthony Burgess' A Clockwork Orange and Henry James' A Turn of the Screw." Diss. New York University, 1978.

Roth's study centers on the use of first person narrative form in the novel and in film. She examines how technique can be used to color time, space, and causal relationships by subjective means. Narrative technique is studied in A Clockwork Orange and The Turn of the Screw and its counterpart is studied in the film versions of the two books.

146. Rothmel, Steven Zachary. "Similarities in the Novelistic Techniques of Jane Austen and Henry James." Diss. University of Utah, 1978.

Rothmel maintains that fictional techniques developed by Jane Austen influenced Henry James. Both interweave disparate narrative methods and experiment with point of view. Both also delve deeply into their characters' lives, public and private, to most fully depict their humanness and thus their motivation and their emotions. Both novelists realize the full potential of the medium, to present fully-developed characters in a believable setting in imaginative and thought-provoking works.

147. Salmon, Rachel. "The Typological Mode and Jamesian Poetics." Diss. Brandeis University, 1978.

Salmon incorporates biblical typology into her study of James to examine how meaning reveals itself in a secular text. Typology is used as a method of examination apart from symbol or allegory. In particular, "The Figure in the Carpet" and "The Beast in the Jungle" are scrutinized by Salmon in an attempt to render James's ambiguity clear.

148. Sallee, Jonel Curtis. "Circles of the Slef." Diss. University of Kentucky, 1977.

Sallee examines the circle metaphor in works by James, Whitman, Norris, and Henry Adams. Usually the self is at the center of the circle the circumference of which represents limits of perception of the self. In *The Ambassadors* Lambert Strether's perceptions are solid rather early in the novel, yet his perception can expand when he becomes aware of the limits.

149. Saner, John Sutherland. "Patterns of Imagery and Figurative Language in the Novels of Henry James, with Special Reference to *The Ambassadors*, *The Wings of the Dove*, and *The Golden Bowl*." Master's Thesis University of Witwatersrand (South Africa), 1976.

The author's primary purpose is to study James's use of the image-pattern as a stylistic device. He maintains that James's imagery progressed from a relatively simple state in his early works to the complex, mature level of his later writings. The author concludes by noting the connection of James's imagery to the central themes of the works in a universal sense that transcends the works themselves.

150. Savarese, John Edmund. "Some Theories of Short Fiction in America in the Nineteenth Century: Poe, Hawthorne and James." Diss. Princeton University, 1975.

Savarese points out that the limits inherent in painting are analogous to the compressed structure essential to short fiction. This is evident in the comparison of James's writings and the art of John Singer Sargent. The same principles apply to Coburn's photographs for the New York Edition. Savarese further says that James manipulates reader reaction differently in different types of tales.

151. Schlib, John Lincoln. "Henry James and the Moral Will." Diss. State University of New York at Binghamton, 1978.

Schlib examines the relationship of will to the lives of the characters. Moral will is defined by action coupled with ethical values. Schlib ficuses on The Princess Casamassima, The Spoils of Poynton, What Maisie Knew, The Awkward Age, and The Wings of the Dove in order to clarify the existence of moral will. He attempts to place this aspect of James's writing in its proper philosophical tradition and so view it as a modern consciousness.

152. Scribner, Margo Parker. "The House of the Imagined Past: Hawthorne, Dickens, and James." Diss. University of Arizona, 1980.

Scribner studies the symbolic uses of the old house, which has definite and firm links to the past and to memory. In particular, she looks at James's The Portrait of a Lady, "The Jolly Corner," and The Sense of the Past. Because of memories evoked by houses, and the former inhabitants, time is not linear within an old house. Houses can also be symbolic of decay (moral and physical), imprisonment, release, or solace. The house is therefore used to understand the self.

153. Seed, D. "The Role of the Narrator in Henry James's Novels, 1896-1901." Diss. University of Hull, 1978.

Seed denies that James's fiction aspires to total scenic objectivity and states that the narrator is very important in James's work. The narrator remains important, even in later fiction. Seed further states that the dramatic analogy does not allow for the effects the narrative voice in the novels. At times, though the narrator begins to analyze, which may threaten the character's autonomy.

154. Serlen, Ellen. "The Rage of Caliban: Realism and Romance in the Nineteenth-Century Novel." Diss. State University of New York at Stony Brook, 1975.

Serlen notes that early in the nineteenth century readers sought an ideal, an escape from reality. Novelists attempted to present a romantic ideal of the sort that was evident in some of the poetry of that time. By the time The Princess Casamassima was written, however, illusion was less able to withstand reality and the conjunction of the two was no longer possible.

155. Sessom, Sandra Lee. "Charlotte in Perspective: A Further Reading of The Golden Bowl." Diss. University of Oregon, 1978.

Sessom surveys the criticism on The Golden Bowl and focuses on the character of Charlotte Stant and her relationship with the other charasters. Sessom then gives a re-reading of the novel, looking at Charlotte's aims and intentions. Sessom concludes that Charlotte is a reasonable moral character, not a monster, who sets the stage for Maggie's and her compromise.

156. Sharma, Jagdish Narain. "The Evolution of the International Theme in the Fiction of Henry James." Diss. Indiana University, 1975.

Because of his penchant for realism and the social and cultural state of America, the international theme in James's work seems to have been inevitable. Some works deal with the cultural and moral contrasts between Europe and America. In later writings national differences give way in part to differences in human nature while the international aspect remains. Sharma concludes that, with the exception of Wharton, few later American writers attempt an international theme, partly because of James's exhaustive treatment of it.

157. Shaw, Jean Barrett. "A Native of the James Family." Diss. University of Louisville, 1977.

Sahw approaches Jamesian study through James's own criticism. In order to most effectively use this approach Shaw considers James's family background and the influences of this on his thinking and writing. The intellectual relationships with Henry, Senior and William are examined in detail. Next Shaw turns attention to specific works and analyzes the effects of the background and acquired values on James's fiction.

158. Shipley, Jeanne Elizabeth. "The Authority of Precision: Essays on Henry James and Robert Musil." Diss. State University of New York at Buffalo, 1979.

Shipley maintains the The Portrait of a Lady is a novel about power and authority, particularly about displacement of authority. The deterioration of authority in writing is evident in James's use of houses haunted by one's double. This is taken as a symbol of an attempt to recapture the past, an attempt doomed to failure. Shipley further maintains that depictions of metaphysical precision tends to erode a rhetoric of authority.

159. Shollenberger, James Edward. "'A Box of Fixed Dimensions': Dramatic Structure and the Plays of Henry James." Diss. Ohio State University, 1977.

Shollenberger begins his study with an examination of James's nonfiction writings on drama and dramatic form. He then looks at the plays under the following divisions: early plays; melodramatic plays; comedies; serious plays; and plays treating societal issues. He concludes that James had some problems with technique and that he did not fully appreciate the interaction between players and audience and the internal logic necessary for favorable response.

160. Sicker, Philip Timothy. "Beyond the Image: Love and the Quest for Identity in the Fiction of Henry James." Diss. University of Virginia, 1977.

Sicker maintains that James's characters seek stable, fully integrated identities through romantic love. For James, love begins with the recognition of another consciousness. The protagonists must realize that there may not be a relationship between their ideal and the person. Failure in love comes about by one consciousness being absorbed by another.

161. Silver, Daniel Jay. "Margin and Mystery: The Fate of Intimacy in the Late Novels of Henry James." Diss. Yale University, 1981.

Silver states that questions of intimacy are of prime importance in The Ambassadors, The Wings of the Dove, and The Golden Bowl. He argues that the grandest emotions and adventures of consciousness are products of an intimacy that includes giving up worldly possessions and and accepting the mystery.

162. Smyth, Paul Rockwood. "Gothic Influences in Henry James's Major Fiction." Diss. Michigan State University, 1980.

Smyth examines James's use of Gothic theme, imagery, and characterization in The American, The Portrait of a

Lady, The Wings of the Dove, and The Golden Bowl. He sees the "international" theme present in many of James's works as a variation on the Gothic theme. The characters embody the sentimental virtues common in Gothic fiction. Smyth sees James's work as a continuation of the Gothic tradition because of the intermingling of art and life and the problem of evil.

163. Spigelmire, W. Lynne. "Daniel Deronda and The Portrait of a Lady: A Revised Estimate of F. R. Leavis' View." Diss. Boston College, 1978.

Spigelmire assesses Leavis' statement that The Portrait of a Lady was greatly influenced by Daniel Deronda. Spigelmire contends that the novels are far more dissimilar than Leavis believes and that the influence of Eliot on James is overstated. The essential difference is that James does not assume that people can be fully known. Thus, James's narrator cannot be omniscient, but in his fallibility he is not deceptive.

164. Sprinker, John Michael. "'Questions of Air and Form': Fictional Paradigms in Jane Austen, George Meredith, and Henry James." Diss. Princeton University, 1975.

Sprinker states that the question of fictional form becomes one of fate with The Portrait of a Lady. James's choce to make the novel conform to fictional restrictions of symmetry and construction is responsible for Isabel's return to Rome. James bases The Wings of the Dove on deception and so reveals the mendacity inherent in the fictional process. His truth is told in the Prefaces, according to Sprinker.

165. Starer, Marilyn Morris. "A Review of Criticism on The Ambassadors, 1903-1972." Diss. State University of New York at Albany, 1977.

Starer focuses her attention on American critical response to The Ambassadors. Scholarly assessments and reviews are examined. The survey is divided into five parts: early acceptance of the novel; response to the language and structure of the novel; criticism of the various characters; themes (such as morality, the transience of life, time, etc.); and the literary method of construction (particularly point of view).

166. Stowe, William Whitfield. "Balzac, James, and the Realistic Novel." Diss. Yale University, 1977.

Balzac and James face the tasks of the realistic writer in similar manner. The tasks, as Stowe sees them, are primarily the realist's understanding of relationship of his view of the world, his presentation of the world, and the world as it exists, and also of how to convince the reader that the realist's view of experience is valid. Stowe takes a chronological approach to the novels of Balzac and James to show the refinement of their expression.

167. Stuchel, Victoria S. "The Child in Nineteenth Century Literature as Seen by Four Representative Authors: William Wordsworth, Charles Dickens, Mark Twain, and Henry James." Master's Thesis. Northeast Missouri State University, 1976.

Stuchel maintains that before the nineteenth century the child served usually as plot device or, at best, a passive observer. During the nineteenth century, however, the role of the child became more active and at times the child actually became a creative agent. There is considerable development in the use of the prophetic child from Wordsworth to James, particularly in James's novels of innocence and corruption. Yet the child is in a position of moral superiority which enables him to convey universal truths.

168. Sutherland, Judith Cleveland. "At the Edge: Problematic Fictions of Poe, James, and Hawthorne." Diss. University of Iowa, 1977.

Works by each of the three writers are problematic fictions that present difficulties in explication, particularly with regard to the nature of analogy. Sutherland examines the artist's role as creator in _The Narrative of Arthur Gordon Pym_, _The Sacred Fount_, and _The Marble Faun_. James sees that the text suffers from the aesthetic concessions made in order for the artist to maintain his position as creator.

169. Taylor, Linda Jennings. "Henry James and the Critics: The 1880s." Diss. Brown University, 1975.

Taylor closely examines criticism written in this century of James's major fiction of the 1880s. She finds, through scrutiny of numerous reviews in newspapers and magazines, that some attention was paid to James in all parts of the United States and that much of the critical attention was favorable. She also finds that his reputation did not decline much after _The Bostonians_. Many contemporary reviewers also saw James as relevant to the concerns of the day.

170. Thomas, Lloyd Spenser. "The Haunts of Language Superstition and Subterfuge in Henry James's Stories of the Supernatural." Diss. State University of New York at Binghamton, 1975.

Thomas examines some Jamesian characters' penchant for verbal deception. Thomas sees much satire in James's work and finds that he continuously parodies the "art for art's sake" doctrine of Wilde, Pater, and others. He claims James relies heavily on puns, conscious narrative plagiarism, double meanings, and sometimes nonsense to display gullibility in characters.

171. Thompson, Robert Bryan. "The Problem of Leisure in Henry James's Novels." Diss. University of Iowa, 1974.

The problem of leisure and people of leisure in three of James's novels is the focus of this dissertation. In Roderick Hudson Thompson considers Mallet's patronage of the sculptor as an attempt by Mallet to reconcile his lack of purpose. In The Portrait of a Lady the freedom of some characters is threatened because convention is threatened. In The Princess Casamassima the Princess leaves the leisure class in an attempt to overcome her own purposelessness.

172. Trotter, Gary Owen. "The Process of Selection in the Art of Henry James." Diss. State University of New York at Buffalo, 1979.

Trotter uses study of James's notebooks, essays, and correspondence to trace the development of his aesthetic theory. Through James's early novels his intentions appear to be unconsciously romantic, but the notoriety and position achieved by the middle phase allowed him to experiment with form. His intentions changed after his disappointments in the theater. He works through the form of the nouvelle to the creation of The Ambassadors, which most completely expresses his evolved intentions.

173. Van Horn, Geraldine Kloos. "The Image of the City in the Early Twentieth-Century Novel: Studies of Conrad, James, Woolf, and Joyce." Diss. Ohio State University, 1978.

Van Horn uses urban sociology to examine how the city embodies the history and psychology of its inhabitants. When focusing on James Van Horn notes that, in The Princess Casamassima, the city cannot be viewed solely as a horror. It contains the good of man as well as the bad. In The Ambassadors James demonstrates the cultural gifts of Paris.

174. Varner, Jeanine Baker. "Henry James and Gustave Flaubert: The Creative Relationship." Diss. University of Tennessee, 1981.

Varner points out James's affinity for French literature and, in particular, for Gustave Flaubert. She concentrates on the six essays James wrote on Flaubert from 1874 to 1902. Varner then compares Madame Bovary with The Portrait of a Lady and L'Education Sentimentale with The Princess Casamassima to show Flaubert's influence on James, noting that James approved of Flaubert's style but disapproved of his limited central characters.

175. Viereck, Helen Raaz. "Intellectual Women in the Early Novels of Henry James." Master's Thesis. University of Houston, 1975.

Viereck studies the intelligent young women of James's novels. Among those focused upon are Kate Croy (The Wings of the Dove), Maria Gostrey (The Ambassadors), Maggie Verver and Charlotte Stant (The Golden Bowl), Christina Light (Roderick Hudson and The Princess Casamassima), Olive Chancellor (The Bostonians), and Julia Dallow (The Tragic Muse). Viereck finds a consistent pattern of characterization which includes the intellectual pursuits as compensation for weakness and reliance on an ill-chosen loved one.

176. Vincec, Mary Barbara. "A Variant Edition of Henry James's The Wings of the Dove." Diss. McMaster University (Canada), 1975.

177. Wessel, Catherine Cox. "Culture and Anarchy: The Survival of the Fittest in the Fiction of Henry James." Diss. Yale University, 1980.

Wessel posits that, in the course of his writing career, James necessarily had to discard the optimistic nineteenth-century notion of the increasing moral development of man for a post-Darwinist view of man as an instictive being. Awareness of base motives is evident in The Golden Bowl, as opposed to the clinging to form in The Portrait of a Lady. The background of the development of James's moral vision is also discussed. Wessel claims that James sees the fittest as not the same as the most moral or ethical.

178. Wicker, Patricia Elizabeth Frazier. "Jamesian Women: A Readers Theatre Adaptation from Selected Novels of Henry James." Master's Thesis. North Texas State University, 1975.

Wicker attempts to study James's female protagonists, particularly with regard to the elements of freedom, power, and destruction that limit an independent person. She focuses on a Readers Theatre adaptation of Daisy Miller, The Wings of the Dove, and The Portrait of a Lady.

179. Wilds, Nancy G. "Rhetorical Strategy in Early Twentieth-Century Fiction: Studies in Henry James, Ford Madox Ford, and James Joyce." Diss. University of South Carolina, 1975.

In the early years of this century narrative technique changed, the effect being that the author no longer overtly imposed his value system upon the reader. James, while operating in this manner, preserved the illusion of internal consistency, thus increasing the responsibility of the reader. In "The Beast in the Jungle" there are three perspectives presented which, with complex imagery and linguistic technique, place a greater burden on the reader.

180. Williams, Michael Gary. "Politics without Love: Anarchism in Turgenev, Dostoevsky, and James." Diss. University of Michigan, 1974.

Williams maintains that politics was conceived by these writers as aggregate morality, so a character's political opinion could be seen in its effect on his or her moral life. The most common effect was a reduction in ability to love. In The Princess Casamassima the loveless characters are Paul Muniment and the Princess and their lovelessness affects everyone in the novel. Williams adds that love cannot be seen as a sole remedy for complex political problems.

181. Wilson, Lois S. "The Stylistics of Henry James: A Linguistic Analysis of Selected Early and Late Novels." Diss. Florida State University, 1974.

Wilson adopts the use of transformation generative grammar for an analysis and comparison of the early and late writing styles of Henry James. James reduces dialogue throughout his career, partly by adding exposition. Also, Wilson notes that the length of James's expository sentences becomes greater because of more dependent clauses and longer independent clauses. These and other changes lead to the increased complexity and intricacy of James's later writing.

182. Wirth-Nesher, Hana. "Limits of Fiction: A Study of the Novels of Henry James and Virginia Woolf." Diss. Columbia University, 1976.

Wirth-Nesher finds similarities between James and Woolf in their use of the imagination in their fiction. Both had a reverence and a mistrust of the imagination and expressed the ambivalence similarly. Both writers rejected many of the conventions of fiction and experimented, though differently, with form, language, and other elements. Both display a move from individual to collective consciousness and from action to perception.

183. Wolk, Merla Samuels. "The Safe Space: The Artist Figure in the Novels of Henry James, 1886-1897." Diss. Wayne State University, 1981.

Wolk studies artist figures in The Bostonians, The Princess Casamassima, The Tragic Muse, and What Maisie Knew. As subject the artist faces the issues of autonomy versus dependency, isolation, and other psychological conflicts. These issues grew from subjects to be absorbed into his technique and imagination.

BOOKS

184. Akiyama, Masayuki. A Rapprochement Study of Yasunari Kawabata's The Sound of the Mountain and Henry James's The Ambassadors. Tokyo: Mishima College, Nihon University, 1976.

185. Anderson, Charles R. Person, Place, and Thing in Henry James's Novels. Durham, NC: Duke University Press, 1977.

Anderson structures his study to contain a chronological sampling of James's novels: Roderick Hudson. The American, The Portrait of a Lady, The Princess Casamassima, The Wings of the Dove, and The Ambassadors. In selecting these titles he purposely chose some set in Italy, in France, and in England. In the course of the study Anderson examines the symbolic relationships of characters to certain objects and certain places and the the development of person-place-thing throughout James's writings.

REVIEWS:
Choice, 15 (1978), 223.
Modern Age, 23 (1979), 106.
Monteiro, George. American Literature, 50 (1979), 656-58.
Puk, Francine Shapiro. Library Journal, 15 January 1978, pp. 167-68.
Stewart, J. I. M. Times Literary Supplement, 25 February 1978, p. 226.
Tintner, Adeline R. Modern Fiction Studies, 24 (1979), 630-31.

186. Asthana, Rama Kant. Henry James: A Study in the Aesthetics of the Novel. New Delhi: Associated Publishing House, 1980.

Asthana's study examines many aspects of James's writing: his introduction of psychological analysis in the novel; the expression he finds in the creation of character; the use of a character as central consciousness; the dynamics, changes, flow of James's form and style; the integral relationship of art and life; and the moral effects of action. These, Asthana says, comprise James's aesthetics of composition.

REVIEWS:
Choice, 19 (1981), 74.
Maini, Darshan Singh. Henry James Review, 3 (1981), 74-75.

187. Auchincloss, Louis. Reading Henry James. Minneapolis: University of Minnesota Press, 1975.

Auchincloss' book is intended as an introduction to the breadth of James's work. He begins by briefly examining James as man and as artist. He then takes a chronological tour through James's work, with numerous stops, such as the early stories, Roderick Hudson, The American, The Portrait of a Lady, the social novels, the ghost stories, the theater years, The Spoils of Poynton, and the major phase, among others. Along with these, Auchincloss looks at James's notebooks, the significance of his last American tour, his autobiographical writings, and his criticism.

REVIEWS:
Breslin, J. B. America, 11 Aoril 1975, p. 309.
Choice, 12 (1975), 678.
Conley, Nancy. Novel: A Forum on Fiction, 10 (1976), 87-91.
Holland, Laurence B. Nineteenth-Century Fiction, 31 (1976), 103-08.
Hughes, James. Antioch Review, 33 (1975), 123.
Kirby, David. Library Journal, 15 March 1975, p. 583.
Meier, T. K. Modern Fiction Studies, 21 (1975-76), 648-49.
Publishers Weekly, 24 March 1975, p. 44.
Rosenberg, V. H. Dalhousie Review, 55 (1975), 577.
Terrie, Henry L. Sewanee Review, 83 (1975), 695-703.
Tintner, Adeline R. Studies in the Novel, 9 (1977), 73-94.
Winner Viola Hopkins. American Literature, 47 (1975), 463-64.

188. Babiiha, Thaddeo K. The James-Hawthorne Relation: Bibliographical Essays. Boston: G. K. Hall, 1980.

This study, based on Babiiha's dissertation (see no. 5), examines first Henry James's writings on Hawthorne. The next chapter approaches generally the James-Hawthorne relationship. Following chapters focus on specific works by Hawthorne (The Scarlett Letter, The Blithedale Romance, The Marble Faun) and how they relate to numerous works by James.

REVIEWS:
Cain, William E. Henry James Review, 2 (1980), 73-75.

189. Beppu, Keiko. The Educated Sensibility in Henry James and Walter Pater. Tokyo: Shohakusha, 1979.

Beppu studies the major concerns of James and Pater and finds that the aesthetic is of foremost importance. James also seeks to unify or to illustrate the relation between the aesthetic and the moral. Beppu stresses that the two also see their roles as artists to include the education or cultivation of aesthetic and moral sensibility. Beppu's discussion includes works by James that approach this differently.

190. Berland, Alwyn. Culture and Conflict in the Novels of Henry James. Cambridge: Cambridge University Press, 1981.

Berland approaches James's fiction with an eye on his view of civilization as culture, civilization which provides a means to measure and arrive at moral value. He begins his study with Roderick Hudson and moves on to selected other novels. This study of civilization is also undertaken in relation to such themes as innocence, experience, and renunciation. The international aspect of much of James's fiction also affects his view of civilization. Berland sees Lambert Strether as the most complete character in terms of James's view of civilization.

REVIEWS:
British Book News, August 1981, p. 498.
Choice, 19 (1981), 376.
Gribben, Alan. American Literature, 54 (1982), 127-28.
Hewitt, Rosalie. Modern Fiction Studies, 27 (1981-82), 719-25.
Mulkey, Christopher. Journal of American Studies, 16 (1982), 136.
Times Literary Supplement, 14 August 1981, p. 939.
Virginia Quarterly Review, 57 (1981), R129.

191. Bradbury, Nicola. Henry James: The Later Novels. Oxford: Clarendon, 1979.

Bradbury initially approaches James by asking two questions--how do we read James and why? She finds that James is also dealing with these issues, but while he stimulates, he does not govern the reader's response. Bradbury maintains that The Portrait of a Lady marks the culmination of James's early career. After acknowledging a transition period to the major phase, she focuses her attention on The Ambassadors, The Wings of the Dove, and The Golden Bowl.

REVIEWS:
Books and Bookmen, 25 (1980), 23.
British Book News, June 1980, p. 368.
Criticism, 26 (1980), 698.
Flint, K. English, 30 (1981), 302-08.
Seed, D. Times Literary Supplement, 27 June 1980, p. 741.
Terrie, H. L., Jr. Sewanee Review, 88 (1980), 623.
Veeder, William. Modern Philology, 79 (1981), 104-09.
Virginia Quarterly Review, 56 (1980), R94.

192. Daugherty, Sarah B. The Literary Criticism of Henry James. Athens, OH: Ohio University Press, 1981.

Daugherty uses the study of James's critical writings to help explain his fiction and its relation to the fiction of earlier writers. She finds that a reading of James's criticism helps to place him in his proper historical context. In his observations and comments on the Naturalists and on his countrymen James's own method becomes clearer. They also help to point out some shortcomings that may be due to the limited scope of his reading. Finally, his later writings display his flexibility and his attempts to come to terms with his era.

REVIEWS:
Eicheberger, Clayton L. American Literature, 54 (1982), 145-46.
Hewitt, Rosalie. Modern Fiction Studies, 27 (1981-82), 719-25.
Long, R. E. American Literary Realism, 1870-1910, 14 (1981), 300-01.
Times Literary Supplement, 14 August 1981, p. 939.

193. Donadio, Stephen. Nietzsche, Henry James, and the Artistic Will. New York: Oxford University Press, 1978.

Donadio's study attempts to link the thought and, to a degree, the aesthetics of James and Nietzsche. In broader terms, it also deals with examination of the American identity and its correlation with the Nietzschean idea of the superman and with the advent of modernism. Donadio approaches James essentially as a novelist of ideas.

REVIEWS:
Bloom, Harold. Commentary, 66 (December, 1978), 85-87.
Brent, Jonathan. Henry James Review, 2 (1980), 70-71.
Choice, 16 (1979), 382.
Gargano, James W. Modern Fiction Studies, 25 (1980), 730-33.
Kirkus Reviews, 1 August 1978, p. 847.

Levinson, Daniel. Library Journal, 1 October 1978, p. 1984.
Shapiro, Gary. Journal of Aesthetics and Art Criticism, 38 (Fall 1979), 83-86.

194. Fogel, Daniel Mark. Henry James and the Structure of the Romantic Imagination. Baton Rouge: Louisiana State University Press, 1981.

Fogel studies James's debt to Romanticism; that is, to the writers of the Romantic period. His hypothesis is based on some observation: the fictions involve a quest for experience that includes an alteration of perception; the quest is usually bipolar; and the protagonists' attitudes result from a synthesis of the polarities. These observations lead Fogel to believe that, primarily in his later fiction, James adopted the Romantic dialectic of spiral return.

REVIEWS:
Choice, 19 (1982), 1068.

195. Furth, David L. The Visionary Betrayed: Aesthetic Discontinuity in Henry James's The American Scene. Cambridge, MA: Harvard University Press, 1979.

Furth notes the importance of James's 1904 visit to America. One effect of the visit was the revitalization of the international theme in his late works. When in America James was struck by new impressions and experiences and The American Scene is, in essence, his attempt to find order in the impressions. Though the style of the book is challenging Furth maintains it is an "act of life" for James.

REVIEWS:
College Literature, 8 (1981), 93.
Hewitt, Rosalie. Modern Fiction Studies, 27 (1981-82), 719-25.

196. Gervais, David. Flaubert and Henry James: A Study in Contrasts. New York: Barnes & Noble, 1978.

Gervais states that he does not apply artificial historical connections between James and Flaubert. It is obvious, however, that James read Flaubert and was influenced by his writings. Though the two writers are very different (indeed, Gervais stresses that this is a study of contrasts), there are vertain connections between the two writers, an awareness of which particularly facilitates readings of James's later novels.

REVIEWS:
Choice, 16 (1979), 382.

L'Esprit Createur, 20 (1980), 77
Journal of American Studies, 14 (1980), 327.
Wegelin, Chistof. American Literature, 52 (1980), 136-37.

197. Graham, [George] Kenneth. Henry James: The Drama of Fulfillment: An Approach to the Novels. Oxford: Clarendon, 1975.

Graham appraoches individual works by James and to avoid generalities made on the basis of the study of these works. He focuses on Madames de Mauves, Daisy Miller, Roderick Hudson, The Aspern Papers, The Tragic Muse, The Spoils of Poynton, and The Wings of the Dove. Graham does examine the characters in these works and the implicit consciousness in the novels.

REVIEWS:
Bradbrook, F. W. Notes & Queries, 23 (1976), 313.
Choice, 12 (1976), 1444.
Cox, C. B. Sewanee Review, 85 (1977), 351-60.
Holland, Laurence B. Nineteenth-Century Fiction, 31 (1976), 105-08.
McLean, Robert C. Modern Fiction Studies, 22 (1976-77), 610-14.
Mull, Donald L. Journal of English and Germanic Philology, 76 (1977), 274-76.
Owen, E. English, 25 (1976), 68.
Stafford, William T. American Literature, 48 (1976), 88-89.
Tintner, Adeline R. Studies in the Novel, 9 (1977), 73-94.
Weinstein, P. M. English Language Notes, 14 (1977), 221.

198. Grandel, Hartmut. Henry James in der Deutschen Literaturkritik. Die zeitgenössische Rezeption von 1875 bis 1916. Berne: Herbert Lang, 1975.

199. Hovanec, Evelyn A. Henry James and Germany. Amsterdam: Rodopi, 1979.

Hovanec acknowledges the importance of the European influence on James's work and focuses on James's views on Germany. She looks at his travel in Germany from schooldays onward and says that his early impressions held throughout his life. Germany does not feature prominently in his fiction but a respect for the German mind and people is evident, yet he considered them "grotesque" in their aggressiveness and lack of polish and grace.

REVIEWS:
Choice, 16 (1979), 832.
Gargano, James W. Modern Fiction Studies, 25 (1980), 730-33.

200. Jones, Granville H. Henry James's Psychology of Experience: Innocence, Responsibility, and Renunciation in the Fiction of Henry James. The Hague: Mouton, 1975.

Jones, in his systematic study of James's fiction, finds innocence and innocents to pervade the works. He finds innocence in James to be absence, negation, a thing to be recognized but not defined. Innocence has many faces and can include children, young adults, the middle-aged, and the elderly. Jones, in view of this, sees innocence is at odds with responsibility, the end result is renunciation.

REVIEWS:
Choice, 12 (1975), 1166.
Holland, Laurence B. Nineteenth-Century Fiction, 31 (1976), 105-08.
Kirschke James J. Journal of Modern Literature, 5 (1976), 726-30.
McLean, Robert C. Modern Fiction Studies, 22 (1976-77), 610-14.

201. Kappeler, Susanne. Writing and Reading in Henry James. New York: Columbia University Press, 1980.

Kappeler attempts to unite literary theory and practical criticism in her study of James. In the course of the book she brings in theory of folklore and its relevance to her study and examines narrative linguistics, society, imagination, the observer. She also pays attention to James as critic and other critics on James.

REVIEWS:
British Book News, May 1981, p. 305.
Choice, 18 (1981), 1261.
Flint, K. English, 30 (1981), 302-08.
Rowe, John Carlos. Henry James Review, 3 (1981), 67-69.
Wilson, A. N. Times Literary Supplement, 6 February 1981, p. 142.

202. Kirschke, James J. Henry James and Impressionism. Troy, NY: Whitson, 1981.

Kirschke conducts a systematic examination of Impressionism (visual and literary) and its effects on James. James's affinity for Impressionism in the visual arts is evident in the influence of the French. The influence of literary Impressionists can be seen in the importance of such writers as Flaubert, Maupassant, Walter Pater, Stephen Crane, and others. All of this played a part in shaping James's artistic sensibilities and enabled him to add depth and breadth to the Impressionistic novel.

REVIEWS:
Choice, 19 (1982), 626.

203. Laitinen, Tuomo. Aspects of Henry James's Style. Helsinki: Suomalainen Tiedeakatemia, 1975.

Laitinen turns particular attention to the following rhetorical figures: exclamation, rhetorical question, emphasis, and hyperbole. He maintains the these devices serve definite functions in James's fiction. He also makes graphic studies of the frequency of use of these devices in The Portrait of a Lady, The Aspern Papers, The Spoils of Poynton, and The Ambassadors.

204. Lee, Brian. The Novels of Henry James: A Study in Culture and Consciousness. New York: St. Martin's, 1979.

Lee attempts to discuss the majority of James's work in one volume. He devotes space and time to discussion of individual novels, with The Ambassadors as the recipient of more attention than any other single work. Lee begins with James as American and progresses to illustrate the changes undergone by James and by America from the 1870s to the twentieth century.

REVIEWS:
Choice, 16 (1979), 530.
Gargano, James W. Modern Fiction Studies, 25 (1980), 730-33.
Jones, Vivien. Review of English Studies, 30 (1979), 366-67.
Lee, H. English, 28 (1979), 83.
Lodge, David, New Statesman, 28 July 1978, p. 125.
Walter, James. Henry James Review, 1 (1980), 198-200.

205. Leeming, Glenda. Who's Who in Henry James. New York: Taplinger, 1976.

Leeming offers an alphabetical listing of the nearly 600 characters that appear in James's novels and longer novellas. A description accompanies each character along with an account of the character's significance in the work. Leeming also adds an appendix that consists of listings of characters by book.

REVIEWS;
ARBA, 8 (1977), 586.
Kirby, David. Library Journal, 101 (1976), 1616.
Lukens, R. RQ, 16 (1977), 258.
Times Literary Supplement, 8 October 1976, p. 1273.

206. Long, Robert Emmet. The Great Succession: Henry James and the Legacy of Hawthorne. Pittsburgh: university of Pittsburgh Press, 1979.

Long examines Hawthorne's influence on James throughout the early part of the latter's career. The influence is particularly evident in James's fiction prior to 1875, a period Long calls James's "apprenticeship." Long views later works by James in terms of Hawthorne's influence, be it overt or subtle, and in terms of James's thoughts on Hawthorne. Works studied include The Europeans, Daisy Miller, Washington Square, Hawthorne, The Portrait of a Lady, and The Bostonians.

REVIEWS:
Booklist, 1 October 1979, p. 210.
Choice, 17 (1980), 673.
Eakin, Paul John. American Literature, 53 (1980), 153-54.
Journal of American Studies, 15 (1981), 255.
McCarthy, Paul. Henry James Review, 3 (1981), 70-71.
Schneider, Daniel J. Modern Fiction Studies, 26 (1980), 646-52.
Terrie, H. L., Jr. Sewanee Review, 88 (1980), 623.
Times Literary Supplement, 8 May 1981, p. 523.
Winchell, Mark Royden. Southern Humanities Review, 15 (1981), 367-69.

207. McColgan, Kristin Pruitt. Henry James 1917-1959: A Reference Guide. Boston: G. K. Hall, 1979.

McColgan presents an annotated bibliography of James criticism from 1917 to 1959. For each year she lists entries under the categories of books (which also includes dissertations) and shorter writings.

REVIEWS:
Cain, William E. Henry James Review, 2 (1980), 73-75.
Choice, 16 (1979), 1288.
Stafford, William T. Analytical & Enumerative Bibliography, 4 (1980), 140-45.

208. Mackenzie, Manfred. Communities of Honor and Love in Henry James. Cambridge, MA: Harvard University Press, 1976.

Mackenzie begins by studying the structure of James's social imagination and determines that society is secret in James's works (regardless if the work has an American theme or an international one). From society Mackenzie moves to psychology in a study of characters. Though the secrecy of society can produce shame in individuals through exposure, the characters still engage in a quest for identity. Mackenzie the examines the presence and effect of love on individuals and their quests.

REVIEWS:
Choice, 13 (1976), 982.
Comley, Nancy. Novel: A Forum on Fiction, 10 (1976), 87-91.
Cox, C. B. Sewanee Review, 85 (1977), 351-60.
Holman, C. Hugh. American Literature, 48 (1977), 602-03.
Kirby, David. Library Journal, 1 June 1976, p. 1288.
Poole, Adrian. Times Literary Supplement, 8 October 1976, p. 1288.
Veeder, William. Modern Fiction Studies, 23 (1977), 258-61.
Yale Review, 66 (October 1976), VI-VIII.

209. Nettels, Elsa. James and Conrad. Athens, GA: University of Georgia Press, 1977.

Nettels studies the relationship between James and Conrad to determine the influence of one on the other. Both writers recognized their committment to the art of fiction. Also, the younger Conrad may have been helped psychologically by James's encouragement. While they both accepted some of the conventions of the nineteenth-century novel, they departed from conventions in the depiction of the perceptions of reflective characters. In this they broke ground for modern fiction.

REVIEWS:
Banta, Martha. American Literature, 49 (1978), 660-61.
Bradbury, Nicola. Times Literary Supplement, 27 May 1977, p. 652.
Choice, 14 (1978), 1498.
Cox, C. B. Sewanee Review, 85 (1977), 351-60.
Kirby, David. Library Journal, 15 June 1977, p. 1383.
McDowell, Frederick P. W. Modern Fiction Studies, 23 (1977-78), 620-28.
Rawson, C. J. Modern Language Review, 74 (1979), 928.
Young, Vernon. Hudson Review, 30 (1977), 475-76.

210. Nierlich, Edmund. Kuriose Wirklichkeit in den Romanen von Henry James: Ein methodischer Beitrag zur Werkanalyse in der Literaturwissenschaft. Bonn: Bouvier, 1973.

211. Norrman, Ralf. The Insecure World of Henry James's Fiction: Intensity and Ambiguity. New York: St. Martin's, 1981.

212. Norrman, Ralf. Techniques of Ambiguity in the Fiction of Henry James: With Special Reference to In the Cage and The Turn of the Screw. Abo: Abo Akademi, 1977.

Norrman studies ambiguity in James from the standpoint of literary criticism, with some attention paid to linguistic aspects. His approach focuses on the differences between vagueness and ambiguity and, in complex ambiguity, the balance and compatibility of alternatives. He examines the ambiguity-creating devices of incomplete reversal, blanks, code and symbol and ambiguity, and misunderstandings. Finally, Norrman looks at ambiguity in In the Cage and The Turn of Screw.

REVIEWS:
Gard, Roger. Notes & Queries, 25 (1978), 375.
Heston, L. Quarterly Journal of Speech, 65 (1979), 341.
Tuttleton, James W. Modern Language Review, 76 (1981), 938-39.
Wegelin, Christof. Modern Fiction Studies, 24 (1978), 261-63.

213. Perosa, Sergio. Henry James and the Experimental Novel. Charlottesville, VA: University of Virginia Press, 1978.

Perosa examines experimental aspects of James's novels from his middle period, particularly the five novels written after his dramatic period. These novels depend upon James's theatrical experience. Also, this experimentation had an effect on theme and presentation of the fiction of his major phase. Perosa also looks at the experimentation in James's two unfinished novels, The Sense of the Past and The Ivory Tower.

REVIEWS:
Choice, 15 (1979), 1519.
Cooley, Thomas. American Literature, 51 (1979), 430-31.
Fogel, Daniel Mark. Modern Fiction Studies, 25 (1979), 315-20.
Virginia Quarterly Review, 55 (1979), R48.
Warren, Austin. Henry James Review, 1 (1979), 107-10.

214. Peterson, Dale E. The Element Vision: Poetic Realism in Turgenev and James. Port Washington, NY: Kennikat, 1975.

Peterson admits that his study is one of the influence of Turgenev on James, particularly in the latter's early writings. He maintains that both writers present a kind of realism based on perception rather than on circumstance. This "poetic realism," as Peterson calls it, has as a basis the assumption that truth is "the revealed truth of perception."

REVIEWS:
Choice, 13 (1976), 360.
Holland, Laurence B. Nineteenth-Century Fiction, 32 (1977), 247-52.

Kirby, D. K. Library Journal, 1 April 1976, p. 902.
Kirschke, James J. Journal of Modern Literature, 5 (1976), 726-30.
Mills, Judith M. Slavic and East European Journal, 20 (1976), 471-72.
Tintner, Adeline R. Studies in the Novel, 9 (1977), 93-94.
Veeder, William. Modern Fiction Studies, 23 (1977), 258-61.

215. Purdy, Strother B. The Hole in the Fabric: Silence, Contemporary Literature and Henry James. Pittsburgh: University of Pittsburgh Press, 1977.

Purdy posits that James has a closer relationship to contemporary writers than does any writer of the past. He states that James "marked out several areas within the novel that have now become central to it." He finds James to be concerned with such things as science fiction, relative time, the erotic, and nothingness and he relates his fiction to that of Beckett, Barth, Nabokov, Vonnegut, Grass, Borges, Robbe-Grillet, and others.

REVIEWS:
Anderson, Quentin. American Literature, 50 (1978), 124-26.
Banta, Martha. Nineteenth-Century Fiction, 33 (1978), 243-48.
Choice, 14 (1977), 1054.
Kirby, David. America, 2-9 July 1977, p. 18.
Kirby, David. Library Journal, 15 December 1976, p. 2580.
Marotta, Kenny. English Language Notes, 16 (1978), 65-69.
Wegelin, Christof. Modern Fiction Studies, 24 (1978), 261-63.
Young, V. Hudson Review, 30 (1977), 471.

216. Ricks, Beatrice. Henry James: A Bibliography of Secondary Works. Metuchen, NJ: Scarecrow, 1975.

Ricks has compiled a bibliography (not annotated) of works on James, consisting of over 4,600 items. It is divided into sections dealing with biography, individual writings by James, general criticism, and bibliography. An author and a subject index are also included.

REVIEWS:
ARBA, 7 (1976), 598.
Choice, 13 (1976), 206.
Kirby, David. Library Journal, 15 February 1976, p. 604.
Kirschke, James J. Journal of Modern Literature, 5 (1976), 730.
Monteiro, George. PBSA, 70 (1976), 552.
W. T. S. Modern Fiction Studies, 22 (1976-77), 629-31.
Wilson Library Bulletin, 50 (1976), 552.

217. Rimmon, Shlomith. The Concept of Ambiguity--The Example of James. Chicago: University of Chicago Press, 1977.

Rimmon begins her study with a theory of narrative and verbal ambiguity to define ambiguity and to describe ways in which ambiguity operates in narrative structure. She then applies her definitions and critical method to "The Lesson of the Master," "The Figure in the Carpet," The Turn of the Screw, and The Sacred Fount. Rimmon applies the methodologies of logic, linguistics, Formalism, and Structuralism to her study of ambiguity in James.

REVIEWS:
Banta, Martha. American Literature. 50 (1978), 486-87.
Choice, 15 (1978), 548.
Schneider, Daniel J. American Literary Realism, 1870-1910, 11 (1978), 322.
Schobert, Timothy. Library Journal, 1 October, 1977, p. 2066.
Tintner, Adeline R. Modern Fiction Studies, 24 (1978-79), 630-31.
Tintner, Adeline R. Studies in the Novel, 11 (1979), 106-15.

218. Rowe, John Carlos. Henry Adams and Henry James: The Emergence of a Modern Consciousness. Ithaca, NY: Cornell University Press, 1976.

Rowe studies Adams and James as representatives of a period of change in American literature. The modern thought embraced by the writers led to modern literature. Adams attempted to organize historical thought and to give coherence to history and aesthetics. James, in his aesthetic of fiction, combined art and historical order to produce a creative imagination.

REVIEWS:
Choice, 13 (1976), 505.
Christian Century, 3 March 1976, p. 203.
Cohen, Lester H. Modern Fiction Studies, 23 (1977), 264-65.
Comley, Nancy. Novel: A Forum on Fiction, 10 (1976), 87-91.
Cooley, Thomas. American Literature, 49)1977), 464-65.
Cox, C. B. Sewanee Review, 85 (1977), 351-60.
Crowley, John W. New England Quarterly, 50 (1977), 184-85.
Doyle, P. A. Best Sellers, 36 (May 1976), 53.
Hoople, Robin. Mosaic, 11, 1 (1977), 165-71.
Kirby, David. Library Journal, 1 February 1976, p. 530.

Michaels, Walter. Georgia Review, 31 (1977), 258-64.
Minter, David. Nineteenth-Century Fiction, 31 (1977), 471-74.
Pickens, D. K. American Quarterly, 33 (1981), 459.
Poole, Adrian. Times Literary Supplement, 8 October 1976, p. 1272.
Stafford, William T. Journal of English and Germanic Philology, 76 (1977), 276-78.
Tintner, Adeline R. Studies in the Novel, 9 (1977), 73-94.
Vandersee, C. English Language Notes, 14 (1977), 308.

219. Schneider, Daniel J. The Crystal Cage: Adventures of the Imagination in the Fiction of Henry James. Lawrence, KS: Regents Press of Kansas, 1978.

Scneider attempts to study the unity of James's imagery and symbolism, to find a system of images that articulate a single vision. He sees a key in "The Figure in the Carpet" to understanding the imagery. He acknowledges that it is not the key, but that it is helpful when examining the fiction chronologically. This study is limited by necessity to major categories of images and their recirrence.

REVIEWS:
Booklist, 1 November 1978, p. 450.
Choice, 15 (1978), 1373.
Fogel, Daniel Mark. Modern Fiction Studies, 25 (1979), 315-20.
Grenander, M. E. American Literature, 51, (1979), 122-24.
Kelly, Richard J. Library Journal, 103 (1978), 1513.
Kirby, David. Henry James Review, 1 (1979), 102-04.
Tintner, Adeline R. Studies in the Novel, 11 (1979), 106-15.

220. Scura, Dorothy McInnis. Henry James 1960-1974: A Reference Guide. Boston: G. K. Hall, 1979.

Scura's work updates McColgan's bibliography (see no. 207). The format is also very similar to McColgan's, but a separate category has been created to handle the increased number of dissertations.

REVIEWS:
Cain, William E. Henry James Review, 2 (1980), 73-75.
Choice, 16 (1979), 1288.
Stafford, William T. Analytical & Enumaerative Bibliography, 4 (1980), 140-45.

221. Sharma, J. N. The International Fiction of Henry James. New Delhi: Macmillan, 1979.

Sharma traces the development of the international theme in James's novels, including the prompting and persistence of the theme throughout James's life. Sharma contends that, in the course of James's writing career, the international theme, while still present, became a forum used to deal with larger themes. There remained an underlying purpose of the attempt to define the American identity.

REVIEWS:
American Literature, 52 (1980), 517.
Choice, 17 (1980), 391.
Middleton, David. Henry James Review, 1 (1980), 269-71.
Schneider, Daniel J. Modern Fiction Studies, 26 (1980), 646-52.

222. Sicker, Philip. Love and the Quest for Identity in the Fiction of Henry James. Princeton, NJ: Princeton University Press, 1979.

Sicker takes a chronological approach to the study of love in James's fiction. He maintains that love as a quest for identity is a result of James's belief in the subjectivity of experience. He notes that the difficulties James faced in the years 1895-1901 led to a solipsistic view during that time. Sicker finally points out that James's vision and depiction of love evolved throughout his career but that obstacles to the full discovery of identity continued to exist.

REVIEWS:
Bellringer, A. W. Modern Language Review, 77 (1982), 429.
Choice, 18 (1980), 96.
Eakin, Paul John. American Literature, 53 (1981), 153-54.
Jacobson, Marcia. Journal of English and Germanic Philology, 80 (1981), 272-73.
Schneider, Daniel J. Modern Fiction Studies, 26 (1981), 646-52.
Spoliar, Nicholas. Times Literary Supplement, 14 November 1980, p. 1304.
Terrie, H. L., Jr. Sewanee Review, 88 (1980), 623.
Veeder, William. Modern Philology, 79 (1981), 104-09.
Winchell, Mark Royden. Southern Humanities Review, 15 (1981), 367-69.
Wright, Walter F. Henry James Review, 3 (1981), 72-73.

223. Springer, Mary Doyle. A Rhetoric of Literary Character: Some Women of Henry James. Chicago: University of Chicago Press, 1978.

Springer takes rhetoric to mean a study of the committed method of an author for revealing character in literature in the light of its function in the fictional work as a whole. She then attempts to define literary character and examines the literary devices used by James in the development of his rhetoric of character as evidenced in several works, particularly with regard to women.

REVIEWS:
Choice, 16 (1979), 82.
Fogel, Daniel Mark. Modern Fiction Studies, 25 (1979), 315-20.
Long, Robert Emmet. American Literature, 51 (1979), 124-25.
Sharp, Sister Corona. Henry James Review, 1 (1979), 104-07.
Tintner, Adeline R. Studies in the Novel, 11 (1979), 106-15.
Virginia Quarterly Review, 55 (1979), R49.

224. Stafford William T. A Name, Title, and Place Index to the Critical Writings of Henry James. Englewood, CO: Microcard Eds., 1975.

Stafford attempts to provide a name, title, and place index to the non-creative writings of James, with the the exception of his letters. He begins with a key to the non-creative writing, corresponding to entries in A Bibliography of Henry James, revised edition, compiled by Edel and Laurence. The entries in the index refer to the key. In the case of authors, such as Trollope or Turgenev, references to individual works are included.

REVIEWS:
ARBA, 7 (1976), 599.
Gale, Robert L. Modern Fiction Studies, 21 (1975-76), 658-59.
Kirschke, James J. Journal of Modern Literature, 5 (1976), 730.
Monteiro, George. PBSA, 70 (1976), 442.

225. Stowell, H. Peter. Literary Impressionism, James and Chekhov. Athens, GA: University of Georgia Press, 1980.

Stowell attempts to define literary impressionism and then to examine it in terms of chekhov and James. He traces impressionism in James from its emergence in The Portrait of a Lady and What Maisie Knew. He then examines The Sacred Fount as a prelude to the major phase and the impressionistic writings of that period. Literary impressionism is more fully developed in The Ambassadors and reaches its culmination in The Golden Bowl. In fact, Stowell maintains it is the impressionistic masterpiece.

REVIEWS:
Armstrong, P. B. Criticism, 22 (1980), 384.
Bellringer, A. W. Modern Language Review, 77 (1982), 429.
Booklist, 1 December 1979, p. 535.
Choice, 18 (1980), 85.
College Literature, 8 (1981), 93.
Flores, Ralph. Library Journal, 1 February 1980, p. 406.
Hay, Eloise Knapp. Journal of English and Germanic Philology, 80 (1981), 603-06.
Kalinalevine, V. Comparative Literature Studies, 19 (1982), 77.
Kennedy, J. Gerald. Henry James Review, 1 (1980), 272-73.
McVay, G. Journal of European Studies, 12 (1982), 72.
Martin, W. R. Germano-Slavico, 3 (1981), 355-57.
Nagel, James. American Literature, 53 (1981), 328-30.
Schneider, Daniel J. Modern Fiction Studies, 26 (1980), 646-52.
Terrie, H. L., Jr. Sewanee Review, 88 (1980), 623.
Western Humanities Review, 36 (1982), 83.
Winchell, Mark Royden. Southern Humanities Review, 15 (1981), 367-69.

226. Styczyńska, Adela. The Art of Henry James's Nouvelle: A Study of Theme and Form. Łódź, Poland: Uniwersytet Łódzki, 1977.

227. Veeder, William R. Henry James--The Lessons of the Master: Popular Fiction and Personal Style in the Nineteenth Century. Chicago: University of Chicago Press, 1975.
Veeder studies the conventions and traditions of fiction in the nineteenth century and how these traditions affected James's style and characters. Since James's career bridged the gap from traditional nineteenth-century fiction to modern fiction, much can be learned from an examination of James. His writing and his life exemplify changes in the role of the artist in society and in the consciousness of the writer. Veeder sees The Portrait of a Lady as the last great Victorian novel even though it in many ways signifies the beginning of modern fiction.

REVIEWS:
Baym, Nina. Journal of English and Germanic Philology, 75 (1976), 465.
Brooks, R. L. Best Sellers, 35 (1976), 348.
Buitenhuis, P. Humanities Association Review, 28 (1977), 368.
Choice, 13 (1976), 74.
Comley, Nancy. Novel: A Forum on Fiction, 10 (1976), 87-91.
Cox, C. B. Sewanee Review, 85 (1977), 351-60.
Heller, T. Arizona Quarterly, 32 (1976), 392.
Keating, Peter. Times Literary Supplement, 28 May 1976, p. 649.
Kirby, David. Library Journal, 15 October 1975, p. 1427.
Kirschke, James J. Journal of Modern Literature, 5 (1976), 726.
McLean, Robert C. Modern Fiction Studies, 22 (1976-77), 610-14.
Michaels, Walter. Georgia Review, 31 (1977), 258-64.
Rinehart, H. Queen's Quarterly, 83 (1976), 683.
Tintner, Adeline R. Studies in the Novel, 9 (1977), 73-94.
Volpe, Edmund L. American Literature, 48 (1976), 392-94.

228. Wagenknecht, Edward. Eve and Henry James: Portraits of Women and Girls in His Fiction. Norman, OK: University of Oklahoma Press, 1978.

Wagenknecht examines a number of female characters he considers particularly interesting. As such his study focuses on various aspects of the characters. In the course of the book he looks at innocence, modernity, destiny, love and honor, and at several types of characters, such as women as victims, women as femme fatales, women as victors, and women as losers.

REVIEWS:
Booklist, 1 November 1978, p. 451.
Choice, 15 (1978), 1375.
Fogel, Daniel Mark. Modern Fiction Studies, 25 (1979), 315-20.
Grenander, M. E. American Literature, 51 (1979), 122-24.
Hewitt, Rosalie. Henry James Review, 1 (1979), 110-12.
Tintner, Adeline R. Studies in the Novel, 11 (1979), 106-15.

229. Wallace, Ronald. Henry James and the Comic Form. Ann Arbor, MI: University of Michigan Press, 1975.

Wallace maintains that the comic elements in James's characters, plots, themes, and style illustrate his relation to the comic tradition of Shakespeare, Cervantes, Moliere, etc. He further states that, while James recognizes society's capability for evil and destruction, he has characters seek power over despair and to realize society's potential for good. It is also noted that the comic elements are not limited to any phase of James's life and writings.

REVIEWS:
Choice, 12 (1976), 1577.
Holland, Laurence B. Nineteenth-Century Fiction, 31 (1976), 105-08.
Kirby, David. Library Journal, 1 December 1975, p. 2251.
Kirschke, James. J. Journal of Modern Literature, 5 (1976), 726.
Levy, Leo B. American Literature, 48 (1976), 87-88.
McLean, Robert C. Modern Fiction Studies, 22 (1976-77), 610-14.
Rinehart, H. Queen's Quarterly, 83 (1976), 683.
Terrie, Henry L., Jr. Sewanee Review, 83 (1975), 695-703.

230. Watanabe, Hisayoshi. Henry James no Gengo: Bungaku no Gengo o sasaeru mono ni tsuite no Shiron. Tokyo: Hokuseido, 1978.

231. Wilson, R. B. J. Henry James's Ultimate Narrative: The Golden Bowl. St. Lucia, Queensland, Australia: University of Queensland Press, 1981.

Wilson maintains that, in The Golden Bowl, James achieves a fusion of form and meaning in the creation of a unified whole. Wilson also chooses the novel for its place in the James canon, coming as it does at the culmination of the major phase. The experimentation of the novel is studied as it simulates poetic figurative language, dramatic scenic art, together with novelistic pace. The key to this creation is James's rhetoric.

REVIEWS:
Choice, 19 (1982), 922.

232. Yeazell, Ruth Bernard. Language and Knowledge in the Late Novels of Henry James. Chicago: University of Chicago Press, 1976.

In concentrating on James's later fiction Yeazell examines various aspects of his use of language. She looks at his syntax in the later fiction, some key metaphors (such as in "The Beast in the Jungle") and their possible origins and uses, James's use of conversation (such as exchanges between Lambert Strether and Maria Gostrey, Merton Densher and Kate Croy, and the Assinghams), and the ending of The Golden Bowl.

REVIEWS:

Bales, K. *Centrum*, 4 (Spring 1976), 50.

Bellringer, A. W. *Modern Language Review*, 74 (1979), 181.

Bradbury, Nicola. *Times Literary Supplement*, 20 May 1977, p. 622.

Buitenhuis, P. *Humanities Association Bulletin*, 28 (1977), 368.

Choice, 13 (1977), 1602.

Cox, C. B. *Sewanee Review*, 85 (1977), 351-60.

Gale, Robert L. *American Literature*, 49 (1977), 128-29.

Kirby, David. *Library Journal*, 15 October 1976, p. 2179.

Tintner, Adeline R. *Studies in the Novel*, 9 (1977), 73-94.

Tompkins, Jane. *Modern Fiction Studies*, 23 (1977), 262-63.

Weinstein, Philip M. *Journal of English and Germanic Philology*, 76 (1977), 577-80.

CHAPTERS AND MATERIALS IN BOOKS

233. Allen, Jeanne. "The Innocents: The Sound of the Turning Screw." In Purdue University Fifth Annual Conference on Film. Ed. Maud Walther. West Lafayette, IN: Department of Foreign Languages and Literatures, Purdue University, 1980, pp. 103-10.

234. Allen, Jeanne Thomas. "Turn of the Screw and The Innocents: Two Types of Ambiguity." In The Classic American Novel and the Movies. Ed. Gerald Peary and Roger Shatzkin. New York: Ungar, 1977, pp. 132-42.

The Film, The Innocents, produces tension by shifting the viewer's attention and sympathy back and forth from the governess to the children. According to Allen, though, the tension does not include the ambiguity of The Turn of the Screw.

235. Auchincloss, Louis. "The Late Jamesing of Early James." In Life, Law, and Letters: Essays and Sketches. New York: Houghton Mifflin, 1979, pp. 91-96.

Auchincloss states that some late revisions of early works are improvements and some are not. Non-dialogue passages were improved by the late style but the personalities of some characters exhibited through dialogue were not.

236. Auerbach, Nina. "Beyond the Self: The Spectacle of History and a New Religion." In Communities of Women: An Idea in Fiction. Cambridge, MA: Harvard University Press, 1978, pp. 115-57.

Auerbach discusses the social and psychological aspects of The Bostonians. She also relates it to James's life, particularly the ambivalence of his youth. She suggests the novel may be something of an anomaly and points out that James did not include it in the New York Edition.

237. Banta, Martha. "About America's 'White Terror': James, Poe, Pynchon, and Others." In Literature and the Occult: Essays in Comparative Literature. Ed. Luanne Frank. Arlington, TX: University of Texas at Arlington Press, 1977, pp. 31-53.

Banta defines the occult in James as "the mystery central to the essential nature--the root meaning--of a person or place that cannot be defined by rational means." She focuses on The Golden Bowl and James's relation to other writers.

238. Beattie, Munro. "Henry James: 'The Voice of Stoicism'." In The Stoic Strain in American Literature: Essays in Honour of Marston LaFrance. Ed. Duane MacMillan. Toronto: University of Toronto Press, 1979, pp. 63-75.

Beattie examines the hardships of James's life, such as the commercial failure of the New York Edition, and how these affected his life, thought, and fiction. He sees in James's characters and in James himself a transcendent stoicism.

239. Berryman, John. "The World of Henry James." In The Freedom of the Poet. New York: Farrar, Straus & Giroux, 1976, pp. 161-67.

Berryman focuses on James's later fiction, particularly the novels and tales he revised for the New York Edition. Berryman also offers a critical appraisal of F. O. Matthiessen's Henry James: The Major Phase.

240. Bersani, Leo. "The Jamesian Lie." In A Future for Astyanax: Character and Desire in Literature. Boston: Little, Brown, 1976, pp. 128-55.

Bersani claims that James's realism lies in the social details and psychological nuances he fills his fiction with. This is at odds with a fantasy of happiness. This tension, Bersani says, is James's "effort to coerce society into becoming an arena for the performance of the passionate fictions of James's heroes."

241. Blake, Nancy. "Hystérie, langue et violence: Les Ailes de la colombe." In Discours de la violence dans la culture américaine. Ed. Régis Durand. Lille: Publications de l'Universite de Lille III, 1979, pp. 37-47.

242. Blasing, Mutlu Konuk. "The Story of the Stories: Henry James's Prefaces as Autobiography." In Approaches to Victorian Autobiography. Ed. George P. Landow. Athens, OH: Ohio University Press, 1979, pp. 311-32.

Blasing sees the Prefaces as autobiographical inasmuch as they reflect his reassessment of his career and his life. Blasing offers that the writing of the Prefaces involved a process of self-consciousness and "re-vision" and so discovery.

243. Briggs, Julia. "Not Without but Within: The Psychological Ghost Story." In Night Visitors: The Rise and Fall of the English Ghost Story. London: Faber & Faber, 1977, pp. 142-64.

In this chapter Briggs focuses her attention on The Turn of the Screw. She notes that the ghosts are central figures and that they are evil. The ambiguity, particularly the question of the existence of the ghosts, makes the book subjective and thus psychologically compelling.

244. Briggs, Julia. "A Sense of the Past: Henry James and Vernon Lee." In Night Visitors: The Rise and Fall of the English Ghost Story. London: Faber & Faber, 1977, pp. 111-23.

Briggs points out that James's debt to Hawthorne is evident in his fiction as is the presence of the romantic. She provides an overview of the supernatural in James's novels and tales.

245. Brooks, Peter. "Henry James and the Melodrama of Consciousness." In The Melodramatic Imagination: Balzac, Henry James, Melodrama, and the Mode of Excess. New Haven: Yale University, 1976, pp. 153-97.

Brooks maintains that James's melodrama (which encompasses his most basic moral concerns, including fear and evil) becomes embodied in consciousness. Using this as a basis of study Brooks examines The Wings of the Dove as a representative of James's later fiction.

246. Bovi-Guerra, Pedro. "Henry James y Carlos Fuentes: Dos cuentos, paralelos, y bifurcaciones." In Estudios de historia, literatura y arte hispánicos ofrecidos a Rodrigo A. Molina. Ed. Wayne H. Finke. Madrid: Insula, 1977, pp. 71-85.

247. Brooke-Rose, Christine. "The Surface Structures in The Turn of the Screw." In A Rhetoric of the Unreal: Studies in Narrative and Structure, Especially the Fantastic. Cambridge: Cambridge University Press, 1981, pp. 188-229.
Reprinted from PTL: A Journal for Descriptive Poetics and Theory, 2 (1977), 517-62. See no. 423.

248. Brooke-Rose, Christine. "The Turn of the Screw and Its Critics: An Essay in Non-Methodology." In A Rhetoric of the Unreal: Studies in Narrative and Structure, Especially the Fantastic. Cambridge: Cambridge University Press, 1981, pp. 128-57.
Reprinted from PTL: A Journal for Descriptive Poetics and Theory, 1 (1976), 265-94. See no. 421.

249. Brooke-Rose, Christine. "The Turn of the Screw: Mirror Structures as Basic Structures." In A Rhetoric of the Unreal: Studies in Narrative and Structure, Especially the Fantastic. Cambridge: Cambridge University Press, 1981, pp. 158-87.
Reprinted from PTL: A Journal for Descriptive Poetics and Theory, 1 (1976), 513-46. See no. 422.

250. Carlson, Jerry W. "Washington Square and The Heiress: Comparing Artistic Forms." In The Classic American Novel and the Movies. Ed. Gerald Peary and Roger Shatzkin. New York: Ungar, 1977, pp. 95-104.
Carlson compares Washington Square with the film, The Heiress, the screenplay of which by Ruth and Augustus Goetz was taken from the play, not from the book. The film sacrifices complexity in the process of adaptation.

251. Caserio, Robert L. "The Story in It: James." In Plot, Story, and the Novel: From Dickens and Poe to the Modern Period. Princeton, NJ: Princeton University Press, 1979, pp. 198-231.
Caserio studies the differences in form, style, and theme between James's earlier writing and his career from The Awkward Age on. Caserio states that James's change of citizenship is indicative of the change in his fiction and his distancing from America that he knew in his youth.

252. Churchill, Kenneth. "The American Novelists in Italy." In Italy and English Literature, 1764-1930. New York: Barnes & Noble, 1980, pp. 147-61.
Churchill, in looking at James's fictional treatment of Italy, determines that it provided a stimulus for James. His view of Italy was more sophisticated than those who had gone before in literature in English.

253. Cockshut, A. O. J. "The Lesbian Theme." In Man and Woman: A Study of Love and the Novel, 1740-1940. New York: Oxford University Press, 1978, pp. 186-208.

Cockshut discusses the lesbian theme in The Bostonians. James manages to depict the confusion and incomplete understanding experienced by the characters. Olive achieves her form of dignity through sexual inversion.

254. Coleman, Basil. "Staging First Productions, 2." In The Operas of Benjamin Britten. Ed. David Herbert. New York: Columbia University Press, 1979, pp. 34-43.

Coleman discusses the staging of Britten's opera, The Turn of the Screw. Design and casting (particularly the children) were especially challenging. The performers must be dependent upon one another because the music and drama are so integrated.

255. Colmer, John. "Political Action and the Crisis of Conscience." In Coleridge to Catch-22: Images of Society. New York: St. Martin's, 1978, pp. 91-104.

Colmer discusses the political aspects of The Princess Casamassima and their effects on the conscience and consciousness of Hyacinth Robinson. Hyacinth's suicide may be due to his loss of faith in the political cause and in the people around him and to determinism.

256. Colmer, John. "Sex, the Family, and the New Women." In Coleridge to Catch-22: Images of Society. New York: St. Martin's, 1978, pp. 105-21.

Colmer states that The Bostonians deals with the women's movement of the 1880s, but centers thematically on the conflict between idealism and corruptive influences. He further states that the tension can have moral and social implications that could be felt today.

257. Cooley, Thomas. "A Sporting Life: Henry James." In Educated Lives: The Rise of Modern Autobiography. Columbus, OH: Ohio State University Press, 1976, pp. 101-24.

Cooley looks at James's autobiographical writings, particularly with an eye to the difficulty James had with delving into his past. The journey into the past was a cause of some "psychic distress" for James, who thought the journey a hazardous one.

258. Dawson, Jan. "An Interview with Peter Bogdanovich." In The Classic American Novel and the Movies. Ed. Gerald Peary and Roger Shat zkin. New York: Ungar, 1977, pp. 83-89.

Bogdanovich discusses his approach to Daisy Miller, the changes he made and the points he emphasized. Reprinted from Sight and Sound, 43 (1973-74), 14-15.

259. Deakin, Motley F. "The Real and Fictive Quest of Henry James." In Makers of the Twentieth-Century Novel. Ed. Henry Raphael Garrin. Lewisburg, PA: Bucknell University Press, 1977, pp. 179-91.
Deakin concentrates on the quest as a means used by James ro express an aspect of experience. Deakin finds it particularly evident in James's travel sketches and in Roderick Hudson, The American, and The Wings of the Dove. James's use of the quest gives the reader an idea of what James views as important.

260. Dennis, Larry R. "Spectres and Spectators in The Turn of the Screw and The Innocents." In Purdue University Fifth Annual Conference on Film. Ed. Maud Walther. West Lafayette, IN: Department of Foreign Languages and Literatures, Purdue University, 1980, pp. 96-102.

261. Dolan, Paul J. "James: The Aesthetics of Politics." In Of War and War's Alarms: Fiction and Politics in the Modern World. New York: Free Press, 1976, pp. 70-95.
Dolan studies the political aspects of The Princess Casamassima and how they relate to emotional and aesthetic aspects. In James it is evident that political events result from the decisions of individuals. Thus, the tale of the aristocracy and the proletariat depends upon the consciousness of the characters.

262. Donaldson, Scott and Ann Massa. "The New World and the Old World." In American Literature: Nineteenth and Early Twentieth Centuries. New York: Barnes & Noble, 1978, pp. 9-46.
Donaldson and Massa approach James as expatriate, as one who has removed himself so that he may observe from a distance. They maintain that exposure to Europe is beneficial to such as Lambert Strether and Christopher Newman.

263. Donoghue, Denis. "The American Style of Failure." In The Sovereign Ghost: Studies in Imagination. Berkeley: University of California Press, 1976, pp. 103-27.
Donoghue examines, particularly in James, the importance of a recognition of failure in the shaping of American literature. In James there is the sense that failure is inevitable, no matter how much time one is given, and that even if one achieves success one may not be able to accept its conditions. Donoghue states that this principle may be a precept of American literature.

264. Dryden, Edgar A. "The Image in the Mirror: The Double Economy of James's Portrait." In Money Talks: Language and Lucre in American Fiction. Ed. Roy R. Male. Norman, OK: University of Oklahoma Press, 1980, pp. 31-49.

Dryden states that James's purpose in The Portrait of a Lady is to make compatible the object of the novel, to represent life, and the effect of the novel, to entertain. This purpose is also to resolve the conflict between the act of writing and the act of reading.

265. Eakin, Paul John. "Henry James and the New England Consciousness: Roderick Hudson, The Europeans, Hawthorne." In The New England Girl: Cultural Ideals in Hawthorne, Stowe, Howells, and James. Athens, GA: University of Georgia Press, 1976, pp. 131-67.

Eakin focuses on James's early writings of the 1870s and 1880s to examine the New England of James. The moral consciousness depicted by James is viewed in the contexts of Roderick Hudson, The Europeans, and Hawthorne.

266. Eakin, Paul John. "New England in Extremis: The Bostonians." In The New England Girl: Cultural Ideal in Hawthorne, Stowe, Howells, and James. Athens, GA: University of Georgia Press, 1976, pp. 195-217.

Eakin offers an explanation of The Bostonians, centering his attention on the female characters. He particularly notes that the novel marks, for James, an end of the innocent American girl and of transcendentalist idealism.

267. Eakin, Paul John. "The Tragedy of Self-Culture: The Portrait of a Lady." In The New England Girl: Cultural Ideals in Hawthorne, Stowe, Howells, and James. Athens, GA: University of Georgia Press, 1976, pp. 168-94.

Eakin states that The Portrait of a Lady " marks a turning point in James's exploration of the redemptive possibilities of American courtship. Isabel Archer fails to find self-expression in travel or in domestic life, so she chooses isolation.

268. Edel, Leon, intoduction. English Hours. By Henry James. Oxford: Oxford University Press, 1981.

Reprinted in Henry James Review, 2 (1981), 167-71. See no. 480.

269. Edel, Leon, introduction. The Europeans. By Henry James. New York: Howard Fertig, 1979.

Edel includes a brief history of the original composition of The Europeans, written at the invitation of William Dean Howells. He also explains the genesis of the facsimile edition of the manuscript, noting the limited possibilities and the method of reproduction.

270. Edel, Leon. "Portrait of the Artist as an Old Man." In Aging, Death, and the Completion of Being. Ed. David D. Van Tassel. Philadelphia: University of Pennsylvania Press, 1979, pp. 193-214.

Edel looks at the aging Henry James and his work. The writing of the later period signified in part a release from the emotions and memories of his youth. The release brought fulfillment for James through his work.

271. Falk, Robert. "Henry James's The American as a Centennial Novel." In Essays in Honor of Russel B. Nye. Ed. Joseph Waldmeir. East Lansing, MI: Michigan State University Press, 1978, pp. 31-41.

Falk looks at the character of Christopher Newman as an amalgamation of many traits along with some autobiographical elements. The first two-thirds of the book present Newman as an idealized but authentic American of 1876.

272. Fergusson, Francis. "James's Dramatic Form." In Literary Landmarks: Essays on the Theory and Practice of Literature. Rutherford, NJ: Rutgers University Press, 1975, pp. 48-61.

Fergusson notes that James's drama was thwarted by the state of British theater at the time he wrote his plays. Fergusson then applies James's theory of writing to his execution of drama.

273. Fetterly, Judith. "The Bostonians: Henry James's Eternal Triangle." In The Resisting Reader: A Feminist Approach to American Fiction. Bloomington, IN: Indiana University Press, 1978, pp. 101-53.

Fetterly states that, while James adopts a type of sexism by romanticizing the suffering he presents in The Bostonians, he presents a glimmering of a breakthrough in the character of Olive Chancellor. She embodies the central elements of radical feminism, primarily freedom from the need for men.

274. Fryer, Judith. "The American Princess: Daisy Miller." In The Faces of Eve: Women in the Nineteenth Century American Novel. New York: Oxford University Press, 1976, pp. 97-101.

Daisy Miller is a new character in American fiction. She is self-reliant, even audacious, and the other characters do not quite know what to make of her.

275. Fryer, Judith. "The American Princess: Isabel Archer." In The Faces of Eve: Women in the Nineteenth Century American Novel. New York: Oxford University Press, 1976, pp. 126-42.

Fryer sees Isabel Archer as James's most fully developed American Princess. Her complexity lies in the ways she responds to her experiences and the changes that result from her responses.

276. Fryer, Judith. "The American Princess: Maggie Verver." In The Faces of Eve: Women in the Nineteenth Century American Novel. New York: Oxford University Press, 1976, pp. 112-26.

Fryer notes that the theme of The Golden Bowl is essentially Maggie Verver's initiation. At the end of the novel Maggie becomes aware of the price she has paid for her victory and, through this, learns compassion.

277. Fryer, Judith. "The American Princess: Milly Theale." In The Faces of Eve: Women in teh Nineteenth Century American Novel. New York: Oxford University Press, 1976, pp. 101-12.

Fryer points out that Milly is more in the tradition of the "good heroine." She is likened to a dove throughout the novel. Fryer states that her character is an idealization of his late cousin, Minny Temple.

278. Fryer, Judith. "The Great Mother: The Archetype: Olive Chancellor." In The Faces of Eve: Women in the Nineteenth Century American Novel. New York: Oxford University Press, 1976, pp. 143-52.

Fryer sees a parallel between Olive Chancellor and Mother Gothel of "Rapunzel." Her characteristics appear in most of James's later mother surrogates.

279. Fryer, Judith. "The Great Mother: The Mother-Surrogates." In The Faces of Eve: Women in the Nineteenth Century American Novel. New York: Oxford University Press, 1976, pp. 153-73.

Fryer discusses the characters of the governess and Mrs. Grose in The Turn of the Screw, Mrs. Bread of The American, and Mrs. Wix of What Maisie Knew.

280. Fryer, Judith. "The Great Mother: The Neglectors." In The Faces of Eve: Women in the Nineteenth Century American Novel. New York: Oxford University Press, 1976, pp. 173-82.

In this section Fryer examines the characters of Ida Farange in What Maisie Knew, Mrs. Moreen in "The Pupil," and Mrs. Touchett in The Portrait of a Lady.

281. Fryer, Judith. The Great Mother: The Real Witchbitches." In The Faces of Eve: Women in the Nineteenth Century American Novel. New York: Oxford University Press, 1976, pp. 182-202.

Some of the Jamesian women are cold-blooded in their destruction of others. Examples are Rose Armiger in The Other House, Madame de Bellegarde in The American, and Serena Merle in The Portrait of a Lady.

282. Fryer, Judith. "The New Woman: The Unnatural Lady Reformers of Boston." In The Faces of Eve: Women in the Nineteenth Century American Novel. New York: Oxford University Press, 1976, pp. 220-34.

In this section Fryer turns to The Bostonians to look at the lady reformer in Boston. In examining the role of the reformer she pays special attention to Olive Chancellor, Miss Birdseye, Mrs. Farrinder, and Dr. Prance.

283. Geary, Edward A. "Morality and Fiction: The Example of Henry James." In "The Need Beyond Reason" and Other Essays: College of Humanities Centennial Lectures 1975-76. Provo, UT: Brigham Young University Press, 1976, pp. 105-15.

Geary states that, for James, the creation of art was a moral act and a reflection of the artist's moral vision. Thus, when the author accepts his moral responsibility, a like responsibility is imposed upon the reader.

284. Gillie, Christopher. "The Early Twentieth-Century Novel: James, Wells, and Conrad." In Movements in English Literature, 1900-1940. Cambridge: Cambridge University Press, 1975, pp. 24-46.

Gillie focuses his attention on The Ambassadors. He maintains that, while it is not as fine as The Portrait of a Lady, it represents a change in narrative technique, that is, James's identification with Strether.

285. Gilmore, Michael T. "Henry James: The Golden Bowl." In The Middle Way: Puritanism and Ideology in American Romantic Fiction. New Brunswick, NJ: Rutgers University Press, 1977, pp. 195-208.

Gilmore examines Puritanism in The Golden Bowl,

particularly the Puritan strain that James noted in Hawthorne. Gilmore likens Maggie to Christ and sees the golden bowl as the loss of paradise.

286. Glasser, William. "The Turn of the Screw." In Essays in Honour of Erwin Stürzl on His Sixtieth Birthday. Ed. James Hogg. Salzburg: Inst. fur Englische Aprache & Literatur, Universitat Salzburg, 1980, Vol. 1, pp. 212-31.

In discussing the controversy surrounding the "reality" of the ghosts in The Turn of the Screw, Glasser states that the fact that controversy exists indicates James's success in presenting the governess' distorted vision and its effects on her and on the reader.

287. Green, André. "The Double and the Absent." In Psychoanalysis, Creativity, and Literature: A French-American Inquiry. Ed. Alan Roland. New York: Columbia University Press, 1978, pp. 271-92.

Green applies psychoanalytical criticism to a study of several texts, among which are James's The Ambassadors and "The Private Life."

288. Grella, George. "The Wings of the Falcon and the Maltese Dove." In A Question of Quality: Popularity and Value in Modern Creative Writing. Ed. Louis Filler. Bowling Green, OH: Bowling Green University Press, 1976, pp. 108-14.

Grella points out the similarities between The Wings of the Dove and The Maltese Falcon, particularly the use of the image of the bird and the sense of renunciation.

289. Gutwinski, Waldemar. "Cohesion in James." In Cohesion in Literary Texts: A Study of Some Grammatical and Lexical Features of English Discourse. The Hague: Mouton, 1977, pp. 83-126.

Gutwinski makes a detailed study of grammatical and lexical cohesion in James's literary structure. He focuses on a paragraph of The Portrait of a Lady and includes charts which illustrate the relationships of the cohesive elements.

290. Habegger, Alfred, introduction. The Bostonians. By Henry James. Indianapolis: Bobbs-Merrill, 1976.

Habegger's introduction to The Bostonians offers a brief biographical sketch of James, a sketch of Boston in the 1880s, and some comments on the novel's place in the women's movement. Habegger also comments on the overall social context of the novel, on the character of Basil Ransom, and on the technique used by James in the novel.

291. Hall, Sallie J. "Henry James and the Bluestockings: Satire and Morality in *The Bostonians*." In *Aeolian Harps: Essays in Litearture in Honor of Maurice Browning Cramer*. Ed. Donna G. Fricke and Douglas C. Fricke. Bowling Green, OH: Bowling Green University Press, 1976, pp. 207-25.

Hall looks at *The Bostonians* in the light of the modern mood of feminism. She maintains that it strikes a balance between and speaks to militant feminists and male chauvinists. In essence, James viewed women as human beings.

292. Hardy, Barbara. "Memory and Memories." In *Tellers and Listeners: The Narrative Imagination*. London: Athlone Press, 1975, pp. 56-101.

Hardy asserts there is a relationship between *The Ambassadors* and Proust's *A la recherche du temps perdu*. She says that *The Ambassadors* prefigures Proust in that the past returns to point out something missed. Strether determines not to live too much in the past or the future and to be wary of memory.

293. Hirsch, Marianne. "*The Ambassadors*: 'A Drama of Discrimination'." In *Beyond the Single Vision: Henry James, Michel Butor, Uwe Johnson*. York, SC: French Literature Publications, 1981, pp. 12-30.

Hirsch studies *The Ambassadors* in terms of the development and education of Lambert Strether. She states that since that is an egocentric process, the two cultures are reduced to abstracts and thus are limited.

294. Hirsch, Marianne. "*The Golden Bowl*: 'That Strange Accepted Finality of Relation'." In *Beyond the Single Vision: Henry James, Michel Butor, Uwe Johnson*. York SC: French Literature Publications, 1981, pp. 57-81.

Hirsch focuses on the international aspects of *The Golden Bowl*, the conflict of the two cultures. In this way James manages to combine the depiction of the personal and the cultural relationships.

295. Holloway, John. "Identity, Inversion, and Density Elements in Narrative: Three Tales by Chekhov, James, and Lawrence." In *Narrative and Structure: Exploratory Essays*. Cambridge: Cambridge University Press, 1979, pp. 53-73.

James's method of narration by "scenes" serves to remove emphasis from plot and place it on items that make up the density of the *nouvelle*. This is evident from an examination of the structure of "The Lesson of the Master."

296. Holman, C. Hugh. "'Of Everything the Unexplained and Irresponsible Specimen': Notes on How to Read American Realism." In Windows on the World: Essays on American Social Fiction. Knoxville, TN: University of Tennessee Press, 1979, pp. 17-26.

Holman notes the importance of Turgenev to the fiction of James and Howells, particularly with regard to literary realism. James, even in his deepest psychological exploration, achieves the mimetic function of the realistic novelist.

297. Howe, Irving. "Henry James as Latter-Day Saint." In Celebrations and Attacks: Thirty Years of Literary and Cultural Commentary. New York: Horizon Press, 1979, pp. 72-79.

Howe examines Quentin Anderson's The American Henry James. He objects to Anderson's relation of James's work to his father which, according to Howe, reduces James to a moral allegorist who reflected his father's ideas.

298. Hutchinson, Stuart. "Beyond the Victorians: The Portrait of a Lady." In Reading the Victorian Novel: Detail into Form. Ed. Ian Gregor. New York: Barnes & Noble, 1980, pp. 274-87.

Hutchinson offers an explication of The Portrait of a Lady. He notes that the novels and Isabel represent a departure from Victorian ideas and portraits. He also finds something of James himself in Isabel.

299. Inglis, Tony. "Reading Late James." In The Modern English Novel: The Reader, the Writer, and the Work. Ed. Gabriel Josipovici. New York: Barnes & Noble, 1976, pp. 77-94.

Inglis points out that James's characters remain within their own experience instead of attacking social questions. He examines James's language to show the cohesion evident in the late fiction and its effects on the characters.

300. Khan, Salamatullah. "The Jamesian View of the American in Europe." In Studies in American Literature: Essays in Honor of William Mulder. Ed. Jagdish Chandler and Narindar S. Pradham. Delhi: Oxford University Press, 1976, pp. 110-18.

In looking at James's Americans in Europe Khan determines that James sought first to present complete characters. He then endowed them with particular qualities he saw as American: moral strength, simplicity, and candor, but he also portrayed their failings.

301. King, Jeanette. "The American." In Tragedy in the Victorian Novel: Theory and Practice in the Novels of George Eliot, Thomas Hardy, and Henry James. Cambridge: Cambridge University Press, 1978, pp. 132-39.

Newman reflects the Jamesian view of heroism--in the lack of publicity of his renunciation there is an absence of triumph and climax. Since there is no climax, continuity is stressed.

302. King, Jeanette. "Henry James: Freedom and Form--The Tragic Conflict and the Novelist's Dilemma: Tragedy and the Novel." In Tragedy in the Victorian Novel: Theory and Practice in the Novels of George Eliot, Thomas Hardy, and Henry James. Cambridge: Cambridge University Press, 1978, pp. 127-32.

James's tragic novels incorporate the principles of inclusiveness and selection. The tension between them reflects the conflict that is the source of tragedy.

303. King, Jeanette. "The Portrait of a Lady." In Tragedy in the Victorian Novel: Theory and Practice in the Novels of George Eliot, Thomas Hardy, and Henry James. Cambridge: Cambridge University Press, 1978, pp. 139-49.

Isabel's story does not have a resolution but the novel does have an aesthetic end in the form of her renunciation. Thus the ending includes both formal finality and realistic continuity, creating a balance between form and freedom.

304. King, Jeanette. "The Wings of the Dove: The Essence of Tragedy?" In Tragedy in the Victorian Novel: Theory and Practice in the Novels of George Eliot, Thomas Hardy, and Henry James. Cambridge: Cambridge University Press, 1978, pp. 149-57.

Milly's death serves a symbolic function--the universality of death and the tragic fate of the individual which can be seen as "death-in-life." The novel includes the immediacy of tragic loss and the living awareness of loss.

305. Knights, Lionel Charles. "Henry James and Human Liberty." In Explorations 3. Pittsburgh: University of Pittsburgh Press, 1976, pp. 24-37.

Knights examines freedom and domination in James, particularly the subtler forms of domination which result in manipulation and victimization. Knights states that James teaches us to use our imaginations in evaluating people.

306. Koljević, Svetozar. "The Pitfalls of Perfection in The Portrait of a Lady." In Yugoslav Perspectives on American Literature: An Anthology. Ed. James L. Thorson. Trans. Natasha Kolchevska. Ann Arbor, MI: Ardis, 1980, pp. 55-68.

Koljević examines The Portrait of a Lady first from the persepective of the death of Minnie Temple. He then views the novel's form and substance and finds that it is representative of the creative and moral force of life.

307. Kono, Yoshio. "H. James: Ecriture no Tankyasha." In America Shosetsu no Tenkai. Ed. Katsuji Takamura and Iwao Iwamoto. Tokyo: Shohakusha, 1977, pp. 122-32.

308. Ledger, Marshall. "Ring around A Christmas Garland." In Aeolian Harps: Essays in Literature in Honor of Maurice Browning Cramer. Ed. Donna G. Fricke and Douglas C. Fricke. Bowling Green, OH: Bowling Green University Press, 1976, pp. 227-46.

Ledger examines Beerbohm's parody of James's "The Mote in the Middle Distance." The piece depicts James's view of art as an expression of his life. Ledger also mentions James's opinion of the parody.

309. Lewis, Wyndham. "Henry James: Excerpt from 'Men without Art'." In Enemy Salvoes: Selected Literary Criticism. Ed. C. J. Fox. New York: Barnes & Noble, 1976, pp. 88-92.

Lewis maintains that James should have left for Europe sooner, that he was "Americanized" before he went. Because of his view of America he conceived of art as abstraction; he did not receive the "sensuous education" his father wanted for him early enough.

310. McLuhan, Marshall. "Canada: The Borderline Case." In The Canadian Imagination: Dimensions of a Literary Culture. Ed. David Staines. Cambridge, MA: Harvard University Press, 1977, pp. 226-48.

McLuhan examines James's search for an American identity. Early in his life James attempted to view America in terms of Europe. He notes that James, late in his life, regreted the mixture of American and European.

311. McMaster, Juliet. "The Portrait of Isabel Archer." In The Novel from Sterne to James: Essays on the Relation of Literature to Life. Ed. Juliet McMaster and Rowland McMaster. New York: Barnes & Noble, 1981, pp. 169-87.

Reprinted from American Literature, 45 (1973), 50-66.

312. McMaster, Juliet. "The Turn of the Screw." In The Novel from Sterne to James: Essays on the Relation of Literature to Life. Ed. Juliet McMaster and Rowland McMaster. New York: Barnes & Noble, 1981, pp. 188-94.

McMaster notes that the reader is to read The Turn of the Screw as a ghost story or as a psychological novel. In terms of the image of the glass the reader may look with the governess or at her.

313. McMaster, Rowland. "'An Honorable Emulation of the Author of The Newcomes': James and Thackeray." In The Novel from Sterne to James: Essays on the Relation of Literature to Life. Ed. Juliet McMaster and Rowland McMaster. New York: Barnes & Noble, 1981, pp. 147-68.

Reprinted from Nineteenth-Century Fiction, 32 (1978), 399-419. See no. 628.

314. McNaughton, W. R. "The Narrator in Henry James's The Sacred Fount." In Literature and Ideas in America: Essays in Memory of Harry Hayden Clark. Ed. Robert Falk. Athens, OH: Ohio University Press, 1976, pp. 155-81.

McNaughton looks at the problems presented in The Sacred Fount by the first-person narration. For instance, there is the heterogeneous tone produced by the narrator being at times observor and at times participant.

315. Mahta, R. N. "Cable's Handling of the Political Theme in The Grandissimes." In Indian Studies in American Fiction. Ed. M. K. Naik, S. K. Desai, and S. Mokashi-Punekar. Dharwar: Karnatak University, 1984, pp. 96-107.

Mehta compares the political theme in The Grandissimes to that in The Princess Casamassima. He maintains that Cable's presentation is more confident and insightful than James's.

316. Melchiori, Giorgio. "James, Joyce e D'Annunzio." In D'Annunzio e il simbolismo europo: Atti del Convegno di Studio, Gardone Riviera, 14-15-16 sett. 1973. Ed Emilio Mariano. Milan: Il Saggiatore, 1976, pp. 299-311.

317. Meyers, Jeffrey. "Bronzino, Veronese and The Wings of the Dove." In Painting and the Novel. New York: Barnes & Noble, 1975, pp. 19-30.

Meyers acknowledges the place of art and James's appreciation of art in the novels and particularly compares the paintings of Bronzino and Veronese to characters in The Wings of the Dove.

318. Milne, Gordon. "Henry James." In The Sense of Society: A History of the American Novel of Manners. Rutherford, NJ: Fairleigh Dickinson University Press, 1977, pp. 43-70.
Cargill defined the "international novel" as one in which a character whose actions are determined by the mores of a particular environment is relocated in another. Milne says that this definition can apply to James's international fiction.

319. Morris, Wright. "Henry James." In Earthly Delights, Unearthly Adornments: American Writers as Image-Makers. New York: Harper& Row, 1978, pp. 43-50.
Morris snatches bits and pieces of The American Scene to depict some of James's views of America, of his place in America, and his life as artist (including his manners and his style) in such an environment.

320. Murphy, Kathleen. "An International Episode." In The Classic American Novel and the Movies. Ed. Gerald Peary and Roger Shatzkin. New York: Ungar, 1977, pp. 90-94.
Murphy examines Bogdanovich's Daisy Miller, focusing primarily on the character of Wihterbourne. She notes that he meticulously follows James, but may have produced too studied a film. Reprinted from Movietone News, No. 33 (July 1974), 13-16.

321. Naik, M. K. "The Draught from The Golden Bowl: The Impact of Europe on American Character in Henry James's Fiction." In Indian Studies in American Fiction. Ed. M. K. Naik, S. K. Desai, and S. Mokashi-Punekar. Dharwar: Karnatak University, 1974, pp. 77-95.
Naik states that the theme of the influence of Europe on the American adds psychological interest to James's fiction. James's American roots are evident in his portrayal of American integrity and European duplicity.

322. Page, Norman. "The Great Tradition Revisited." In Jane Austen's Achievement. Papers Delivered at the Jane Austen Bicentennial Conference at the University of Alberta. New York: Barnes & Noble, 1976, pp. 44-63.
Page assesses contentions made in F. R. Leavis' The Great Tradition. He particularly concerns himself with Jane Austen's influence on James. He finds that there are similarities between the two in structure, as well as subject.

323. Pilling, John. "Henry James: A Small Boy and Others." In Autobiography and Imagination: Studies in Self-Scrutiny. London: Routledge & Kegan Paul, 1981, pp. 23-35.

Pilling states that James's autobiographical writing is a fine example of his later writing. The attempt is made to tie memory to experience and development. James also relates the development of a generation and how he fits into it.

324. Piper, Myfawny. "Writing for Britten." In The Operas of Benjamin Britten. Ed. David Herbert. New York: Columbia University Press, 1979, pp. 8-21.

Piper discusses the making of The Turn of the Screw and Owen Wingrave into operas. The Turn of the Screw proved to be particularly adaptable because of the theme and James's stylistic elaboration which suits dramatic action.

325. Porter, Carolyn. "Henry James: Visionary Being." In Seeing and Being: The Plight of the Participant Observer in Emerson, James, Adams, and Faulkner. Middletown, CT: Wesleyan, 1981, pp. 121-64.

Porter examines James's works with the problem of seer as doer in mind. James as visionary naturally depicted the visionary in his works. Porter states that doers must be seers, so vision is limited and thus the limits of knowledge are reached.

326. Pritchett, V. S. "Henry James: Birth of a Hermaphrodite." In The Tale Bearers: Literary Essays. New York: Random House, 1980, pp. 120-37.

Pritchett looks at the period of James's life covered by the second volume of Leon Edel's biography of James. Pritchett also pays some attention to The American Scene and determines that it is a work of creation because of the self-creation involved.

327. Rahv, Philip. "The Heiress of All the Ages." In Essays on Literature and Politics, 1932-1972. Ed. Arabel J. Porter and Andrew J. Dvosin. New York: Houghton Mifflin, 1978, pp. 43-61.

Rahv points out through a study of several of James's works that the heroine, particularly the young American woman in Europe, is the most dominant figure of the American-European world of James. Though the characters differ in disposition and perception, they share, to a degree, James's vision of the American abroad.

328. Rahv, Philip. "Henry James and His Cult." In Essays on Literature and Politics, 1932-1972. Ed. Arabel J. Porter and Andrew J. Dvosin. New York: Houghton Mifflin, 1978, pp. 93-104.

Rahv maintains that James is peculiarly American in his portrayals of naiveté and his romanticizing of Europe. Rahv also attacks James cultists for, among other things, reading the Prefaces to the New York Edition too literally and for ignoring James's snobbery.

329. Riese, Teut Andreas. "Henry James: The Golden Bowl." In Der amerikanische Roman im 19. und 20. Jahrhundert: Interpretationen. Ed. Edgar Lohner. Berlin: Erich Schmidt, 1974, pp. 92-105.

330. Rihoit, Catherine. "The Bostonians: An Investigation of the Female Feature in James's Cosmogony." In Myth and Ideology in American Culture. Ed Régis Durand. Villeneuve-d'Ascq: Univ. de Lille III, 1976, pp. 81-110.

Rihoit carefully studies the semantic significance of the title, the human relationships (male versus female), and the features of the male and female characters (including positive and negative attributes of individuals and of sex groups).

331. Rihoit, Catherine. "Waiting for Isabel: An Analysis of the Levels of Significance in the First Fifteen Sentences of The Portrait of a Lady." In Studies in English Grammar. In André Joly and Thomas K. H. Fraser. Lille: Univ. de Lille III, 1975, pp. 185-225.

Rihoit approaches the beginning of The Portrait of a Lady linguistically. The textual analysis provides a sentence-by-sentence examination of James's complex syntactic construction. She recognizes the difficulty of the linguistic analysis of a novel by looking at a portion of the text.

332. Rubinstein, Annette T. "Henry James, American Novelist, or: Isabel Archer, Emerson's Grand-Daughter." In Weapons of Criticism: Marxism in America and the Literary Tradition. Ed. Norman Rudich. Palo Alto, CA: Ramparts Press, 1976, pp. 311-26.

Rubinstein maintains that James is a representative American novelist in more than subject matter or viewpoint. His roots , in The Portrait of a Lady for instance, are in Emerson rather than in Austen or Eliot. As such, it springs from the tradition of Melville and Hawthorne.

333. Sarbu, Aladár. "Some Aspects of the Changing Nature of Twentieth Century English Fiction." In Studies in English and American. Vol. II. Ed. Erzsébet Perényi and Tibor Frank. Budapest: Department of English, Eötrös University, 1975, pp. 91-119.

Sarbu concentrates on James's experimentation which helped bridge the gap between nineteenth- and twentieth-century writing. Some experimentation is with narrative, as in The Ambassadors, and some is in the area of the psychological examination of characters, as in The Golden Bowl.

334. Sarotte, Georges Michel. "Latent Homosexuality: Short of and Beyond True Heterosexuality: Hnery James; The Feminine Masochist Syndrome." In Like a Brother, Like a Lover: Male Homosexuality in the American Novel and Theater from Herman Melville to James Baldwin. Garden City, NY: Anchor Press/Doubleday, 1978, pp. 197-211.

Sarotte reads The Ambassadors as an allegory for James's own life. Sarotte reads homosexuality into the character of Lambert Strether (for instance, in Strether's wanting to be one of Chad's "feeders") and into the life of James.

335. Schneider, Daniel J. "'A Terrible Mixture in Things': The Symbolism of Henry James." In Symbolism: The Manichean Vision: A Study in the Art of James, Conrad, Woolf and Stevens. Lincoln: NE: University of Nebraska Press, 1975, pp. 62-117.

Scneider states that with the writings of his major phase James is able to capture through symbolism apparent opposites--the poetic and the prosaic, the ideal and the material, etc. His later style and symbolism help James to attain a full view and grasp of reality.

336. Schor, Naomi. "Fiction as Interpretation/Interpretation as Fiction." In The Reader in the Text: Essays on Audience and Interpretation. Ed. Susan R. Suleiman and Inge Crosman. Princeton, NJ: Princeton University Press, 1980, pp. 165-82.

James's central characters are frequently involved in the act of interpretation. Schor uses In the Cage as an example of such an instance and states that, in this case, the interpretive activity is creative and risks excessiveness.

337. Schug, Charles. "Henry James." In The Romantic Genesis of the Modern Novel. Pittsburgh: University of Pittsburgh Press, 1979, pp. 74-132.

Schug points out that James's fiction represents a transition from the traditional nineteenth-century novel to the modern novel. In particular he examines Romantic form in three novels of James's later phase, concentrating on structure in The Wings of the Dove, imagery in The Golden Bowl, and freedom in The Ambassadors.

338. Shuey, William A., III. "From Renunciation to Rebellion: The Female in Literature." In The Evolving Female: Women in Psychosocial Context. Ed. Carol Landau Heckerman. New York: Human Sciences Press, 1980, pp. 138-57.

Shuey maintains that Isabel Archer is a renunciatory heroine, possibly one of the greatest in American literature. Her renunciation appears to be submission, but it is self-denying and suffering is her choice.

339. Skilton, David. "Late-Victorian Choices: James, Wilde, Gissing and Moore." In The English Novel: Defoe to the Victorians. New York: Barnes & Noble, 1977, pp. 178-91.

James introduced what were to become important twentieth-century concepts in his later works, among which was the subjectivity inherent in his style of that period. His attention to the psychological makeup of his characters, however, preclude detailed examination of the working class and politics, for example.

340. Smith, Henry Nash, "Henry James I: Sows' Ears and Silk Purses." In Democracy and the Novel: Popular Resistance to Classic American Writers. New York: Oxford University Press, 1978, pp. 128-42.

Nash, assuming that James read a great deal of the popular fiction of his day, examine James's relation to popular culture, especially as it is expressed in his works.

341. Smith, Henry Nash. "Henry James II: The Problem of an Audience." In Democracy and the Novel: Popular Resistance to Classic American Writers. New York: Oxford University Press, 1978, pp. 143-65.

Smith studies James's impression of the size of his audience and of his financial state as a writer. James probably overstated his lack of an audience but his books did not sell as well as those by some of his contemporaries. In the last decade of his life some of his beliefs were tested by changing times.

342. Smith, Henry Nash. "On Henry James and 'The Jolly Corner'." In The American Short Story. Ed. Calvin Skaggs. New York: Dell, 1977, pp. 122-28.

Smith gives a brief critical background on "The Jolly Corner" to accompany tales included in The American Short Story series filmed with the aid of the National Endowment for the Humanities.

343. Snow, C. P. "Henry James." In The Realists: Eight Portraits. New York: Scribner's, 1978, pp. 256-96.

Snow provides an overview of James's professional (writing) life. He points out that James was never wealthy; that his biggest commercial success came early in his career with Daisy Miller. He also notes James's failure in the theater and his desire to preserve "civilization" in England.

344. Spengemann, William C. "Henry James." In The Adventurous Muse: The Poetics of American Fiction. New Haven, CT: Yale University Press, 1977, pp. 241-63.

James, in developing his art over the whole of his career, was ultimately dependent upon those who had gone before. Ground broken by such writers as Thoreau, Melville, Hawthorne, and even Twain, allowed James to let his art seek its own direction.

345. Spilka, Mark. "Henry James and Walter Besant: 'The Art of Fiction' Controversy." In Towards a Poetics of Fiction. Bloomington, IN: Indiana University Press, 1977, pp. 190-208.

Spilka states that Besant's lecture, "The Art of Fiction," prompted James's work of the same title. He then compares the two, illustrating some similarities, but pointing out that James's observations were much more astute than Besant's and had a great influence on literary history.

346. Stafford, William T. "'The Birthplace': James's Fable for Critics?" In Books Speaking to Books: A Contextual Approach to American Fiction. Chapel Hill, NC: University of North Carolina Press, 1981, pp. 114-19.

Noting the plethora of criticism on James, Stafford looks at "The Birthplace," which about literary greatness and its related industry. He stresses James's distinctions between the artist and the critic evident in "The Birthplace" and states that they (the distinctions) should be maintained.

347. Stafford, William T. "An 'Easy Ride' for Henry James." In Books Speaking to Books: A Contextual Approach to American Fiction. Chapel Hill, NC: University of North Carolina Press, 1981, pp. 54-59.

It is the unlikely combination of the movie Easy Rider and James's The American that attracts Stafford's attention. He does not suggest that the film is a conscious update or imitation of the novel, but both works deal with the westerner turning eastward in a quest for an extension of horizons.

348. Stafford, William T. "'Knower, Doer, and Sayer'--The James Family View of Emerson." In Books Speaking to Books: A Contextual Approach to American Fiction. Chapel Hill, NC: University of North Carolina Press, 1981, pp. 127-50.

Stafford examines the opinions of Emerson held by the elder Henry James, William James, and Henry James, Jr. He carefully differentiates the views held by the father and his younger son. Henry James, Jr. was able to praise Emerson's conception of good while noting that it was not balanced with a conception of evil. The novelist looked at Emerson as artist, and especially at the moral aspect of his art.

349. Stafford, William T. "Milly Theale as America." In Books Speaking to Books: A Contextual Approach to American Fiction. Chapel Hill, NC: University of North Carolina Press, 1981, pp. 19-22.

Stafford looks at Milly Theale as an American idea, as a force and power exerted as an American over Kate and Densher. That idea lives on in Densher after, and because of, her death.

350. Stineback, David C. "'Hurried Particles in the Stream': Henry James's The Bostonians." In Shifting World: Social Change and Nostalgia in the American Novel. Lewisburg, PA: Bucknell University Press, 1976, pp. 75-86.

Stineback sees The Bostonians as depicting the changes of the world that preclude the ideals of the aristocracy. The fact that Ransom is the loser and Olive is the winner reflects the changing order.

351. Stocking, Marion Kingston. "Miss Tina and Miss Plin: The Papers behind The Aspern Papers." In The Evidence of the Imagination: Studies of Interactions Between Life and Art in English Romantic Literature. Ed. Donald H. Rieman, Michael C. Jaye, Betty T. Bennett, Doucet Devin Fischer, and Ricki B. Herzfeld. New York: New York University Press, 1978, pp. 372-84.

Stocking provides a bit of background information

on The Aspern Papers and possible sources for Juliana Bordereau and Miss Tina in the persons of Claire Clairmont and her niece Pauline (Plin).

352. Stone, Albert E. "Henry James and Childhood: The Turn of the Screw." In American Character and Culture in a Changing World: Some Twentieth-Century Perspectives. Ed. John A. Hague. Westport, CT: Greenwood Press, 1979, pp. 279-92.
Stone notes that The Turn of the Screw signifies an end in literature of equating childhood and innocence. While the tale realizes that the child, limited in experience, has limited vision, it does childhood the service of taking it seriously.

353. Strout, Cushing. "Psyche, Clio, and the Artist." In New Directions in Psychohistory: The Adelphi Papers in Honor of Erik H. Erikson. Ed. Mel Albin. Lexington, MA: Heath, 1980, pp. 97-115.
Strout takes a psychoanalytical approach in his look at "The Jolly Corner." He pays special attention to the dream-adventure and Edel's treatment of this aspect of the tale.

354. Tatar, Mary Magdelene. "From Science Fiction to Psychoanalysis: Henry James's 'Bostonians,' D. H. Lawrence's 'Women in Love.' and Thomas Mann's 'Mario and the Magician'." In Spellbound: Studies on Mesmerism and Literature. Princeton, NJ: Princeton University Press, 1978, pp. 230-71.
In her study of The Bostonians Tatar states that with its publication, "the nineteenth-century tradition of the mesmerist novel came to an end." James incorporated psychological analysis rather than mesmerism or spiritualism to explain the actions and reactions of the characters.

355. Tate, Allen. "Three Commentaries: Poe, James, and Joyce." In Memoirs and Opinions, 1926-1974. Chicago: Swallow Press, 1975, pp. 155-69.
Tate examines the method James used to tell the tale of "The Beast in the Jungle," the nouvelle. He compares James's method to Poe's in "The Fall of the House of Usher" and Joyce's "The Dead."

356. Taylor, Anne Robinson. "Henry James: The Penalties of Action." In Male Novelists and Their Female Voices: Literary Masquerades. Troy, NY: Whitson, 1981, pp. 157-87.
Taylor maintains that James's female characters are, on the whole, more aggressive, more "masculine," than his male characters.

357. Tomlinson, Thomas Brian. "'Fits of Spiritual Dread': George Eliot and Later Novelists." In The English Middle-Class Novel. New York: Barnes & Noble, 1976, pp. 114-30.

Tomlinson examines The Awkward Age, particularly with an eye on the characters' self-consciousness and introversion, and also the same characteristics of James. He pays special attention to Nanda's excluding herself from society.

358. Tomlinson, Thomas Brian. "Henry James: The Ambassadors." In The English Middle-Class Novel. New York: Barnes & Noble, 1976, pp. 148-65.

Tomlinson here notes that The Ambassadors brought something new to English fiction--the recognition of the gap between Europe and America. He states that it incorporates a kind of irrepressable cheerful honesty peculiar to Americans.

359. Vann, Barbara. "A Psychological Interpretation of Daisy Miller." In A Festschrift for Professor Marguerite Roberts, on the Occasion of Her Retirement from Westhampton College, University of Richmond, Virginia. Ed. Frieda Elaine Penninger. Richmond, VA: University of Richmond, 1976, pp. 205-08.

Vann approaches Daisy Miller from a Jungian point of view, focusing primarily on repressed libidinal energy and the masculine-feminine aspect (conflict) of the individual psyche.

360. Winks, Robin W. Modus Operandi: An Excursion into Detective Fiction. Boston: David R. Godine, 1981.

Winks chooses to look at The Turn of the Screw as an example of a kind detective story. He turns his attention to the tale at scattered location throughout his book (hence no page numbers are included in the citation). In the course of his examination he notes the many possibilities for solution of the mystery available to the reader.

361. Wyatt, David. "Modernity and Paternity: James's The American." In Prodigal Sons: A Study in Authorship and Authority. Baltimore: Johns Hopkins University Press, 1980, pp. 1-25.

Wyatt maintains that when James re-approached The American in the course of preparing the New York Edition of his novels and tales he did so with the feeling that he had left a gap between experience and the understanding of it. His family life, as he looked back on it, influenced his revision of the novel.

362. Yoshida, Yasua. "To the Lighthouse to The Portrait of a Lady." In Gengo to Bu-tai: Higashida Chiaki Kyoju Kanreki Kinen Ronbunshu. Ed. Higashida Chiak. Osaka: Osaka Kyoiku Tosho, 1975, pp. 218-28.

ARTICLES

363. Akiyama, Masayuki. "The American Image in Kafū Nagai and Henry James." Comparative Literature Studies, 18 (1981), 95-103.

Akiyama states that Kafū Nagai visited America at about the same time James did (prior to his publication of The American Scene). Akiyama then discusses some similarities between Kafu's Tales of America and The American Scene.

364. Aldaz, Anna Maria. "Tiger, Tiger Burning Bright: A Study of Theme and Symbol in Henry James' 'The Beast in the Jungle'." ITA Humanidades, 12 (1976), 83-85.

Aldaz examines James's symbolism in "The Beast in the Jungle" with particular regard to May Bratram and John Marcher and their relationship.

365. Alexander, Charlotte. "Henry James and 'Hot Corn'." American Notes & Queries, 14 (1975), 52-53.

Alexander relates a recollection of James of a novel by Solon Richardson entitled "Hot Corn," particularly of its suggestiveness.

366. Allen, John J. "The Governess and the Ghosts in The Turn of the Screw." Henry James Review, 1 (1979), 73-80.

Allen maintains that the governess is mistaken in not realizing that the ghosts appear to some characters and not others. This causes her uncertainty, her relentless questions of the children, and the tale's ultimate ambiguity.

367. Altenbernd, Lynn. "A Dispassionate Pilgrim: Henry James's Early Travel in Sketch and Stodry." Exploration, 5, i (1977), 1-14.

Altenbernd looks at the European travel of the young Henry James as evidenced in his fiction, such as "A Passionate Pilgri," and in his autobiographical writings and travel sketches. The conflict within him over America and Europe was responsible for some of his greatest work.

368. Anand, Mulk Raj. "A Note on Henry James and the Art of Fiction in India." Commonwealth Quarterly, 2, vii (1978), 3-7.

Anand discusses James's desire to create based on "pure form," but he mentions that the social aspect also enters into James's fiction. He concludes by saying that the people of India cannot accept the subjects of Western novels but can accept the form.

369. Anderson, Charles R. "A Henry James Centenary." Georgia Review, 30 (1976), 34-52.

Anderson makes a case for the inclusion of Henry James in America's bicentennial celebrations. 1875 and 1876 marked the years that James came upon the literary scene. Since England shares in the celebration it seems fitting that the first great Anglo-American man of letters be honored.

370. Anderson, Quentin. "Practical and Visionary Americans." American Scholar, 45 (1976), 405-18.

In speaking of the acquisitive nature of the American Anderson notes that James intimates that there is no other way to possession of consciousness than through "guilty acquisition."

371. Andrews, Nigel. "Henry James on Location." Sight & Sound, 43 (1974), 215-16.

Anderson discusses the filming for television of "The Author of Beltraffio," directed by Tony Scott. He also states that it, unfortunately, did not enjoy very wide distribution.

372. Aoki, Tsugio. "Kenkyu no genjyo to Kadai: Henry James." Eigo Seinen, 126 (1980), 168-69.

373. Armistead, J. M. "Henry James for the Cinematic Mind." English Record, 26, iii (1975), 27-33.

Armistead discusses the difficulties students have with James, particularly with his style and he suggests the accompaniment of film to illustrate James's narrative structure.

374. Armstrong, Nancy. "Character, Closure, and Impressionist Fiction." Criticism, 19 (1977), 317-37.
Ambiguity is produced in The Turn of the Screw when the reader, realizing the unreliability of the governess' narrative, seeks to decipher what her connotative code might be.

375. Armstrong, Paul B. "How Maisie Knows: The Phenomenology of James's Moral Vision." Texas Studies in Literature and Language, 20 (1978), 517-37.
Armstrong applies existential phenomenology to the study of the relation of consciousness and morality in What Maisie Knew. Armstrong maintains that morality is sought after, but cannot be found because it is constantly challenged.

376. Armstrong, Paul B. "Knowing in James: A Phenomenological View." Novel: A Forum on Fiction 12 (1978), 5-20.
Armstrong states that James invites a phenomenological reading of his works because of his affinity for his brother's philosophical thought. This another means by which James provides a link between America and Europe. The "house of fiction" metaphor is a key to knowing in James.

377. Ashton, Jean. "Reflecting Consciousness: Three Approaches to Henry James." Literature/Film Quarterly, 4 (1976), 230-39.
Ashton examines three cinematic approaches to James: Jacques Rivette's Celine et Julie vont en bateau (based on The Other House), Peter Bogdanovich's Daisy Miller, and Claude Chabrol's The Bench of Desolation.

378. Auchincloss, Louis. "Henry James's Literary Use of His American Tour (1904)." South Atlantic Quarterly, 74 (1975), 45-52.
Auchincloss examines James's impressions of America at a later stage of life as reported in The American Scene. Auchincloss sees the book as an attempt at literary impressionism and as an observation of the American psyche and what it could become.

379. Babiiha, Thaddeo Kitasimbwa. "James's Washington Square: More on the Hawthorne Relation." Nathaniel Hawthorne Journal, 1974, pp. 270-72.
Babiiha quotes passages from Washington Square and works by Hawthorne to show that there is a strong Hawthorne background in James's novel.

380. Babiiha, Thaddeo K. "A Note on the James and Hawthorne Sections in Leary's Articles on American Literature, 1968-1975." Henry James Review, 1 (1980), 267-68.

Babiiha states that he carefully examined the entries on the two writers and points out some errors in the entries in Leary's work. The errors concern the Hawthorne-James relationship and are present in listings for both authors.

381. Babin, James L. "Henry James's 'Middle Years' in Fiction and Autobiography." Southern Review, 13 (1977), 505-17.

Babin offers an analysis of the tale, "The Middle Years," particularly of Dencombe's assessment and comments on the life and work of an artist. Babin also examines James's own reflections of his "middle years" and his life and work.

382. Badger, Reid. "The Character and Myth of Hyacinth: A Key to The Princess Casamassima." Arizona Quarterly, 32 (1976), 316-26.

There is a correlation between the story of Hyacinth and the myth of Hyacinthus, according to Badger. A parallel may be drawn between classical civilization and its downfall and the society that James depicts in the novel.

383. Banta, Martha. "James and Stein on 'Being American' and 'Having France'." The French-American Review, 3 (1979), 63-84.

Banta compares some of the differences and similarities of views on expatriation of James and Gertrude Stein. Her comments on the two writers include analyses of their opinions of America and France and also of a concept of "modernity."

384. Bargainnier, Earl F. "Browning, James, and 'The Private Life'." Studies in Short Fiction, 14 (1977), 151-58.

Bargainnier negates the contention by some that "The Private Life" is disguised autobiography. He reads James's notebook entries as accurate accounts of his conscious intent in the story.

385. Barnett, Louise K. "Displacement of Kin in the Fiction of Henry James." Criticism, 22 (1980), 140-55.

In James's fiction the displaced relative is a rather common occurrence, due to absence, irresponsibility, or benign neglect. Because of this James takes the opportunity to examine the relationship of a surrogate to his or her charge.

386. Barnett, Louise K. "Jamesian Feminism: Women in Daisy Miller." Studies in Short Fiction, 16 (1979), 281-87.
James has portraits of many women seeking freedom. usually unsuccessfully. Barnett maintains that Daisy is not resistent to the social force that would have her compromise her principles. She never gives in to the societal pressure.

387. Barry, Peter. "In Fairness to the Master's Wife: A Re-Interpretation of The Lesson of the Master." Studies in Short Fiction, 15 (1978), 385-89.
Barry offers evidence to show that Overt is unable to prove that Mrs. St. George is a malignant influence on her husband and his writing, as he thinks. The reader is then prompted to look to St. George as responsible for his own decline.

388. Barry, P. T. "Physical Descriptions in the International Tales of Henry James." Orbis Litterarum, 35 (1980), 47-58.
Barry maintains that James's physical descriptions of his characters provides some moral guides to the reading of the tales. Physical types are used for Americans and Europeans and belie James's feelings about the two continents.

389. Barstow, Jane Missner. "Originality and Conventionality in The Princess Casamassima." Genre, 11 (1978), 445-58.
Barstow states that there is a strangeness about The Princess Casamassima that is due to a number of dichotomies: politics and culture; social involvement and sensibility; and originality and conventionality. The last pervades the novel and provides a key to creativity.

390. Baxter, Charles. "'Wanting in Taste': The Sacred Fount and the Morality of Reading." Centennial Review, 25 (1981), 314-29.
Baxter sees The Sacred Fount as aggrssive act, an assault, by James on the part of the novel's audience. To James the novel is a joke played on readers following the failure of The Awkward Age, as Baxter sees it. As fiction The Sacred Fount purposely does not work, thus sending a messages to the reader not to read it.

391. Baym, Nina. "Revisions and Thematic Change in The Portrait of a Lady." Modern Fiction Studies, 22 (1976), 183-200.
Baym studies the revisions of The Portrait of a Lady James made in 1908 for the New York Edition. She contends that the later text, while not revised enough to approximate the late style, is more problematical than the 1881 version, and the revisions result in important thematic changes.

392. Beauchamp, Andrea Roberts. "'Isabel Archer': A Possible Source for The Portrait of a Lady." American Literature, 49 (1977), 267-71.

Beauchamp posits that James could have read a story by Professor Alden, D. D., entitled "Isabel Archer." There are similarities in the character and the fate of the two Isabels that suggest Alden's tale may have been a source for James's novel.

393. Beit-Hallahmi, Benjamin. "The Turn of the Screw and The Exorcist: Demoniacal Possession and Childhood Purity." American Imago, 33 (1976), 296-303.

Beit-Hallahmi examines evil in The Turn of the Screw and The Exorcist. The primary difference, as Beit-Hallahmi sees it is that The Exorcist leaves one feeling innocent and James's ambiguity of The Turn of the Screw leaves the reader involved and possibly feeling guilty.

394. Bell, Barbara Currier. "Beyond Irony in Henry James: The Aspern Papers." Studies in the Novel, 13 (1981), 282-93.

Bell argues that James uses irony "only as an artistic means for highlighting an unqualified moral value." In The Aspern Papers the complex process of morality passing through art becomes evident, according to Bell.

395. Bell, Millicent. "Jamesian Being." Virginia Quarterly Review, 52 (1976), 115-32.

Bell examines the conflict of being and doing in James's fiction and his life. The conflict in his life had its roots in his father's philosophy. He sought to merge the two in his fiction and was most successful in The Ambassadors.

396. Bell, Millicent. "Style as Subject: Washington Square." Sewanee Review, 83 (1975), 19-38.

Bell concentrates on Washington Square as style, in the sense of behavior as well as literary tone. Washington Square marks the beginning of literary independence for James and its moral and stylistic discoveries presage works to come.

397. Bellringer, Alan W. "Henry James's The Sense of the Past: The Backward Vision." Forum for Modern Language Studies, 17 (1981), 201-16.

Bellringer recounts the history of James's composition of The Sense of the Past and argues that it has more in common with the supernatural fiction of the late nineteenth century than with The Ivory Tower, which was also left unfinished.

398. Bellringer, Alan W. "The Ivory Tower: The Cessation of Concern." Journal of American Studies, 10 (1976), 241-55.

James's stopped composition of The Ivory Tower that came at the time war broke because, Bellringer says, war showed James that life had been different and worse than he had believed or depicted.

399. Bellringer, Alan W. "The Wings of the Dove: The Main Image." Modern Language Review, 74 (1979), 12-25.

Bellringer states that Milly is not to be thought of as saintly, and that she is not, for all her complexity, a rounded character. James focuses more on the relationships than on Milly's character.

400. Bender, Bert. "Henry James's Late Lyric Meditations upon the Mysteries of Fate and Self Sacrifice." Genre, 9 (1976), 247-62.

Bender focuses on James's late tales, which differ from most of the "short" stories published at the time. They represent a unique narrative form but one that is able to justify itself. They are explorations of consciousness and embody James's own sensibility.

401. Benert, Annette Larson. "The Dark Sources of Love: A Jungian Reading of Two Early James Novels." University of Hartford Studies in Literature, 12 (1980), 99-123.

Benert states that James's writing is not explainable solely in literary terms, but can be made clearer by Jung's writings on nature and the psyche. By using the parallels between the two writers Benert examines the psychology of James's Roderick Hudson and The Portrait of a Lady.

402. Bengels, Barbara. "Flights into the Unknown: Structural Similarities in Two Works by H. G. Wells and Henry James." Extrapolation, 21 (1980), 361-66.

Bengels examines Wells' The Time Machine and The Turn of the Screw and finds similarities in setting, style, and the handling of the major characters. She then notes a fine line between what she sees as science fiction and psychology.

403. Bengels, Barbara. "The Term of the 'Screw': Key to Imagery in Henry James's 'The Turn of the Screw'." Studies in Short Fiction, 15 (1978), 323-27.

Bengels examines the many possibilities that lie in the image of the screw: the twists and turns of the plot, the jailer, the physical stress, and the latent sexual connotations.

404. Berkove, Lawrence. "Henry James and Sir Walter Scott: A 'Virtuous Attachment'?" Studies in Scottish Literature, 15 (1980), 43-52.

Berkove examines the phrase "virtuous attachment" referring to Chad Newsome and Madame de Vionnet in The Ambassadors and traces the phrase to a Scott review of Austen's Emma. He then notes other connections between the essay and the novel.

405. Berkson. Dorothy. "Tender-Minded Idealism and Erotic Repression in James's 'Madame de Mauves' and 'The Last of the Valerii'." Henry James Review, 2 (1980), 78-86.

Berkson notes that the idealism of the tender-minded philosophers, as described by William James, was instrumental in creating the sexual malaise of the last century. "Madame de Mauves" and "The Last of the Valerii" illustrate the failure of this idealism and the consequences of such an attitude not tempered with a grasp of reality.

406. Bier, Jesse. "Henry James's 'The Jolly Corner': The Writer's Fable and the Deeper Matter." Arizona Quarterly, 35 (1979), 321-34.

Bier looks at James's debt to Hawthorne and the ways James used him as a model in "The Jolly Corner." In the same tale, Bier says, James also used Poe as an "antimodel," as a means to get at the universal.

407. Birje-Patil, J. "The Beast in the Jungle and The Portrait of a Lady." Literary Criterion, 11, iv (1975), 45-52.

Birje-Patil suggests that Eliot's poem, "Portrait of a Lady," is most evocative of "The Beast in the Jungle." Birje-Patil sees a common experience linking the two works and states that Eliot may have viewed himself somewhat as Marcher.

408. Birrell, T. A. "The Greatness of The Bostonians." Dutch Quarterly Review of Anglo-American Letters, 7 (1977), 242-64.

Birrell attempts to study many aspects of The Bostonians: James's artistic stance in creating it; the social background and plot of the novel; how it is executed; and its place in the totality of James's works. He concludes that The Bostonians is a great achievement, the finest example of the novel as dramatic poem.

409. Blackall, Jean Frantz. "The Case for Mrs. Brookenham." Henry James Review, 2 (1981), 155-61.
Blackall states that the case for Mrs. Brookenham is not as apparent as that for Langdon. She can, however, be seen as a heroine if The Awkward Age is read as an entertainment, a game of wits. She knows how to live by her wits and, despite her faults, is successful as an actress.

410. Blackall, Jean Frantz. "Cruikshank's Oliver and The Turn of the Screw." American Literature, 51 (1979), 161-78.
The Turn of the Screw succeeds in tapping primitive fears and emotions perhaps in part, according to Blackall, due to James's early reading of Oliver Twist and his reaction to Cruikshank's illustrations for the novel.

411. Blackall, Jean Frantz. "Literary Allusion as Imaginative Event in The Awkward Age." Modern Fiction Studies, 26 (1980), 179-97.
Blackall focuses on a passage in the last Book of The Awkward Age to illustrate James's most complex use of literary allusion and indirect narration. The allusions show Vanderbank's alternatives and provides questions for him and for the reader.

412. Blackall, Jean Frantz. "Moral Geography in What Maisie Knew." University of Toronto Quarterly, 48 (1978/79), 130-48.
Blackall maintains that the theme of the novel becomes clearer when one examines Maisie's mental development. He also states that the novel is similar, especially near the end, to a morality play.

413. Blodgett, Harriet. "Verbal Clues in The Portrait of a Lady: A Note in Defense of Isabel Archer." Studies in American Fiction, 7 (1979), 27-36.
Blodgett says that James uses his verbal dexterity, especially with repititions and parallelisms, to emphasize Isabel's admirable qualities and her development as a person. This culminates in her making a painful but free decision that is consistent with the character she has become.

414. Bluefarb, Sam. "The Middle-Aged Man in Contemporary Literature: Bloom to Herzog." College Language Association Journal, 20 (1976), 1-13.
In his study of middle-aged men in literature Bluefarb adds Lambert Strether who, Bluefarb notes, becomes less passive as the novel progresses.

415. Bock, Darilyn W. "From Reflective Narrators to James: The Coloring Medium of the Mind." Modern Philology, 76 (1979), 259-72.

Bock notes that James criticized the narrative conventions of the typical Victorian novel. In order that fiction might be more meaningful, James experimented with narrative technique. James thus serves as a link between between Victorian and modern fiction.

416. Bogardus, Ralph F. "Henry James and the Art of Illustration." Centennial Review, 22 (1978), 77-94.

Bogardus studies James's opinions about illustration, which he could appreciate while at the same time believing that they could be detrimental to the literature they accompany. Bogardus focuses primarily on James's statements in Picture and Text

417. Boland, Dorothy M. "Henry James's 'The Figure in the Carpet': A Fabric of the East." Papers on Language and Literature, 13 (1977), 424-29.

Boland notes the significance of Eastern thought and imagery in "The Figure in the Carpet." She says the perception of the individual characters is limited by karmic law.

418. Bradbury, Nicola. "Filming James." Essays in Criticism, 29 (1979), 293-301.

Bradbury, writing of James Ivory's film The Europeans, says that it is good cinema and is Jamesian in tone, but it does not capture such aspects as aging, failure, and isolation that are present in the book.

419. Brasch, James D. "Hemingway's Words: Enduring James's Thoughts: A Review Essay." Modernist Studies: Literature and Culture, 1920-1940, 2, ii (1976), 45-51.

In reviewing several books on Hemingway, Brasch notes the extent of the influence of Hawthorne on James. Brasch then points out Hemingway's rather extensive reading of James and the shared approach to literature as art.

420. Briden, E. F. "James's Miss Churm: Another of Eliza's Prototypes?" Shaw Review, 19 (1976), 17-21.

Briden posits that Miss Churm of "The Real Thing" may be a prototype for Eliza Doolittle. Briden sees parallels in the personalities of the two and also in their transformations.

421. Brooke-Rose, Christine. "The Squirm of the True: An Essay in Non-Methodology." PTL: A Journal for Descriptive Poetics and Theory, 1 (1976), 265-94.

Brooke-Rose attempts to clarify critical concern for The Turn of the Screw by adhering to some principles: respect for the genre, respect for the textuality of the text, and distinction between the language of the critic and the language of the linguistic object examined.

422. Brooke-Rose, Christine. "The Squirm of the True: A Structural Analysis of Henry James's The Turn of the Screw." PTL: A Journal for Descriptive Poetics and Theory, 1 (1976), 513-46.

Brooke-Rose presents the second part of her discussion of The Turn of the Screw, concentrating on the structure of the tale. She looks at it in terms of poetic principles that function to retain the ambiguity of the tale.

423. Brooke-Rose, Christine. "Surface Structure in Narrative: The Squirm of the True, Part III." PTL: A Journal for Descriptive Poetics and Theory, 2 (1977), 517-62.

Brooke-Rose completes her discussion of The Turn of the Screw and attempts to produce a "semantic grammar of a piece of discourse." Specifically, she applies principles of Transformational Grammar to the discourse and examines the structure of The Turn of the Screw, according to her stated principles.

424. Buitenhuis, Peter. "Exiles at Home and Abroad: Henry Adams and Henry James." English Studies in Canada, 1 (1975), 74-85.

Buitenhuis examines the impact of expatriation of James and Henry Adams. More than that, he shows that the exile was as much mental and psychological as it was physical and that it affected their lives and, as a result, their art.

425. Burde, Edgar J. "The Ambassadors and the Double Vision of Henry James." Essays in Literature, 4 (1977), 59-77.

Burde sees the meaning of The Ambassadors as resting in the conflict between spirit and matter. The novel is more complex than the character of Lambert Strether, who, according to Burde, does not really grow in knowledge. Strether and the novel are seen in the light of this double vision.

426. Burlui, Irina. "Narrative Patterns in Henry James' Short Novels The Spoils of Poynton and What Maisie Knew." Analele Ştiintifice ale Universităţii Iaşi, 22 (1976), 60-63.

427. Byers, John R., Jr. "Alice Staverton's Redemption of Spenser Brydon in James' 'The Jolly Corner'." South Atlantic Bulletin, 41, ii (1976), 90-99.

Byers notes that Alice provides a contrast to Bryden as a balanced character. She then influences him and shows him not only the past but the possibilities of the future. Byers says she fills out and completes the story.

428. Chapman, Sara S. "Stalking the Beast: Egomania and Redemptive Suffering in James's 'Major Phase'." Colby Library Quarterly, 11 (1975), 50-66.

Chapman refutes charges that James's short fiction is about people without self-awareness. She says that his late fiction shows that he has matured, citing particularly "The Beast in the Jungle," "The Jolly Corner," and "The Bench of Desolation."

429. Clark, Susan. "A Note on The Turn of the Screw: Death from Natural Causes." Studies in Short Fiction, 15 (1978), 110-12.

Assuming the governess is an unreliable narrator, Clark suggests that perhaps Miles suffers from some illness unbeknownst to the governess and dies of natural causes.

430. Cohen, Paula Marantz. "Feats of Heroism in The Spoils of Poynton." Henry James Review, 3 (1982), 108-16.

Cohen notes that through the first part of the novel the focus is on the material. It is Fleda's character that raises the level to a higher plane. The emphasis is shifted from an attitude of win or lose to one of freedom, which, Cohen says, Fleda achieves at the end of the novel through the burning of Poynton.

431. Colaco, Jill. "Henry James and Mrs. Humphrey Ward: A Misunderstanding." Notes & Queries, 23 (1976), 408-10.

Colaco examines Eleanor, a novel by Mrs. Humphrey Ward and is able to find a partial portrait of James embedded in it.

432. Collins, Martha. "The Center of Consciousness on Stage: Henry James's Confidence." Studies in American Fiction, 3 (1975), 39-50.

Collins observes the strange and sometimes erratic behavior of the characters in Confidence and attributes this behavior to love. The artistic reason, she says, is the attempted but failed fusion of narrative techniques.

433. Collins, Martha. "The Narrator, the Satellites, and Isabel Archer: Point of View in The Portrait of a Lady." Studies in the Novel, 8 (1976), 142-57.

The Portrait of a Lady presents particular difficulty from the standpoint of point of view in the novel. Isabel is presented as she sees, with her consciousness explored, and also as she is seen, from the narrator's point of view.

434. Collister, Peter. "Mrs. Humphrey Ward, Vernon Lee, and Henry James." Review of English Studies, 31 (1980), 315-21.

Collister traces in part the genesis of Mrs. Ward's novel, Miss Bretherton, and James's role in its composition.

435. Connaughton, Michael E. "American English and the International Theme in The Portrait of a Lady." Midwest Quarterly, 22 (1981), 137-46.

The Portrait of a Lady contains the speech of Americans, Anglo-Americans, and Englishmen. Connaughton contends that James is able to capture subtle distinctions in usage and use them in defining his characters.

436. Cook, David A. and Timothy J. Corrigan. "Narrative Structure in The Turn of the Screw: A New Approach to Meaning." Studies in Short Fiction, 17 (1980), 55-65.

Cook and Corrigan study James's narrative technique with relation to meaning in The Turn of the Screw. They find that James gives the governess credibility and takes it away and that the structure of the narrative admits two opposite interpretations.

437. Cook, Eleanor. "Portraits of Ladies." Notes & Queries, 27 (1980), 533-34.

Cook attributes a quoted phrase in Eliot's "Portrait of a Lady" to James's novel The Portrait of a Lady, linking James's influence on Eliot.

438. Corse, Sandra. "From Narrative to Music: Benjamin Britten's The Turn of the Screw." University of Toronto Quarterly, 51 (1981-82), 161-74.
Corse studies the narrative and musical structures of the two versions of The Turn of the Screw. She maintains that Britten created a new and different Turn of the Screw, one that blends music and text into a single fluid structure.

439. Cosgrove, William and Irene Mathees. "'To See Life Reflected': Seeing as Living in The Ambassadors." Henry James Review, 1 (1980), 204-10.
The authors state that Lambert Strether's observation of life in Paris actually becomes a creative act. In fact, his "seeing" life is possibly more effective than any attempt would be at trying to live the kind of life he observes.

440. Costa, Richard Hauer. "Edwardian Intimations of the Shape of Fiction to Come: Mr. Britling/Job Huss as Wellsian Central Intelligences." English Literature in Transition (1880-1920), 18 (1975), 229-42.
Costa focuses on The Ambassadors and Mr. Britling in order to examine and comment on the debate between James and Wells on the distinction between literature and journalism.

441. Cowdery, Lauren T. "Henry James and the 'Transcendent Adventure': The Search for the Self in the Introduction to The Tempest." Henry James Review, 3 (1982), 145-53.
Cowdery examines the introduction to The Tempest James wrote at the request of Sidney Lee. James looks at Shakespeare's imagination, which he sees as very different from his own. Cowdery sees this effort by James as an attempt to capture the elusive spirit of art at a time very late in his life.

442. Coy, Javier. "A Thematic and Character Approach to Henry James." Studi Americani, 21-22 (1976), 109-27.
Coy maintains that James uses only two types of characters which are, essentially, victim and executioner. In addition to this, the subject matter of James's fiction is likewise severly limited in its scope, according to Coy.

443. Craig, David M. "The Indeterminacy of the End: Maggie Verver and the Limits of Imagination." Henry James Review, 3 (1982), 133-44.
Craig looks at the closing paragraphs of The Golden Bowl. The ending is inconclusive although Maggie's effort

produces a reunion with her husband. Craig says that the nature of the reunion necessitates consciousness and Maggie must continuously explore the new territory she has found.

444. Craig, Randall. "'Read[ing] the Unspoken into the Spoken': Interpreting What Maisie Knew." Henry James Review, 2 (1981), 204-12.

Craig looks at Maisie's perception, which is limited early in the book. As the limitation diminishes, Maisie's powers of understanding develop. Eventually Maisie is able to translate experience into dialogue, a process that applies analogously to the reader, in order to produce a more complete understanding.

445. Crawford, Fred D. and Bruce Morton. "Hemingway and Brooks: The Mystery of 'Henry's Bicycle'." Studies in American Fiction, 6 (1978), 106-09.

Crawford and Morton note the place of James in Hemingway's fiction, particularly as a fellow expatriate writer.

446. Cross, Mary. "Henry James and the Grammar of the Modern." Henry James Review, 3 (1981), 33-43.

Cross states that James devises a literary language that encompasses the complexity of reality, a language that many modernists are indebted to. She then examines that language as medium and as action in The Portrait of a Lady.

447. Crowley, Francis E. "Henry James' The Beast in the Jungle and The Ambassadors." Psychoanalytic Review, 62 (1975), 154-63.

Crowley looks at Strether and Marcher as older, nonaggressive heroes of James's later years. He then notes the many and varied psychological images in the two works.

448. Crowley, John W. "The Wiles of a 'Witless'Woman: Tina in The Aspern Papers." ESQ, 22 (1976), 159-68.

Crowley states that the narrator of The Aspern Papers, commonly acknowledged by critics to be unreliable, is mistaken about the character of Tina, who is more resourceful and complex than the narrator imagines or allows for.

449. Curtsinger, E. C., Jr. "Henry James's Farewell in 'The Velvet Glove'." Studies in Short Fiction, 18 (1981), 163-69.

Curtsinger sees "The Velvet Glove," particularly Barridge's goodbye to Amy Evans as a final tribute to Edith Wharton.

450. Curtsinger, E. C. "James's Writer at the Scared Fount." Henry James Review, 3 (1982), 117-28.

Curtsinger looks at the role and activity of the narrator in The Sacred Fount. Curtsinger maintains that the narrator succeeds in his creative role of discovery and does produce a work of art. The narrator, realizing the force of love affecting imagination, moves towards a truth that he can give order and form to.

451. Dahl, Curtis. "The Swiss Cottage's Owner: A Model for J. L. Westgate in James's An International Episode." American Notes & Queries, 17 (1978), 58-70.

Dahl offers a possible model for Westgate and certainly for an American type in the person of Col. George T. M. Harris.

452. Daugherty, Sarah B. "James, Renan, and the Religion of Consciousness." Comparative Literature Studies, 16 (1979), 318-31.

James was influenced by the idealist, Ernest Renan, according to Daugherty. Of particular interest to James was Renan's writing on consciousness that he retained in an adapted form throughout his fiction.

453. Daugherty, Sarah B. "Taine, James, and Balzac: Toward an Aesthetic of Romantic Realism." Henry James Review, 2 (1980), 12-24.

Daugherty examines James's opinions of Hyppolyte Taine. James took an early interest in Taine's travel writings but at first did not accept his critical judgment. He came to accept Taine's criticism of Balzac, incorporating the spirit of Taine's essay into his own.

454. Davidson, Cathy N. "'Circumsexualocution' in Henry James's Daisy Miller." Arizona Quarterly, 32 (1976), 353-66.

Davidson examines the uses of verbalization as opposed to action in Daisy Miller and finds that deviant speech may in fact result from deviant perception. She also says that Winterbourne is a victim of James's parody.

455. Davis, Sara deSaussure. "The Bostonians Reconsidered." Tulane Studies in English, 23 (1978), 39-60.

Davis studies The Bostonians in its entirety, examining the characters and their interactions (particularly the two worlds represented by Basil and Olive and Verena's struggle between them), and the historical surroundings of the feminist theme.

456. Davis, Sara deSaussure. "Feminist Sources in The Bostonians." American Literature, 50 (1979), 570-87.

Davis sees Verena and Olive as James's first political characters. In presenting women in political affairs James illustrates both the public and the personal aspects of feminism. Unfriendly reception of the novel may have been due to a temporary lull in women's suffrage activity and interest.

457. Davis, Sara deSaussure. "Two Portraits of a Lady: Henry James and T. S. Eliot." Arizona Quarterly, 32 (1976), 367-80.

Davis finds that Eliot adapts technique, substance, and attitude in his "Portrait of a Lady" from James's novel. Eliot then added some ironic reversals to the story for his poem.

458. Dawson, Anthony B. "The Reader and the Measurement of Time in 'The Beast in the Jungle'." English Studies in Canada, 3 (1977), 458-65.

Dawson points out that James makes the reader of "The Beast in the Jungle" go through Marcher's ordeal. He has the reader waiting for some culmination and thus creates the same kind of conflict and tension that Marcher struggles with.

459. Dean, Sharon. "Constance Fenimore Woolson and Henry James: The Literary Relationship." Massachusetts Studies in English, 7, iii (1980), 1-9.

Dean notes Woolson's debt to James and, in more detail, James's indebtedness to Woolson. She cites "A Transplanted Boy," "The Street of the Hyacinth," and "Miss Grief" to illustrate how closely James read and appreciated Woolson.

460. Dean, Sharon. "James' The Golden Bowl." Explicator, 35, iv (1977), 8-9.

Dean addresses the question of the apparent inability of Adam and Charlotte to have children of their own in The Golden Bowl.

461. Dean, Sharon. "The Principino and the Ending of James's The Golden Bowl." American Notes & Notes, 16 (1977), 43-44.

Dean posits that the Principino serves to note that parenthood is a reason for the preservation of the marriage.

462. Delfattore, Joan. The 'Other' Spencer Brydon." Arizona Quarterly, 35 (1979), 335-41.

Delfattore exmaines James's representation of Brydon as he is and as he sees himself, but also as he might have been and the effects of these various perceptions on Brydon.

463. DeLoach, William. "The Influence of William James on the Composition of The American." Interpretations, 7 (1975), 38-43.

DeLoach finds aspects of William James in some characters in The American. He contends that the brothers at times looked up to one another, sometimes down at one another, and that theirs was a relatively normal sibling relationship.

464. De Rose, Peter L. "The Experience of Perception: A Reading of The Ambassadors." Publications of the Arkansas Philological Association, 2, iii (1976), 1-8.

De Rose examines The Ambassadors as Strether journeys from innocence to experience. The change is both apparent in and a product of his perception and its development. He grows throughout the novel in his vision and appreciation of life.

465. Dupperay, Annick. "Henry James et The Yellow Book." Confluents, 1975, i, pp. 153-75.

466. Durand, Régis. "The Turn of the Screw: le déni de la fiction." Études Anglaises, 31 (1978), 176-87.

467. Duthie, Enid L. "Henry James's 'The Turn of the Screw' and Mrs. Gaskell's 'The Old Nurse's Story'." Brontë Society Transactions, 17 (1977), 133-37.

Duthie sees similarities of the use of the supernatural and the presence of evil in The Turn of the Screw and "The Old Nurse's Story." She notes particularly the responses to evil of both the nurse and the governess and the likenesses of the ttransmission of the tales by different authors.

468. Dyson, J. Peter. "Bartolozzi and Henry James's 'Mora Montravers'." Henry James Review, 1 (1980), 264-66.

James makes a statement about the characters in "Mora Montravers" by connecting them with Bartolozzi, an Italian engraver whose work was not held in high critical regard.

469. Dyson, J. Peter. "Death and Separation in 'Fordham Castle'." Studies in Short Fiction, 16 (1979), 41-47.

Dyson examines the genesis of "Fordham Castle" from James's notebook entries through the execution of the tale. He finds that themes of death and separation were on James's mind early and permeate the story under consideration.

470. Dyson, J. Peter. "James' 'The Turn of the Screw'." Explicator, 36, iii (1978), 9.

Regarding the image of the beast in The Turn of the Screw, Dyson suggests that it springs from the governess herself.

471. Dyson, J. Peter. "Perfection, Beauty and Suffering in 'The Two Faces'." Henry James Review, 2 (1980), 116-25.

Dyson says the theme of "The Two Faces" involves the vulnerability of the self without its protective consciousness. He states that consciousness can be a source of evil whereas unconsciousness can achieve a value that makes suffering and beauty possible. The perfection sought by consciousness thus becomes an enemy of beauty. Therefore, the perfection of Mrs. Grantham is the means of Lady Gwyther's triumph.

472. Dyson, J. Peter. "Romance Elements in Three Late Tales of Henry James: 'Mora Montravers,' 'The Velvet Glove,' and 'The Bench of Desolation'." English Studies in Canada, 5 (1979), 66-77.

Dyson maintains that the three tales follow in the English and American traditions of Romance. He particularly addresses verisimilitude in the tales--the "tension between form and content" or "between imagination and reality."

473. Eakin, Paul John. "Margaret Fuller, Hawthorne, James and Sexual Politics." South Atlantic Quarterly, 75 (1976), 323-38.

Eakin examines the feminist movement in terms of the three personalities. He focuses on The Bostonians as portrait of Margaret Fuller and as comment on a social order that has no apparent escape from the sexual politics that victimizes both men and women.

474. Ebine, Shizue. "The Central Theme of Henry James." Studies in English Literature, 51, i-ii (1974), 53-66.
In Japanese.

475. Edel, Leon. "A Bibliography of the Writings on Henry James by Leon Edel, With Some Annotations." Compiled by Vivian Cadbury and William Laskowski, Jr. Annotated by Adeline R. Tintner. Henry James Review, 3 (1982), 176-99.
This is a 196-item bibliography of Edel's writings, including translations of his works. The bibliography is presented in chronological order, beginning with Edel's first publication on James in 1930 and is selectively annotated.

476. Edel, Leon. "Henry James in the Abbey." Times Literary Supplement, 18 June 1976, pp. 741.
Edel pays homage to James on the event of the dedication of a stone commemorating his memory in Westminster Abbey.

477. Edel, Leon. "How I Came to Henry James." Henry James Review, 3 (1982), 160-64.
Edel describes how he first became interested in James through the study of Joyce. He found out the modern novel he was studying in Joyce had roots in James and so he turned first to The Wings of the Dove to begin his examination of James, which led to a lifetime devoted in considerable measure to the study of James.

478. Edel, Leon. "Portrait of the Artist as an Old Man." American Scholar, 47 (1977-78), 52-68.
In writing of James's old age Edel notes that James released the anxiety built up through his youth by working. he was able to face aging and his solitude and to realize that creativity need not wither with the passage of time.

479. Edel, Leon. "Shaping and Telling: The Biographer at Work." Henry James Review, 3 (1982), 165-75.
Edel tells, not only the circumstances surrounding his endeavor to write the biography of James, but also his method and approach to such a work. The appearance of many letters by James was, in large part, responsible for the enlargement of a one-volume factual biography to a five-volume work.

480. Edel, Leon. "The Three Travelers in English Hours." Henry James Review, 2 (1981), 167-71.

Edel observes that evident in The English Hours is the awareness that the observer (James) is actually three different people, each corresponding with a stage of James's life. This leads to a cognizance of the autobiographical element of the book, which is an account of his own admiration of his adopted country.

481. Edel, Leon. "Westminster Abbey Address." Henry James Review, 1 (1979), 5-9.

In 1976 a memorial stone honoring Henry James waa unveiled in Westminster Abbey. Edel says that James was able to link the language of America with Britain. Because of his contributions to art he is a treasure claimed by both nations.

482. Eggenschwiler, David. "James's 'The Pupil': A Moral Tale without a Moral." Studies in Short Fiction, 15 (1978), 435-44.

Eggenschwiler maintains that "The Pupil" is a moral tale, one that prompts the reader to make moral judgments. James does make it simple, though. He adds complications and complexities that make it more revealing than a straightforward moral lesson.

483. Empet, Carol J. "James' Portrait of a Lady and Browning's 'My Last Duchess': A Comparison." DeKalb Literary Arts Journal, 13, i-ii (1978-79), 79-84.

In comparing The Portrait of a Lady with "My Last Duchess" Empet finds a number of similarities in characterization and plot. She notes that there is evidence James read Browning and borrowed from other works which supports Empet's theory that James borrowed from "My Last Duchess."

484. Evans, T. Jeff. "F. Scott Fitzgerald and Henry James: The Raw Material of American Innocence." NMAL: Notes on Modern American Literature, 4 (1980), Item 8.

Evans point out a possible link between Daisy Miller and The Great Gatsby, especially regarding innocence. Evans particularly notices this link after the deaths of Daisy and Gatsby.

485. Ewell, Barbara C. "Parodic Echoes of The Portrait of a Lady in Howell's Indian Summer." Tulane Studies in English, 22 (1977), 117-31.

Ewell notes that there are strong similarities in plot, character, and theme in The Portrait of a Lady and

Indian Summer. Ewell maintains that where James's view is dark and tragic, though, Howell's attitude is one of parody.

486. Faber, M. D. "Henry James: Revolutionary Involvement, the Princess, and the Hero." American Imago, 37 (1980), 245-77.

Faber concentrates on The Princess Casamassima because he finds it a revealing study of the revolutionary within the individual, particularly those psychological factors. He says that in James the aim of violent reform has an irrational side.

487. Faderman, Lillian. "Female Same-Sex Relationships in Novels by Longfellow, Holmes, and James." New England Quarterly, 51 (1978), 309-32.

Faderman studies the relationship of Olive and Verena in The Bostonians. She notes that, while Verena seems content when with Olive, there is no indication that she will be able to find contentment with Basil.

488. Felman, Shoshana. "Turning the Screw of Interpretation." Yale French Studies, 55-56 (1977), 94-207.

In this lengthy study of The Turn of the Screw Felman addresses the issues of readings of text and critics, Freudian analysis of the tale, conflicting interpretations, the importance of the narrative of the tale, the act of reading and writing the letter that comprises the tale the complexity of the ghosts, and others.

489. Ferguson, Suzanne. "The Face in the Mirror: Authorial Presence in the Multiple Vision of Third-Person Impressionist Narrative." Criticism, 21 (1979), 230-50.

Ferguson notes that, in The Ambassadors, James does not allow the reader to immerse himself in Strether's consciousness. Authorial intrusions create a split perspective that complicates and sometimes obscures the reader's point of reference.

490. Field, Mary Lee. "'Nervous Anglo-Saxon Apprehensions': Henry James and the French." The French-American Review, 5 (1981), 1-13.

Field surveys James's comments on French literature made in various publications throughout his lifetime. Though reticent about the apparent seeminess he saw in it as a young man he grew to see the need to formulate a critical theory that can accept the art of a work, regardless of its subject matter.

491. Field, Mary Lee. "'The unmitigated "business man" face': Portraits of American Business Men by Henry James." Chu-Shikoku Studies in American Literature, 15 (1979), 1-16.

492. Fincham, Gail. "'The Alchemy of Art': Henry James's The Europeans." English Studies in Africa, 23 (1980), 83-92.
Fincham looks at the juxtaposition of the American and the European and finds that the differences of the two can be reconciled by art. She finds the novel to be optimistic in its unification of the aesthetic and the moral.

493. Fogel, Danial Mark. "The Jamesian Dialectic in The Ambassadors." Southern Review, 13 (1977), 468-91.
Fogel contends the The Ambassadors is essentially the establishment of polarities and the exploration of possibilities for resolving them. It is based on the dialectic of spiral return and shares this with many works of the Romantic period.

494. Fowler, Virginia C. "Milly Theale's Malady of Self." Novel: A Forum on Fiction, 14 (1980), 57-74.
Fowler examines the deficiencies of Milly that include her illness and go beyond it. She rejects love, which could have saved her, and embraces the physical illness because she sees it giving her a definition of self. Ultimately, she lacks a sense of self and is unable to achieve identity.

495. Frank, Albert J. von. "James Studies 1980: An Analytical Bibliographical Essay." Henry James Review, 3 (1982), 210-28.
Von Frank takes a look at the year's work on James in 1980. He examines books, general articles, articles on single works, and miscellaneous articles. He notes that some of the approaches to James are purposely nontraditional.

496. Franklin, Rosemary F. "Military Metaphors and the Organic Structure of Henry James's 'The Aspern Papers'." Arizona Quarterly, 32 (1976), 327-40.
Franklin focuses on the structure of The Aspern Papers, examining its aesthetic unity and consistency of imagery. She finds it a technical masterpiece, satiric and profound.

497. Friedel, Herwig. "Problemgeschichtliche Überlegungen zum Stellenwert der Kunst in amerikanischen künstlererzählungen." Anglia: Zeitschrift für Englische Philologie, 97 (1979), 153-67.

498. Friedrich, Otto. "A Little Tour with Henry James." American Scholar, 44 (1975), 643-52.

Friedrich relates his own travel experiences in Europe as he visits spots along the route James took when he wrote of his Little Tour.

499. Fryer, Judith. "The Other Victoria: 'The Woodhull' and Her Times." Old Northwest, 4 (1978), 219-40.

Judith Fryer examines the notorious life of Victoria Woodhull and some of the effects of her radical ideas. She also looks at two literary views of Woodhull: Harriet Beecher Stowe's harsh satire in My Wife and I and Henry James's ironic novel, The Siege of London.

500. Fussell, Edwin. "The Ontology of The Turn of the Screw." Journal of Modern Literature, 8 (1980), 118-28.

Fussell examines the use of the governess as teller of the tale, the form and style of her tale, and the implications of the governess as novelist for The Turn of the Screw itself.

501. Fussell, Edwin Sill. "Sympathy in The Portrait of a Lady and The Golden Bowl." Henry James Review, 2 (1981), 161-66.

Sympathy was an important concept to Adam Smith's philosophy and that of others and found literary expression in James and many American writers, Fussell notes. Isabel is a sympathetic character and is desirous of sympathy from all, but her sympathizing contains a sadness. In The Golden Bowl sympathy is comic with respect to Fanny Assingham, but signals tragedy for others, such as Charlotte.

502. Gale, Robert, Robert L. "H. J.'s J. H. in 'The Real Thing'." Studies in Short Fiction, 14 (1977), 396-98.

Gale posits that Jack Hawley of "The Real Thing" is the reverse of James and is much like his contemporary, John Hay.

503. Gale, Robert L. "Henry James." American Literary Scholarship: An Annual/1977, 99-118.

504. Gale, Robert L. "Henry James." American Literary Scholarship: An Annual/1978, 91-110.

505. Gale, Robert L. "Henry James." American Literary Scholarship: An Annual/1979, 93-113.

506. Gale, Robert L. "Henry James." American Literary Scholarship: An Annual/1980, 103-20.
In this and the above three entries Gale analyzes the year's work on James. For earlier bibliographic essays on James in American Literary Scholarship see entries in this section under William T. Stafford.

507. Gale, Robert L. "An Unpublished Letter from Henry James to F. Marion Crawford." Revue des Langues Vivante, 42 (1976), 179-82.
Gale offers a brief look at James's relationship with Francis Marion Crawford and adds a previously unpublished letter from James to Crawford.

508. Galloway, David. "Henry James: Daisy Miller and the International Novel." Dutch Quarterly Review of Anglo-American Letters, 6 (1976), 304-17.
Galloway examines events of James's life and the nature of his art which make the international theme so fitting to his work. He focuses on Daisy Miller and the development of the complex theme that recurred and became more sophisticated in the course of his life.

509. Gargano, James W. "James's Stories in 'The Story in It'." NMAL: Notes on Modern American Literature, 1 (1976), Item 2.
Gargano maintains that there certainly is a story in "The Story in It," and it is a complex story because of its double concern with life and art.

510. Gargano, James W. "James's The Sacred Fount: The Phantasmagorical Made Evidential." Henry James Review, 2 (1980), 49-60.
Gargano notes that the narrator is sometimes seen as a madman, but he states that the narrator is a sane but self-doubting analyst of the human condition who suffers for what he learns. He knows that his theorizing would be seen as madness, so by his renunciation he attains attributes of some of James's most admired chararcters.

511. Gargano, JamesW. "The 'Look' as a Major Event in James's Short Fiction." Arizona Quarterly, 35 (1979), 303-20.
Gargano examines the importance of looking, staring, gazing, glancing, and so forth in several of James's works. These looks are used by James as a means of communication, that can sometimes be even more important than verbal communication.

512. Gargano, James W. "Washington Square: A Study in the Growth of an Inner Self." Studies in Short Fiction, 13 (1976), 355-62.

Gargano focuses on Catherine Sloper and her renunciation in Washington Square. While she does not have the assurances that Lambert Strether has, she does show that she has matured by the end of the novel.

513. Gervais, David. "James's Reading of Madame Bovary." Cambridge Quarterly, 7 (1976), 1-26.

Gervais points out the Victorian background of criticism of Flaubert that James absorbed and incorporated, to a degree, into his reading. James rejects the moral position of Madame Bovary but he is also attracted to it. The energy of pessimism of the novel is most disturbing to James.

514. Gill, Richard. "Letter from L. P. Hartley." Journal of Modern Literature, 5 (1976), 529-31.

Gill notes correspondence from Hartley regarding the place of the country house in his fiction, noting similarity to James's use of the same.

515. Girling, Harry K. "On Editing a Paragraph of The Princess Casamassima." Languange and Style, 8 (1976), 243-63.

Girling collated a paragraph of the manuscript of The Princess Casamassima (using the holograph manuscript at the Houghton Library, Harvard) with the various editions of the novel to show the many difficulties James's revisions present.

516. Girling, Harry Knowles. "A Toot of the Trumpet against the Scholarly Regiment of Editors." Bulletin of Research in the Humanities, 81 (1978), 297-323.

Girling studies some revisions, primarily in puncuation, that the Atlantic made to The Princess Casamassima and that James removed or left in some of the later editions and other changes that James made to his own text of the novel.

517. Goetz, William R. "The Allegory of Representation in The Tragic Muse." Journal of Narrative Technique, 8 (1978), 151-64.

The Tragic Muse, Goetz notes, bridges two phases of James's creative life. It comes at the end of his pictorial phase and at the beginning of the time he would devote to writing for the stage and then writing dramatic novels.

518. Goetz, William R. "The 'Frame' of The Turn of the Screw: Framing the Reader In." Studies in Short Fiction, 18 (1981), 71-74.

Goetz offers another use for the "frame" of the opening section of The Turn of the Screw. It can serve as an instruction from James on how to read the tale, but it is not a means of interpretation.

519. Goetz, William R. "Criticism and Autobiography in James's Prefaces." American Literature, 51 (1979), 333-48.

Goetz states that James's Prefaces should be read as more than the author's critical commentary on his work. They form a narrative that serves to continue the work on which it comments and also presents a kind of autobiography. In this way the Prefaces constitute an amalgamation of critical and literary texts.

520. Goldfarb, Clare R. "Matriarchy in the Late Novels of Henry James." Research Studies, 49 (1981), 231-41.

Goldfarb begins her study of the matriarch in James's fiction with Maud Lowder of The Wings of the Dove and Mrs. Newsome of The Ambassadors. She then moves on to the matriarchal view James developed with Charlotte and Maggie in The Golden Bowl.

521. Goodman, Charlotte. "Henry James, D. H. Lawrence, and the Victimized Child." Modern Language Studies, 10, i (1979-80), 43-51.

Goodman states that Lawrence' short fiction is linked to James, not just by craftsmanship. She compares "England, My England" with "The Author of Beltraffio," with particular interest in the child as a source of conflict between the man and woman.

522. Greenstein, Susan M. "The Ambassadors: The Man of Imagination Encaged and Provided for." Studies in the Novel, 9 (1977), 137-53.

Greenstein observes the likenesses of Strether and James and links The Ambassadors to some of James's autobiographical writings. Particularly noted is the development of what it means to "live," ultimately asserted by James as the imagination.

523. Grenander, M. E. "Benjamin Franklin's Glass Armonica and Henry James's 'Jolly Corner'." Papers on Language and Literature, 11 (1975), 415-17.

Grenander, in looking at Franklin, notes the hypnotic effect the glass armonica can have on listeners. He says that this may provide a clue to what Brydon sees in "The Jolly Corner."

524. Grenander, M. E. "Henrietta Stackpole and Olive Harper: Emanations of the Great Democracy." Bulletin of Research in the Humanities, 83 (1980), 406-22.
Grenander provides evidence that the character of Henrietta Stackpole in The Portrait of a Lady was based on Olive Harper (whose real name was Helen Burrell).

525. Griggs, Quay. "The Novel in John Gabriel Borkman: Henry James's The Ambassadors." Henry James Review, 1 (1980), 211-18.
Griggs maintains that Ibsen's play, John Gabriel Borkman, is a possible source for The Ambassadors. They share a carpe diem theme and James's characters and their relations and the use of Strether as central consciousness are indebted to Ibsen.

526. Grindea, Miron, ed. "Letters to the London Library: Edmund Gosse, J. M. Barrie, Henry James, George Moore, T. E. Lawrence, Aldous Huxley." Adam International Review, 397-400 (1976-77), 26-29.
Grindea offers reprints of some letters by distinguished members of the London Library, including one by Henry James.

527. Grove, James. "The Neglected Dinner in James's The Wings of the Dove." American Notes & Queries, 18 (1979), 5-6.
Grove cites the thematic importance, particularly regarding the perspectives concerning Milly, of the dinner at Aunt Maud's.

528. Grubman, G. B. "Amerikankaja monografia o Turgenev: Genri Džejmse." Russkaja Literatra, 22, i (1979), 211-16.

529. Grunes, Dennis. "The Demonic Child in The Turn of the Screw." Psychocultural Review, 2 (1978), 221-39.
Grunes examines the vulnerability of the child, the susceptibility to corruption or possession by demonic forces. He looks at the Christian context of the tale and at the literary tradition regarding demonic possession.

530. Gustafson, Judith A. "The Wings of the Dove: Or, A Gathering of Pigeons." Gypsy Scholar, 3 (1975), 13-19.
Gustafson states that The Wings of the Dove has been misread as a tale about a Fair Maiden who, on her deathbed,

induces nobility in a former cad. She maintains that Milly Theale is really the manipulator of Kate Croy, with Merton Densher as a "sacrificial lamb."

531. Gvozdeva, G. A. "G. Dzheims ob Isskustve Romana." Sbornik Nauchnykh Trudov Moskovskoyo Pedagogicheskogo Instituta Inostrannykh Yazykov, 84 (1975), 299-307.

532. Habegger, Alfred. "Autistic Tyrant: Howell's Self-Sacrificial Woman and Jamesian Renunciation." Novel: A Forum on Fiction, 10 (1976), 27-39.

Habegger offers explanations for the differences between James's version of renunciation and Howell's. In James's earlier works the renunciation is a bit pathological, whereas in later works it is a conscious act of withdrawal.

533. Haddick, Vern. "Colors in the Carpet." Gay Literature, 5 (1976), 19-21.

Haddick uses textual study to pursue the possibility that James was homosexual.

534. Haddick, Vern. "Fear and Growth: Reflections on 'The Beast in the Jungle'." Journal of the Otto Rank Association, 9, ii (1974-75), 38-42.

Haddick applies some Rankian thought, particularly the ideas of dual forces (fear and love), to a study of "The Beast in the Jungle."

535. Hall, Richard. "An Oscure Hurt: The Sexuality of Henry James." New Republic, 28 April 1979, pp. 25-31; 5 May 1979, pp. 25-29.

Hall examines James's sexual life through psychocritical techniques. He finds that James's relationship with William was the important relationship of his life. Hall then posits that there is evidence in James's writing of the betrayal he felt when William married.

536. Hall, William F. "Henry James and the Picturesque Mode." English Studies in Canada, 1 (1975), 326-43.

Hall looks at James's use of the picturesque tradition in Roderick Hudson and The Portrait of a Lady in particular. He sees it especially as derived from Hawthorne's Blithedale Romance. Hall examines the elements of caricature, melodrama, and also the use of myth and art.

537. Hall, William F. "The Meaning of *The Sacred Fount*: 'Its Own Little Law of Composition'." *Modern Language Quarterly*, 37 (1976), 168-78.

Hall takes issue with the psychological interpretation of *The Sacred Fount*. He states that, for the narrator, the fount siginifies Egeria and, for James and the reader, the fount has the connations of secular love. He also notes that the narrator comes to confuse what he has created with reality.

538. Hallab, Mary Y. "*The Turn of the Screw* Squared." *Southern Review*, 13 (1977), 492-504.

Hallab states that there are archetypal elements evident in *The Turn of the Screw*: innocence, evil, salvation, and so on. She applies Jungian principles to demonstrate the tale's reliance on myth and its effects on personal consciousness.

539. Halperin, John. "Trollope, James, and the International Theme." *Yearbook of English Studies*, 7 (1977), 141-47.

Halperin looks at the international theme in both James and Trollope. He notes that Trollope was probably influenced by *Daisy Miller* and "An International Episode," but also that James was probably influenced in his composition of *The Portrait of a Lady* by Trollope's *The Duke's Children*.

540. Hanley, Lynne T. "The Eagle and the Hen: Edith Wharton and Henry James." *Research Studies*, 49 (1981), 143-53.

Hanley looks at the relationship between the two writers in terms of Wharton's reaction to James's theorizing. She was wary of his preoccupation with theory and design, because of which, she said, verisimilitude suffered.

541. Harris, Janice H. "Bushes, Bears, and 'The Beast in the Jungle'." *Studies in Short Fiction*, 18 (1981), 147-54.

Harris contends that close attention to the language and imagery of "The Beast in the Jungle" and to May being given, it becomes evident that Marcher has been active, but he has not realized the extent of the impact of his actions.

542. Hartsock, Mildred. "Another Way to Heightened Consciousness." *Humanist*, 37 (July/August 1977), 26-30.

In "The Great Good Place" George Dane seeks out fulfillment first in negatives, according to Hartsock. He retreats from those things he can live without in order to achieve a heightened awareness.

543. Hartsock, Mildred. "The Most Valuable Thing: James on Death." Modern Fiction Studies, 22 (1976-77), 507-24.

Hartsock sees a consistency in James's view of death throughout his works. He sees death as termination and, as such, is an enemy to be confronted. This is a modern view, but he does not let it alter his urge to hold on to life.

544. Hartsock, Mildred E. "Time for Comedy: The Late Novels of Henry James." English Studies, 56 (1975), 114-28.

Hartsock makes a case for the comic in James's late fiction, particularly in The Ambassadors, The Wings of the Dove, and The Golden Bowl. The comedy serves to complement the seriousness of the three and gives them deeper meaning.

545. Heaton, Daniel H. "The Altered Characterizations of Miss Birdseye in Henry James's The Bostonians." American Literature, 50 (1979), 588-603.

Heaton notes that James treats Miss Birdseye negatively in the early chapters of The Bostonians but in a more positive light for the remainder of the book. One reason for the change may have been a letter from William upbraiding Henry for an unflattering caricature of Elizabeth Peabody, on whom Miss Birdseye was to have been based.

546. Hewitt, Rosalie. "Henry James's The American Scene: Its Genesis and Its Reception, 1905-1977." Henry James Review, 1 (1980), 179-96.

Hewitt examines and lists criticism of The American Scene. She says that some early critics wrote negatively of the stylistic difficulty, that later criticism overemphasized its content, and that recent criticism resembles that of the time of the book's publication.

547. Higgins, Joanna A. "The Ambassadorial Motif in The Ambassadors." Journal of Narrative Technique, 8 (1978), 165-75.

Higgins looks at Strether's renunciation of Maria Gostrey in terms of the ambassadorial motif--the representation of a character to another to elicit perceptual changes in others.

548. Hill, Robert W., Jr. "A Counterclockwise Turn in James's The Turn of the Screw." Twentieth Century Literature, 27 (1981), 53-71.

Hill states that Miles' apparent awareness of carnality coupled with his youth produces confusion for the boy, particularly in his relationship with the governess. The governess's hallucinations prompt turmoil in her relationship with Miles. The two invent worlds, each inhabited by the other, and the dual confusion is fatal to Miles.

549. Hoag, Gerald. "The Death of the Paper Lion." Studies in Short Fiction, 12 (1975), 163-72.
Hoag examines James's story "The Death of the Lion." He contends that the character of Neil Paraday is not completely drawn and his greatness is not established. It may be more parody than serious.

550. Hochman, Baruch. "From Middlemarch to The Portrait of a Lady: Some Reflections on Henry James and the Traditions of the Novel." Hebrew University Studies in Literature, 5 (1977), 102-26.
Hochman notes that there are similarities between Middlemarch and The Portrait of a Lady but that there are also basic differences in the outlooks on life and art. For instance, James's work concedes the existence of evil, but Eliot's characters intend nothing malevolent. Hochman contends that James does not probe for motives and that his works are severely limited.

551. Hochman, Baruch. "The Jamesian Situation: World as Spectacle." Denver Quarterly, 11, i (1976), 48-66.
Hochman maintains that James treats the world as spectacle, that characters have a childlike relation to the world. Though James's children (in What Maisie Knew, The Turn of the Screw, and others) fit this mold, so too do Isabel Archer. Milly Theale, and Maggie Verver. Hochman also says that this tendency of James limits him to surfaces.

552. Hocks, Richard A. "Daisy Miller, Backward into the Past: A Centennial Essay." Henry James Review, 1 (1980), 164-78.
Hocks states that Daisy Miller presaged James's later international fiction. It is a success of American literary realism and represents James's early examination of the relationship of American to European.

553. Hocks, Richard A. and John S. Hardt. "James Studies 1978-1979: An Analytic Bibliographical Essay." Henry James Review, 2 (1980), 132-52.
Hocks and Hardt examine some of the work on James published in 1978 and 1979 in their bibliographical essay. They note that James's middle period received more attention than any other.

554. Hoile, Christopher. "Lambert Strether and the Boaters--Tonio Kroger and the Dancers: Confrontation and Self-Acceptance." Canadian Review of Comparative Literature, 2 (1975), 243-61.
Hoile endeavors to examine the awakening consciousness and awareness of Strether through his reaction to the pairing of Chad Newsome and Madame de Vionnet, both of whom he is introduced individually. He compares this aspect of The Ambassadors to Tonio Kroger.

555. Holloway, Marcella M. "Another Turn to James' The Turn of the Screw." CEA Critic, 41, ii (1979), 9-17.
Holloway stresses the importance of looking at the entirety of The Turn of the Screw. The governess's manuscript is seen by Holloway as a confession to its recipient.

556. Horwitz, B. D. "The Sense of Desolation in Henry James." Psychocultural Review, 1 (1977), 466-92.
Horwitz examines some forms of desolation in various works by James. Complex relationships and their effects on the ego are looked at in "The Pupil." Horwitz also pays attention to James's investigation of the many forms of perception and consciousness and James's depiction of the family.

557. Houston, Neal B. "A Footnote to the Death of Miles." Re: Artes Liberales, 3, ii (1977), 25-27.
Houston agress with Muriel West in stating that the governess's physical assault of Miles may be the cause of his death.

558. Hubert, Thomas. "The Princess Casamassima: Ideas against Persons." Arizona Quarterly, 32 (1976), 341-52.
Hubert examines the conflict between allegiance to ideology and devotion to persons in The Princess Casamassima. The conflict exists in Hyacinth Robinson and James favors placing individuals above ideas.

559. Hudspeth, Robert N. "A Hard, Shining Sonnet: The Art of Short Fiction in James's 'Europe'." Studies in Short Fiction, 12 (1975), 387-95.
In "Europe" James observes some of the American, particularly the New England, culture that he dislikes most. The form of the short story provides sharp focus for this moral drama.

560. Hunting, Constance. "The Identity of Miss Tina in The Aspern Papers." Studies in the Humanities, 5, ii (1976), 28-31.
Hunting examines the place of Miss Tina in the tale, particularly her relation to Juliana. Hunting concludes that Miss Tina is the illegitimate child of Jeffrey Aspern by Juliana's younger sister.

561. Huntley, H. Robert. "James's 'The Turn of the Screw': Its 'Fine Machinery'." American Imago, 34 (1977), 224-37.
There is the possibility, according to Huntley, that James was experimenting with the Doppelganger, or double, motif in The Turn of the Screw, though in an ambiguous and muted manner.

562. Hutchison, Stuart. "James's Medal: Optimism in The Wings of the Dove." Essays in Criticism, 27 (1977), 315-35.
Hutchison says there is a humanity evident in The Wings of the Dove. James does not allow the reader to feel too superior to the characters so that the reader (and James himself) shares in their failure, thus humanizing the novel.

563. Hyde, H. Montgomery. "Henry James at Home." Essays by Divers Hands, 38 (1975), 58-77.
Hyde recounts James's years at his home, Lamb House, Rye.

564. Hynes, Joseph. "The Transparent Shroud: Henry James and William Story." American Literature, 46 (1975), 506-27.
James knew William Wetmore Story and, Hynes contends, James owes something of a debt to Story and his generation. James learned, by writing Story's biography, some of the dangers to creativity that the previous heneration did not avoid.

565. Itagaki, Konomu. "The Progress of Seeing in The Portrait of a Lady." Studies in English Literature, 54 (1977), 83-98.

566. Jacobs, Edward Craney. "James's 'Amiable Auditress': An Ironic Pun." Studies in the Novel, 9 (1977), 311.
Jacobs briefly notes a perceived pun in The Portrait of a Lady.

567. Jacobson, Marcia. "Convention and Innovation in The Princess Casamassima." Journal of English and Germanic Philology, 76, (1977), 238-54.
The Princess Casamassima marks a departure for James in that it deals with the working class. Jacobson notes that it is not falsely optimistic but that it fails to address the real discontents of the working class in England in the 1880s.

568. Jabobson, Marcia. "Literary Convention and Social Criticism in Henry James's The Awkward Age." Philological Quarterly, 54 (1975), 633-46.
While contemporary reviewers wrote harshly about The Awkward Age, some noted that the dialogue captured the conversation of the intellectually acute but morally indifferent. James used conversation in the novel to expose social foibles rather than to affirm the values of the society.

569. Jacobson, Marcia. "Popular Fiction and Henry James's Unpopular Bostonians." Modern Philology, 73 (1976), 264-75.
Jacobson looks at The Bostonians along with other fiction of the day and maintains that The Bostonians is a political novel. It contends that the war produced irreconcilable differences and that the women's movement produced further difficulties.

570. Jeffers, Thomas L. "Maisie's Moral Sense: Finding Out for Herself." Nineteenth-Century Fiction, 34 (1979), 154-72.
Jeffers examines the possible sources of Maisie's moral consciousness. In spite of adversity and lack of proper and strong moral direction, she is able to learn a considerable amount on her own and to assimilate that learning.

571. Jeffrey, David K. "On Henry James." Scholia Satyrica, 1, i (1975), 13-18.
Jeffrey offers this satirical piece, his notion of what Twain's criticism of James would have been. "James's Literary Offenses" is presented as a newly discovered work by Twain.

572. Jensen-Osinski, Barbara. "The Key to the Palpable Past: A Study of Miss Tina in The Aspern Papers." Henry James Review, 3 (1981), 4-10.
Jensen-Osinski offers that Tina proposes marriage to the narrator to resolve her inner conflict and to give the narrator an opportunity to prove his humanity by joining the Venice family. She focuses on Tina's strength of character and her action.

573. Johnson, D. Barton. "A Henry James Parody in Ada." Vladimir Nabokov Research Newsletter, 3 (1979), 33-34.
Johnson notes some parallels between Ada and Daisy Miller, with Nabokov parodying James's prose style in Ada.

574. Jones, O. P. "The Cool World of London in 'The Beast in the Jungle'." Studies in American Fiction, 6 (1978), 227-35.
Jones states that, in reading "The Beast in the Jungle" one must be aware of the threatening presence of London and the effects it has on Marcher's world and his consciousness.

575. Jones, Peter. "Pragmatism and The Portrait of a Lady." Philosophy and Literature, 5 (1981), 49-61.
Jones sees The Portrait of a Lady as consistent with William James's view of pragmatism as method, although the novel predates by many years the publication of Pragmatism.

576. Jungman, Robert E. "A Mock-Heroic Reference in The Ambassadors." Modern British Literature, 3 (1978), 79-80.
Jungman cites a brief passage in The Ambassadors that may be a parody of Julius Caesar's statement, "I came, I saw, I conquered,"

577. Kadir, Djelal. "Another Sense of the Past: Henry James' The Aspern Papers and Carlos Fuentes' Aura." Revue de Littérature Comparée, 50 (1976), 448-54.
James follows an American line of thought in depicting the past as allowing no redemption, though itself not irredeemable. As opposed to Mexican tradition represented here by Fuentes, there is a finality to James's work.

578. Kantrow, Alan M. "Anglican Custom, American Consciousness." New England Quarterly, 52 (1979), 307-25.
Kantrow states that Newman rediscovers himself in Catholic Europe in The American. Also, Catholic Europe serves as an analogy to the Anglican consciousness of Newman's fellow Americans. The American thus serves as a cautionary tale for Americans.

579. Kaston, Carren O. "Emersonian Consciousness and The Spoils of Poynton." ESQ, 26 (1980), 88-99.
Kaston, while not attempting to demonstrate a direct influence of Emerson on James's composition of The Spoils of Poynton, does attempt to show the impact of Emersonian thought, familiar to James, on the consciousnesses of James's characters, not surprising considering James's family background.

580. Kaston, Carren Osna. "Houses of Fiction in What Maisie Knew." Criticism, 18 (1976), 27-42.

Kaston says that in the course of What Maisie Knew Maisie escapes from the custodial houses that define her existence and from the fictional "house" James creates for her as a narrative device.

581. Kauffman, Linda S. "The Author of Our Woe: Virtue Recorded in The Turn of the Screw." Nineteenth-Century Fiction, 36 (1981), 176-92

Kauffman maintains that the object of the governess's love is the uncle in Harley Street to whom the manuscript is addressed. She further states that the tragedy of the tale is the inconfirmed and denied love of the governess.

582. Kaufman, Jule S. "The Spoils of Poynton: In Defense of Fleda Vetch." Arizona Quarterly, 35 (1979), 342-56.

Kaufman attempts to examine Fleda as an individual struggling to attain freedom. She is the most "human" character of the novel and, although she fails, there is hope in her humanity.

583. Kaul, R. K. "The Jamesian Hero." Indian Journal of American Studies, 6, i (1976), 65-71.

Kaul uses James's autobiographical writings and Roderick Hudson in his study of the hero in James, which he sees as a man of imagination. James strives to place the artist in the heroic role once occupied by the inspired prophet.

584. Keefe, Carolyn. "Mystic Experience in Till We Have Faces." Bulletin of the New York C. S. Lewis Society, 7, i (1975), 4-7.

585. Keyser, Elizabeth. "Veils and Masks: The Blithedale Romance and The Sacred Fount." Henry James Review, 2 (1980), 101-10.

Keyser says Miles Coverdale provides James with a model for some of his observers, among whom is the narrator of The Sacred Fount. The two characters can be seen in terms of failure to accept life or the triumph of life in the face of death. Death, or death in life, is the predominate image of both novels.

586. Kimmey, John L. "The 'London' Book." Henry James Review, 1 (1979), 61-72.

Kimmey finds numerous references to the architecture and cultural life of London in James's Notebooks and

Autobiography. These notes, Kimmey observes, were written in preparation for a books on London which James was never able to write.

587. Kirchhoff, Frederick. "City as Self: Henry James's Travel Sketches of Venice." Prose Studies 1800-1900, 2 (1979), 73-87.

Kirchhoff recognizes James's precarious position in his travel sketches of being an outsider trying to place himself on the inside. Focusing on sketches of Venice in Italian Hours, Kirchhoff notes a link between James and the city, the discovery of his identity and the discovery of Venice.

588. Kirk, Carey H. "Daisy Miller: The Reader's Choice." Studies in Short Fiction, 17 (1980), 275-83.

Kirk offers some textual evidence in favor of Winterbourne and against Daisy to illustrate the choices that are available to the reader of Daisy Miller. James purposely places the reader in the position of being responsible for the choice.

589. Knights, L. C. "Henry James and Human Liberty." Sewanee Review, 83 (1975), 1-18.

Knights looks at the theme of domination (physical and psychological) in James and the conflict with human liberty. In this, as in other aspects of his writing, James wants the reader to eschew generalization and to pay attention to the specific.

590. Kondo, Keiko. "A Comparative Study of Eliot's Early Poems and James's Work." Sophia English Studies, 1 (1976), 53-70.

591. Korenmen, Joan S. "Henry James and the Murderous Mind." Essays in Literature, 4 (1977), 198-211.

Korenman recognizes the importance of consciousness in James, observes that his characters experience life largely through the mind. At time, though, the mind can be the cause of retreat from experience, and the ultimate retreat is death.

592. Kotzin, Michael. "The American and The Newcomes." Études Anglaises, 30 (1977), 420-29.

Kotizin sees the influence of Thackeray's novel, The Newcomes, on The American. Newman's reception in Paris is similar to that of Thomas Newcome by his relatives. Other similarities and James's own comments point to James's reading of Thackeray.

593. Kozikowski, Stanley J. "Unreliable Narration in Henry James's 'The Two Faces' and Edith Wharton's 'The Dilettante'." Arizona Quarterly, 35 (1979), 357-72.
Kozikowski looks at the related stories, "The Two Faces" and "The Dilettante," especially in terms of the use of the narrator. He also looks at Wharton's attempt to free herself of the accusation that she imitates James.

594. Krenn, Sister Heliena. "The American Identity in the 'Novels of Manners'." Fu Jen Studies, 10 (1977), 41-57.
Krenn studies the international theme in James from the standpoint of manners. She focuses on the women of James's novels and the differences between American manners and European manners.

595. Kreyling, Michael. "Nationalizing the Southern Hero: Adams and James." Mississippi Quarterly, 34 (1981), 383-402.
Kreyling examines the Southern hero in the person of Basil Ransom of The Bostonians. Ransom is not a "nationalized" Southern hero; such characteristics as chivalry and a desire for national unity are not claimed by him. Rather, in appetite and expression Ransom most closely resembles Wilbur J. Cash's "savage ideal." As such, he was an anomaly in popular fiction.

596. Krier, William J. "The 'Latent Extravagance' of The Portrait of a Lady." Mosaic, 9, iii (1976), 57-65.
Krier examines the development of the character of Isabel Archer throughout the novel. He maintains that she is eventually emancipated; she becomes her own author. At that point the narrative must perforce come to an end.

597. Krupnick, Mark L. "The Golden Bowl: Henry James's Novel about Nothing." English Studies, 57 (1976), 533-40.
Krupnick says that the plot, imagery, characters, and moral purpose of The Golden Bowl are secondary to its language and the study of aesthetics within the novel.

598. Krupnick, Mark [L.] "Playing with the Silence: Henry James's Poetics of Loss." Forum, 13, iii (1976), 37-42.
Krupnick investigates James's method of using silence to signify the "loss of the actual and the instinctual," and also to signify the psychology behind this method of composition.

599. Kudo, Yoshimi. "Mizu no Image wo Megatte: Mill on the Floss to The Ambassadors." Eigo Seinen, 121 (1976), 439-42.

600. Kudo, Yoshimi. "Shiten to ishiki to kotoba: Henry James no The Golden Bowl o megatte." Eigo Seinen, 125 (1979), 122-24, 152, 200-02, 250-53.

601. Kummings, Donald D. "The Issue of Mrality in James's The Golden Bowl." Arizona Quarterly, 32 (1976), 381-91.

Kummings looks at Maggie and the Prince as a pair and as the only two who achieve a moral awareness by the end of the novel.

602. Labatt, Blair P. "The Exploring Logic of Henry James." Cahiers d'études et de recherches victoriennes et édouardiennes, 7 (1978), 67-81.

Labatt sees the search for meaning in James as an attempt to discover the persona implicit in the text. He also says that James replaces the logic of organization with a logic of language, significant objects, and structure.

603. Labrie, Ross. "The Good and the Beautiful in Henry James." Greyfriar, 16 (1975), 3-15.

Labrie states that, in many of James's works, there are characters who are governed by either aesthetic or moral awareness. These are juxtaposed with characters with somewhat more complete, but not perfect, perception and awareness.

604. Labrie, Ross. "The Other House: A Jamesian Thriller." North Dakota Quarterly, 45 (1977), 23-30.

Labrie examines The Other House as a psychological thriller. Rather than relying on characterization, this novel centers on dramatic and narrative development, particularly on James's deft foreshadowing of what is to come.

605. Laird, J. T. "Cracks in Precious Objects: Aestheticism and Humanity in The Portrait of a Lady." American Literature, 52 (1981), 643-48.

Laird maintains that, while James does frequently incorporate the theme of the conflict of the aesthetic and the moral, the conflict of aestheticism and humanity is more centralto The Portrait of a Lady than most of his other works.

606. Landiera, Ricardo López. "Aura, The Aspern Papers, 'A Rose for Emily': A Literary Relationship." Journal of Spanish Studies: Twentieth Century, 3 (1975), 125-43.

Landiera points out some similarities of the three works: each has a character who is a widow (figuratively or literally); these characters are heiresses who live in old houses; and in each there is a degree of misanthropy. Landiera states that his comparison is not meant to imply interdependence.

607. Lang, Hans-Joachim. "The Making of Henry James's 'The American': The Contribution of Four Literatures." Amerikastudien, 20 (1975), 55-71.

Lang focuses on the basis of inspiration and sources for The American. James's inspiration came from many places, including Turgenev and French literature, and particularly (according to Lang) from Hawthorne's The House of the Seven Gables.

608. Lavers, Norman. "Art and Reality: The Theme of The Sacred Fount." Publications of the Arkansas Philological Association, 4, ii (1978), 37-44.

Lavers notes that The Sacred Fount may be infrequently studied because of its ambiguity. The novel focuses on the creative process which can be analogous to James's novelistic effort put forth in the creation of a work of art.

609. Lay, Mary M. "Parallels: Henry James's The Portrait of a Lady and Nella Larsen's Quicksand." College Language Association Journal, 20 (1977), 475-86.

Lay notes similarities of characters and plot between The Portrait of a Lady and Larsen's Quicksand. Lay particularly notes personality parallels between Isabel Archer and the heroine of Quicksand, Helga crane, along with plot parallels.

610. Lay, Mary M. "The Real Beasts: Surrogate Brothers in James's 'The Pupil' and The Princess Casamassima." American Literary Realism, 1870-1910, 13 (1980), 73-84.

Lay notes in this article some similarities in the disillusionment and frustration of "The Pupil" and The Princess Casamassima, precipitated in large part according to Lay by what she sees as the generally unsatisfactory relationships between the male characters in each of the works.

611. Lees, Francis Noel. "Isabel Clarendon and Henry James." Gissing Newsletter, 11, i (1975), 12-14.
Lees suggests that James influenced George Gissing in his composition of his novel, Isabel Clarendon.

612. Leitch, Thomas M. "The Editor as Hero: Henry James and the New York Edition." Henry James Review, 3 (1981), 24-32.
With the New York Edition James stressed both his mature style and his mature aesthetic in his choice of selections to be included and in his revisions, according to Leitch. Leitch also says that the most important legacy of the New York Edition is the shift of hero from character to author and from author to reader.

613. Lester, Pauline. "James's Use of Comedy in 'The Real Thing'." Studies in Short Fiction, 15 (1978), 33-38.
Lester looks at the place of the comic in "The Real Thing," particularly as provided by Miss Churm and Oronte. Comedy, though limited, is a means of shaping meaning and rendering experience.

614. Leverentz, David. "Reflections on Two Henries: James and Kissinger." Soundings, 59 (1976), 374-95.
Leverentz's study compares the theory and work of James with the public life of Kissinger. Both attempt to manipulate. James's ironic perspective endures, and Kissinger illustrates the effect of structure for the sake of structure.

615. Levy, Leo B. "The Golden Bowl and 'the Voice of Blood'." Henry James Review, 1 (1980), 154-63.
Levy says The Golden Bowl is a novel of relationships: the ties between Adam and Maggie; the social relationships exterior to those involving the four main characters; and the sexual relationships of various sorts among the four. The relationships are in flux and compromise is the only possible resolution.

616. Levy, Leo B. "Consciousness in Three Early Tales of Henry James." Studies in Short Fiction, 18 (1981), 407-12.
Levy looks at James's early treatment of the subject of consciousness (including its various limitations and its convolutions). Levy focuses his attention on "A Landscape Painter," "My Friend Bingham," and "Osborne's Revenge."

617. Levy, Leo B. "Henry James and the Image of Franklin." Southern Review, 16 (1980), 552-59.

Levy maintains that James was attracted to Benjamin Franklin, particularly to Poor Richard. He sees in Franklin's Autobiography a struggle to control externals that is similar to James's struggles. Levy also finds traces of Franklin in James's fiction.

618. Lewis, Paul. "Beyond Mystery: Emergence from Delausion as a Pattern in Gothic Fiction." Gothic, 2 (1980), 7-13.

Lewis examines the Gothic aspect of a number of works, including "The Beast in the Jungle." He focuses on the mysterious horror of the awaited occurrence as the element that makes the tale Gothic.

619. Lock, Peter W. "'The Figure in the Carpet': The Text as Riddle and Force." Nineteenth-Century Fiction, 36 (1981), 157-75.

Lock looks upon the literary text as a dynamic force that cannot be dominated or even seen as a unified whole. A text such as "The Figure in the Carpet," that Lock focuses his attention on may reveal nothing more than its own force.

620. Long, Robert Emmet. "Henry James's Apprenticeship: The Hawthorne Aspect." American Literature, 48 (1976), 194-216.

When James began writing fiction there was a scant tradition of American fiction. Long says that James read Hawthorne and adapted his realistic tendencies to themes derived from Hawthorne. Clues to psychological insight also have their henesis in Hawthorne.

621. Long, Robert Emmet. "James's Roderick Hudson: The End of the Apprenticeship: Hawthorne and Turgenev." American Literature, 48 (1976), 312-26.

James's early fiction owes much to Hawthorne and also to Turgenev, but Roderick Hudson, which includes elements of both mentors, marks a move toward independence for James in his fiction. James provides a clear and specific working of a theme similar to that of The Marble Faun.

622. Long, Robert Emmet. "Transformations: The Blithedale Romance to Howells and James." American Literature, 47 (1976), 552-71.

Long sees a line of descent from The Blithedale Romance to Howells' The Undiscovered Country and James's

The Bostonians. James takes his inspiration from Hawthorne but subjects his story to a more modern understanding based on the possibility of living life fully or failing to do so.

623. Lycette, Ronald L. "Perceptual Touchstones for the Jamesian Artist-Hero." Studies in Short Fiction, 14 (1977), 55-62.

Lycette examines "The Real Thing" and "The Middle Years," particularly the relationship between James's pictorial and dramatic modes of story-telling. These modes provide a gateway to the inner lives and experiences of the characters.

624. MacAdam, Alfred. "La figura en el tapiz: La coincidencia de Cortázar y James." Inti: Revista de Literatura Hispánica et Luso-Brasilera, 10-11 (1979-80), 173-78.

625. McCullough, Joseph B. "Madame Merle: Henry James's 'White Blackbird'." Papers on Language and Literature, 11 (1975), 312-16.

McCullough notes the significance of Madame Merle's name, which means "blackbird." He states that its allusions and James's descriptions of her give clues to her character.

626. McFee, Michael. "The Church Scenes in The Ambassadors, The American, and The Wings of the Dove." Papers on Language and Literature, 16 (1980), 325-28.

McFee exmaines the different thematic uses of the church, chapel, and other significant religious places in The Ambassadors, The American, and The Wings of the Dove.

627. McMahan, Elizabeth. "Sexual Desire and Illusion in The Bostonians." Modern Fiction Studies, 25 (1979), 241-51.

McMahan notes that Ransom's attitude is that of the "classic male supremisist." He is enormously attractive to Verena who has a penchant for confusing illusion with reality. She gives in to her sexual desires, which are part of the source of illusion for her.

628. McMaster R[owland] D. "'An Honorable Emulation of the Author of The Newcomes': James and Thackeray." Nineteenth-Century Fiction, 32 (1978), 399-419.

Early in James's career, Thackeray was one of the major influences on his writing, according to McMaster. In particular, The Newcomes influenced the composition of both <u>Roderick Hudson</u> and <u>The American</u>. McMaster points out there is evidence for these claims in James's autobiographical writings.

629. McMurray, William. "Reality in Henry James's 'The Birthplace'." <u>Explicator</u>, 35, i (1976), 10-11.
McMurray maintains that the author in "The Birthplace" exists within the life and the experience of Morris Gedge.

630. McMurray, William. "Reality in James' 'The Great Good Place'." <u>Studies in Short Fiction</u>, 14 (1977), 82-83.
McMurray proposes that, in "The Great Good Place," the material world and the inner world are aspects of a single reality.

631. McNaughton, W. R. "Maisie's Grace under Pressure: Some Thoughts on James and Hemingway." <u>Modern Fiction Studies</u>, 22 (1976), 153-64.
McNaughton sees some parallels between <u>What Maisie Knew</u> and <u>The Sun Also Rises</u>. McNaughton maintains that, while both books deal in part with squalor and difficulty, James and Hemingway are positive writers, expressing hope and endurance.

632. Mack, Stanley Thomas. "The Narrator in James's 'The Death of the Lion': A Religious Conversion of Sorts." <u>Thoth</u>, 16, i (1975-76), 19-25.
Mack looks at the fate of Neil Paraday in "The Death of the Lion" and the lessons learned by the narrator. He contends that the narrator chronicles the events as a personal witness of the action and also out of a personal need.

633. Mackle, Elliott. "Two Mistakes by Henry James in <u>The American Scene</u>." <u>American Literary Realism, 1870-1910</u>, 10 (1977), 211-12.
Mackle notes some errors of James in <u>The American Scene</u> regarding his descriptions of the state of Florida.

634. Maini, Darshan Singh. "<u>Washington Square</u>: A Centennial Essay." <u>Henry James Review</u>, 1 (1979), 81-101.
Maini points out that <u>Washington Square</u> marks a point of transition for James. The influence of French novelists is now fading and his style is more markedly his own. It combines the scenic methods and omniscient-author narration with good effect.

635. Malmgren, Carl. "Henry James's Major Phase: Making Room for the Reader." Henry James Review, 3 (1981), 17-23.
With the fiction of the major phase James signals the beginning of modern fiction, according to Malmgren. For instance, interpretation becomes the responsibility of the reader. The Author is less dominant, thus resulting in more reader initiative.

636. Manolesu, Nicolae. "Donă femei." Steaua, 28, viii (1977), 20.

637. Marks, Patricia. "Culture and Rhetoric in Henry James's 'Poor Richard' and 'Eugene Pickering'." South Atlantic Bulletin, 44, i (1979), 61-72.
Marks examines the cultural background of romanticism, aestheticism, and puritanism that comes into play in James's composition of "Eugene Pickering" and Poor Richard: A Tragedy."

638. Marotta, Kenny. "What Maisie Knew: The Question of Our Speech." ELH, 46 (1979), 495-508.
Marotta examines the language of What Maisie Knew, which is one of the first novels of his late style and which is distinctly different from earlier narratives in the added responsibility placed on the reader. In the novel the manipulative aspect of language is especially evident.

639. Martin Robert K. "The 'High Felicity' of Comradeship: A New Reading of Roderick Hudson." American Literary Realism, 1870-1910, 11 (1978) 100-08.
Martin's reading of Roderick Hudson focuses on the relationship of Roderick Rowland Mallet. Martin contends that there is especially evident the presence of Rowland's homosexual love for Roderick.

640. Martin, Timothy P. "Henry James and Percy Lubbock: From Mimesis to Formalism." Novel: A Forum on Fiction, 14 (1980), 20-29.
While acknowledging Lubbock's debt to James the critic, Martin notes differences in their theories. James, he says, is a mimetic critic, for whom art has a moral end. Lubbock is a formalist who seeks to confront art on its own terms. The difference is based, according to Martin, on a shift toward experimentation in twentirth-century fiction.

641. Martin, W. R. "The Narrator's 'Retreat' in James's 'Four Meetings'." Studies in Short Fiction, 17 (1980), 497-99.
Martin offers more evidence of the narrator's irritability in "Four Meetings."

642. Martin, W. R. and Warren U. Ober. "'Crapy Cornelia': James's Self-Vindication?" Ariel: A Review of International English Literature, 11, iv (1980), 57-68.
The images of the dance and the fire are significant in their connection with the writer and his reader. Through "Crapy Cornelia" James conveys the sympathetic relationship between the two images established by the telling.

643. Matthews, Robert J. "Describing and Interpreting a Work of Art." Journal of Aesthetics and Art Criticism, 36 (1977), 5-14.
Using a panel discussion of The Turn of the Screw as an example, Matthews points out that sometimes certain aspects of a work of art can be described and others cannot. Attempts to describe the latter can result in interpretation that may be neither false nor true.

644. Mayer, Charles W. "Henry James's 'Discriminated Occasion': A Determination of Form." Journal of Narrative Technique, 9 (1979), 133-46.
Mayer examines the background of the term "discriminated occasion" that appears in the preface to The Wings of the Dove. He relates this to structure, citing specific relationships among occasions in The Wings of the Dove.

645. Mayer, Charles W. "Henry James's 'Indispensable Centre': The Search for Compositional Unity." Essays in Literature, 3 (1976), 97-104.
Mayer states that unity for James consisted of the successful marriage of subject and form, with the consciousness of the characters as a cohesive force. He further states that The Spoils of Poynton and What Maisie Knew achieve integration of the elements necessary for unity.

646. Mayer, Charles W. "Isabel Archer, Edna Pontellier, and the Romantic Self." Research Studies, 47 (1979), 89-97.
Though there are a number of obvious differences, Mayer finds some similarities between James's Isabel Archer and Kate Chopin's Edna Pontellier, most notably Emersonian idealism and a romantic idea of self. James realizes the importance of consciousness, though, while action in The Awakening is governed by mood.

647. Mayer, Charles W. "The Triumph of Honor: James and Hemingway." Arizona Quarterly, 35 (1979), 373-91.
Both James and Hemingway attest that there is no victory possible, but that man and their characters can retain honor through adherence to a personal moral code, says Mayer.

648. Maynard, Reid N. "Autotelism in Henry James's Aestheticism." Tennessee Studies in Literature, 21 (1976), 35-42.
Maynard notes that James believed art could exist of itself and by itself. This belief is evident in James's contention that art is of the artist's mind and thus of experience and that it should be realistic as part of the artist's consciousness.

649. Mazzella, Anthony J. "An Answer to the Mystery of The Turn of the Screw." Studies in Short Fiction, 17 (1980), 327-33.
Mazzella states that he tries to use the methods of the detective to solve the mystery of The Turn of the Screw. He says that the act of writing down the events creates a distance from them, as does the act of reading a text.

650. Mazzella, Anthony J. "'The Illumination [That] Was All for the Mind': The BBC Video Adaptation of The Golden Bowl." Henry James Review, 2 (1981), 213-27.
Mazzella states that the BBC adaptation of The Golden Bowl is a sensitive translation of the novel to another medium. Jack Pulman's script and James Cellan Jones' direction manage to capture James's language and discrimination in the action of the visual form. Some alterations are inevitable, though, and the effect is a different reader-viewer experience.

651. Mazzella, Anthony J. "A Selected Henry James Artsography." Henry James Review, 3 (1981), 44-58.
Mazzella provides a list of James's works adapted for dance, film, radio, television, opera, and spoken-word recording.

652. Manikoff, Barry. "A House Divided: A New Reading of The Bostonians." College Language Association Journal, 20 (1977), 459-74.
Manikoff shares with William Dean Howells and William James every high esteem for The Bostonians. He sees the contest for Verena as one for the heart of America and the conflict is not resolved since America has yet to resolve its difficulties.

653. Merivale, Patricia. "The Esthetics of Perversion: Gothic Artifice in Henry James and Witold Gombrowicz." PMLA, 93 (1978), 992-1002.
Merivale compares The Sacred Fount with Gombrowicz' Cosmos and The Turn of the Screw with Pornografia. The Turn of the Screw, according to Merivale, is more obviously Gothic; The Sacred Fount links Gothic with the nouveau roman.

654. Meyers, Jeffrey. "Velázquez and 'Daisy Miller'." Studies in Short Fiction, 16 (1979), 171-78.
Meyers sees an important connection between Velazquez' painting of Pope Innocent X and the meaning of Daisy Miller. Velázquez' portrait conveys an idealistic vision while Winterbourne is mired in his narrowly superficial vision.

655. Michaels, Walter Benn. "Writers Reading: James and Eliot." MLN, 91 (1976), 827-49.
Michaels notes James's claim that the writer must also be the reader of his works. The reader projects himself onto the work and so becomes responsible for it. In this way the act of reading is not a passive one but an active one.

656. Milicia, Joseph. "Henry James' Winter's Tale: 'The Bench of Desolation'." Studies in American Fiction, 6 (1978), 141-56.
Milicia offers a detailed examination of "The Bench of Desolation," noting its themes of weariness and reconciliation (as a positive but costly act) and its many ambiguities, including the ending.

657. Miller, J. Hillis. "The Figure in the Carpet." Poetics Today, 1, iii (1980), 107-18.
Miller discusses the narrative problem approached by James of producing continuity while dealing with finite form. He states that the artist must act as a kind of father, a benevolent overseer, controlling himself and his own power as an artist.

658. Miller, James E., Jr. "Henry James in Reality." Critical Inquiry, 2 (1976), 585-604.
James, the critic and theorist, has proven to be rather immune to much attack because of the unity of his theory with his language. James recognizes that reality in literature is not single because it is born of the varied forms of the writer's consciousness.

659. Miller, Nancy K. "Novels of Innocence: Fictions of Loss." Eighteenth-Century Studies, 11 (1978), 325-39.
Miller studies The Portrait of a Lady and The Wings of the Dove as novels about the loss of innocence. She says the loss is more than sexual but also attacks illusions and threatens characters' concepts of self.

660. Miller, Vivienne. "Henry James and the Alienation of the Artist: 'The Lesson of the Master'." English Studies in Africa, 23 (1980), 9-20.
Miller states that, for James, the paradox of the artist's life is the same as the paradox of art and the reconciliation of Artist and Life is the same as that for Art and Life. She examines this stance as evidenced in "The Lesson of the Master."

661. Milne, Fred L. "Atmosphere as Triggering Device in The Turn of the Screw." Studies in Short Fiction, 18 (1981), 293-99.
Milne states that the atmosphere of The Turn of the Screw is not just a background or accompaniment to the governess's hallucinations. Atmosphere, especially light and sound help to induce these hallucinations in the governess.

662. Minnick, Thomas L. "'The Light of Deepening Experience' in the Major Novels of Henry James." Rendezvous, 10, ii (1975), 37-51.
Minnick examines images of light and dark in James's later fiction in terms of their prefigurement of characters' experiences and their relation to characters' perception and awareness.

663. Mochi Gioli, Giovanna. "'The Beast in the Jungle' e l'assenza del referente." Paragone, 314 (1976), 51-76.

664. Mogen, David. "Agonies of Innocence: The Governess and Maggie Verver." American Literary Realism, 1870-1910, 9 (1976), 231-42.
Mogen examines James's characterizations of the governess and Maggie Verver as products of the Victorian age, noting the conflict of emotion and society and the problems of Victorian innocence.

665. Monteiro, George. "Henry James and Scott Fitzgerald: A Source." Notes on Contemporary Literature, 6, ii (1976), 4-6.
Monteiro examines similarities between Daisy Miller and

Tender Is the Night. He pays particular attention to the narration of the encounter of the two young people in each.

666. Monteiro, George. "Henry James and the Lessons of Sordello." Western Humanities Review, 31 (1977), 69-78.

Monteiro examines the relationship of some stories by James and some poems by Browning, particularly as he sees Browning having influenced James's composition of "The Lesson of the Master."

667. Monteiro, George. "Innocence and Experience: The Adolescent Child in the Works of Mark Twain, Henry James, and Ernest Hemingway." Estudos Anglo-American, 1 (1977), 39-57.

668. Monteiro, George. "'The Items of High Civilization': Hawthorne, Henry James, and George Parsons Lathrop." Nathaniel Hawthorne Journal, 1975, pp. 146-55.

Monteiro looks at James's publication of Hawthorne, and particularly at the reception of the book by George Parsons Lathrop. Monteiro includes a long letter by Lathrop to the New York Tribune. He also notes that, while Lathrop disagreed with James, he defended him against "outsiders" to the literary community.

669. Monteiro, George. "Washington Friends and National Reviewers: Henry James's 'Pandora'." Research Studies, 43 (1975), 38-44.

Monteiro, noting the success of Daisy Miller and James's visit to America in 1881-1882, looks at James's story about Washington, "Pandora." The story was not well-received, but it is James's response to his impressions of the Washington world and to reviewers of Daisy Miller.

670. Moon, Heath. "James's 'A London Life' and the Campbell Divorce Scandal." American Literary Realism, 1870-1910, 13 (1980), 246-58.

London is equated with "society" in "A London Life," so it is a social tale based on the protracted legal history of the Campbell divorce case and the scrutiny of society when such an occurrence is thrust into the social arena.

671. Moore, Rayburn S. "The Strange Irregular Rhythm of Life: James's Late Tales and Constance Woolson." South Atlantic Bulletin, 41, iv (1976), 86-93.

Moore examines "The Beast in the Jungle," "The Jolly

Corner," and "The Bench of Desolation" in terms of James's friendship with Constance Fenimore Woolson and his response to her death in 1894.

672. Morales, Peter. "The Novel as Social Theory: Models, Explanation and Values in Henry James and William Dean Howells." CLIO, 5 (1976), 331-44.
Morales looks at the novel as presentation and explanation of social ideas. He focuses on The Bostonians and A Hazard of New Fortunes. He finds James's approach essentially Freudian and states that the novel displays James's distaste for some extremes of the women's movement.

673. Mori, Mihoko. "Meian to The Golden Bowl." Eigo Seinen, 121 (1975), 212-12.

674. Mori, Mihoko. "'Meian' to The Golden Bowl: Saisetsu." Eigo Seinen, 122 (1976), 74-76.

675. Morsiani, Giovanni. "Un anarchico fallito." Paragone, 324 (1977), 115-23.

676. Murphy, Brenda. "The Problem of Validity in the Critical Controversy over The Turn of the Screw." Research Studies, 47 (1979), 191-201.
Murphy focuses her attention on the critics of The Turn of the Screw and the many (and sometimes contradictory) interpretations. She looks especially at Hirsch's claim that valid interpretation has consensus as its goal. Consensus is a problem of perception and epistemology, though, and is not likely to be resolved.

677. Murphy, Kevin. "The Unfixable Text: Bewilderment of Vision in The Turn of the Screw." Texas Studies in Literature and Language, 20 (1978), 538-51.
Murphy points out that there is fragmentary evidence that the governess sees ghosts and that she hallucinates. This leads to a duplicity that is not resolvable unless the reader interpolates extraneous evidence.

678. Nance, William. "'The Beast in the Jungle': Two Versions of Oedipus." Studies in Short Fiction, 13 (1976), 433-40.
Nance examines "The Beast in the Jungle" in terms of the Oedipus myth, particularly the conflict between Oedipus as hero and Oedipus as complex.

679. Nance, William L. "What Maisie Knew: The Myth of the Artist." Studies in the Novel, 8 (1976), 88-102.

Nance examines What Maisie Knew as a work of art and as an insight into James's vision of life and art. He then turns his attention to Maisie's acquisition of knowledge and the effects it has on her and her fate.

680. Nardin, Jane. "The Turn of the Screw: The Victorian Background." Mosaic, 12, i (1978), 131-42.

Nardin examines thequestion of ambiguity in The Turn of the Screw by focusing on the societal influences on the characters, particularly on the governess, who hallucinates in an attempt to solve the mystery of the behavior of the others.

681. Nash, Christopher. "Henry James, Puppetmaster: The Narrative Status of Maria Gostrey, Susan Stringham, and Fanny Assingham as Ficelles." Studies in the Novel, 9 (1977), 297-310.

Nash observes James's use of the French stage convention, the ficelle, to observe and comment in his fiction. The ficelle is separate from the action, she aligns herself with a lie, and she suffers the hazards of detachment.

682. Nettels, Elsa. "'A Frugal Splendour': Thoreau and James and the Principles of Economy." Colby Library Quarterly, 12 (1976), 5-13.

The most obvious bond between James and Thoreau is the imporatnce of the concept of economy in the work of each. Economy, as Nettels takes it to mean, is the compressing of as much life as one can into the little space available.

683. Nettels, Elsa. "Henry James and the Art of Biography." South Atlantic Bulletin, 43, iv (1978), 107-24.

Nettels looks at James's biographical writings, particularly Hawthorne and William Wetmore Story and His Friends, and determines James made important contributions to biography.

684. Nettels, Elsa. "Henry James and the Idea of Race." English Studies, 59 (1978), 35-47.

Nettels examines James's treatment of race (that is, national types) in his works. James was influenced in his thinking on this sublect by the writings of Hyppolyte Taine. In his fiction, however, all of his characters were endowed with the power of choice.

685. Nettels, Elsa. "Poe and James on the Art of Fiction." Poe Studies, 13 (1980), 4-8.

Nettels looks at the critical theories of both Poe and James. She notes that Poe, as the first American to formulate an extensive theory of literary art, anticipated some of James's criticism and served to break ground for James.

686. Nettels, Elsa. "Vision and Knowledge in The Ambassadors and Lord Jim." English Literature in Transition (1880-1920), 18 (1975), 181-93.

There are some similarities between the fiction of James and that of Conrad: for instance, psychological and moral questions merge and consciousness and action are primary values. They differ on a number of principles and the execution of those principles.

687. "New York: 'Accessibility to Experience'." Marianne Moore Newsletter, 4, i (1980), 13-14.

The author identifies the source of the last line of Moore's "New York," which was taken from a letter from James to his publisher and was reprinted on the dust jacket of the English edition of The Finer Grain.

688. Newberry, Frederick. "A Note on the Horror in James's Revision of Daisy Miller." Henry James Review, 3 (1982), 229-32.

Newberry examines James's revisions of Daisy Miller for the New York Edition, commenting especially on James's use of the word "horror" in the later version. Newberry says it has sexual connotations when used about Daisy and emphasizes Winterbourne's misinterpretation of the girl.

689. Niemtzow, Annette. "Marriage and the New Woman in The Portrait of a Lady." American Literature, 47 (1975), 377-95.

James's ideas of the inviolability of marriage had roots in his father's Swedenborgian thought. Still, The Portrait of a Lady is a different kind of marriage novel and stands on the brink of modernism in its treatment of women and marriage.

690. Norrman, Ralf. "End-Linking as an Intensity-Creating Device in the Dialogue of Henry James's The Golden Bowl." English Studies, 61 (1980), 236-51.

Norrman studies the intensity of the dialogue in The Golden Bowl, particularly in light of textual links in James's sentence structure based on repitition.

691. Norrman, Ralf. "The Intercepted Telegram Plot in Henry James's In the Cage." Notes & Queries, 24 (1977), 425-27.
Norrman looks at the telegram plot in In the Cage as another of James's examinations of knowledge, in this case subjective truth versus objective reality.

692. Norrman, Ralf. "Referential Ambiguity in Pronouns as a Literary Device in Henry James's The Golden Bowl." Studia Neophilologica, 51 (1979), 31-71.
Norrman recognizes the magnitude of the games (à quartre) that James plays in The Golden Bowl. The possible relationships are numerous, so there is considerable room for confusion. The uncertainty of James's use of referential pronouns adds to the ambiguity of the various relationships.

693. Obuchowski, Peter A. "Technique and Meaning in James's The Turn of the Screw." College Language Association Journal, 21 (1978), 380-89.
James's technique is deliberatly used to add to the ambiguity of The Turn of the Screw according to Obuchowski. Thus the meaning is not in the theme or the incidents, but in the technique.

694. O'Connor, Dennis L. "Intimacy and Spectatorship in The Portrait of a Lady." Henry James Review, 2 (1980), 25-35.
O'Connor suggests that Isabel fears the sexuality of Caspar Goodwood, so she rejects him for Osmond. By rejecting intimacy Isabel limits her intelligence and increases her solipsistic aspect. Her solitude leads to her narcissism and her renunciation of all but the spectator's role.

695. O'Donnell, Patrick. "Between Life and Art: Structures of Realism in the Fiction of Howells and James." Etudes Anglaises, 33 (1980), 142-55.
Though Howells and James are seen as realist writers, their approaches to realism are different. Howells' heroes leave decisions unmade and have no control over their futures. James's heroes and heroines face alternatives, make decisions, and attempt to look toward the future.

696. O'Gorman, Donal. "Henry James's Reading of The Turn of the Screw." Henry James Review, 1 (1980), 228-56.
O'Gorman comments on many aspects of the tale, among which is the combination of Christmas and Saturnalian aspects, notable role-reversal (adult-child, servant-master).

He also notes that the governess is not a reliable gauge of perception and that evil distorts perception and thus action (witness numerous allusions to the Devil). It is the force of evil that devastates the characters and frightens the reader.

697. Oku, Suzuo. "Meian to The Golden Bowl: Mohititsu no kanei." Eigo Seinen, 123 (1977), 68-69.

698. Otsu, E., E. Beppu, N. Ebi, and A. Namegata. "Henry James: Reading The Portrait of a Lady." Studies in English Literature, 57 (1980), 324-25.

699. Ott, Josephine. "Henry James, critique de Balzac." L'Anée Balzacienne, 1977, pp. 273-81.

700. Page, Philip. "The Princess Casamassima: Suicide and 'The Penetrating Imagination'." Tennessee Studies in Literature, 22 (1977), 162-69.

Page states that, for James, much rests on the "penetrating imagination," the ability to project one's imagination beyond oneself. Hyacinth's suicide is the culmination of his penetrations of imagination and the reader must then exercise his imagination.

701. Palliser, Charles. "'A Conscious Prize': Moral and Aesthetic Value in The Spoils of Poynton." Modern Language Quarterly, 40 (1979), 37-52.

Palliser maintains that for Fleda, the spoils represent a time and place of tranquility--one that is more certain than that of human relationships. Throughout, Fleda deludes herself about Owen, Mrs. Gereth, and about certain elements within herself.

702. Palmer, James W. "Cinematic Ambiguity: James's The Turn of the Screw and Clayton's The Innocents." Literature/Film Quarterly, 5 (1977), 198-215.

Palmer writes about Jack Clayton's film, The Innocents, an adaptation of James's The Turn of the Screw. He states that Clayton successfully uses film to simulate James's shifts in point of view and to maintain the ambiguity of the tale, especially pointing out the presence of evil without offering a simplified reason for its presence.

703. Pancost, David W. "Henry James and Julian Hawthorne." American Literature, 50 (1978), 461-65.

James and Julian Hawthorne established a tenuous relationship while James was writing Hawthorne. Though never very friendly and occasionally critical of one another, each had a grudging respect for the other.

704. Parrill, Anna S. "Portraits of Ladies." Tennessee Studies in Literature, 20 (1975), 92-99.
Using The Portrait of a Lady and Meredith's The Egoist as examples, Parrill illustrates how two writers depicted women's frustrations. They recognize the repression of society and women's problems with the conventions of that society.

705. Parrill, William. "Peter Milton, Henry James, and 'The Jolly Corner'." Innisfree, 4 (1977), 16-25.
Perrill studies Milton's illustrations of "The Jolly Corner" as art and as interpretation. Rather than illustrating scenes from the tale Milton chooses to include illustrations that are more suggestive of meaning.

706. Patnode, Darwin. "The Quality of Life in The Ambassadors." DeKalb Literary Arts Journal, 13, i-ii (1978-79), 99-108.
Patnode examines The Ambassadors in terms of Strether's words, "Live all you can." He sees it as James's advice to the individual to assert one's independence and to observe and relish the experience of observing. Strether's life has too long been spent in not living.

707. Paton, Wayne. "Henry James and Alfred de Musset: A Possible Misattribution." Long Room, 16/17 (1978), 35-36.
Paton suggests that a review of Selections from the Prose and Poetry of Alfred de Musset may be erroneously attributed to James in A Bibliography of Henry James by Edel and Laurence.

708. Pauly, Thomas H. "Henry James and the Travel Sketch: The Artistry of Italian Hours." Centennial Review, 19 (1975), 108-20.
Pauly examines James's art of the travel sketch, focusing on Italian Hours. He notes James's ability to capture the pictorial in his descriptions and the combination of this with his fondness for Italy.

709. Pauly, Thomas H. "The Literary Sketch in Nineteenth Century America." Texas Studies in Literature and Language, 17 (1975), 489-503.
Transatlantic Sketches helped to launch James's literary career and he continued the writing of travel sketches with English Hours and Italian Hours. In these he managed to write the classic and the romantic into his sketches and to unite them into a single creative spirit.

710. Pearce, Howard. "Henry James's Pastoral Fallacy." PMLA, 90 (1975), 834-47.

Pearce notes the tendency of Jamesian characters to create a "pastoral fallacy" for themselves, an ideal that may or may not relate to the actual world. The effects of this creation may be both good and bad, but usually signifies denial.

711. Peinovich, Michael P. and Richard F. Patterson. "The Cognitive Beast in the Syntactic Jungle: A Study of James's Language." Language and Style, 11 (1978), 82-93.

Peinovich and Patterson look at "The Beast in the Jungle" as an example of James's late style. They attempt to link thematic significance with certain stylistic features.

712. Perrot, Jean. "L'Anamorphose dans les romans de Henry James." Critique: Revue Générale des Publications Françaises et Etrangères, 35 (1979), 334-54.

713. Perrot, Jean. "Henry James: Strategie litteraire et constitution de l'homme de lettres." Litterature, 33 (1979), 37-57.

714. Person, Leland, Jr. "Aesthetic Headaches and European Women in The Marble Faun and The American." Studies in American Fiction, 4 (1976), 65-79.

Person states that Hawthorne and James paint a similar portrait of the European woman in the two works. He sees the woman as a danger to Christopher Newman and it is with some loss that he emerges once again his own person.

715. Peterson, Carla L. "Dialogue and Characterization in The Portrait of a Lady." Studies in American Fiction, 8 (1980), 13-22.

Peterson states that quite a good deal can be learned from the characters in The Portrait of a Lady by giving a close reading to the dialogue. Differences in language and individual usage hint at differences in personality that otherwise might remain hidden.

716. Phillips, Kathy J. "Conversion to Text, Initiation to Symbolism, in Mann's Der Tod in Venedig and James's The Ambassadors." Canadian Review of Comparative Literature, 6 (1979), 376-88.

Phillips notes similarities between Der Tod in Venedig and The Ambassadors. She observes that the situations of the two novels are somewhat similar and that they share aspects of imagery, narrative voice, narrative technique, and especially symbolism.

717. Porat, Zephyra. "The Madonna and the Cat: Transcendental Idealism and Tragic Realism in Henry James's The Portrait of a Lady." Hebrew University Studies in Literature, 5 (1977), 67-101.

Porat examines the Emersonian tradition of Transcendentalism and James's negative attitude toward it, particularly as expressed in The Portrait of a Lady. In the case of Isabel James takes Emersonian self-reliance and turns it into its reverse, anti-Emersonian self-denial.

718. Posnock, Ross. "'The Novel in The Ring and the Book': Henry James's Energetic 'Appropriation' of Browning." Centennial Review, 25 (1981), 277-93.

Posnock examines James's essay on Browning's poem, The Ring and the Book, in which James states that the poem could have been improved had he redone it as a novel. Posnock maintains that James "appropriated" more than the poem; he incorporates Browning's lessons of art.

719. Purton, Valerie. "James's The Turn of the Screw, Chapter 9." Explicator, 34, iii (1975), Item 24.

A key to the governess' character, including her moral struggle and her emotion, can be found in her reading of Amelia.

720. Putt, S. Gorley. "Henry James, Radical Gentleman." Massachusetts Review, 18 (1977), 179-86.

Putt offers a sketch of James following his tribute in the form of the memorial stone in Westminster Abbey dedicated in 1976.

721. Quartermain, Peter. "'Blocked. Make a Song out of That': Pound's 'E. P. Ode pour l'election de son sepulchre'." Kentucky Review, 1, i (1980), 32-48.

In his essay focusing on Pound, Quartermain comments on James's view of language and its use. James's opinions on the sounds of American speech are evident in his 1905 address delivered to the graduating class of Bryn Mawr, according to Quartermain.

722. Quebe, Ruth Evelyn. "The Bostonians: Some Historical Sources and Their Implications." Centennial Review, 25 (1981), 80-100.
Quebe examines the historical background of The Bostonians: it was published as part of Century's "War Series;" it conveys the attitudes and aspirations of the young Southerner in post-war society; and it looks at many aspects of the women's movement. James illustrates fictionally an increasing formalization of society.

723. Ray, Laura. "Childhood and the English Novel: Two English Girls." Genre, 8 (1975), 89-106.
Ray examines the child's importance in the novel, focusing on Daisy Ashford's The Young Visitors and What Maisie Knew. Maisie learns, despite many barriers, to infer moral value from a world in which it is not immediately visible.

724. Reddick, Bryan. "The Control of Distance in The Golden Bowl." Modern British Literature, 1 (1976), 46-55.
Reddick maintains that James uses distance in The Golden Bowl through such techniques as varying point of view. Primarily distance is a result of James's complex form, abstractions, extended metaphors, and tempered uncertainty.

725. Richards, Bernard. "James and His Sources: The Spoils of Poynton." Essays in Criticism, 29 (1979), 302-22.
Richards examines James's source for The Spoils of Poynton, first noting his notebook entry on the subject. He further cites incidents that could have provided background and identifies James's model for the setting, Fox Warren.

726. Richards, Bernard. "The Sources of Henry James's 'Mrs. Medwin'." Notes & Queries, 27 (1980), 226-30.
Richards offers a possible source for the characters in "Mrs. Medwin," including Elizabeth Balch, Lady Grantley, and Robert Temple.

727. Richards, Bernard. "The Sources of Henry James's 'The Marriages'." Review of English Studies, 30 (1979), 316-22.
Citing the Notebooks and Alice James's diary, Richards notes a possible source for "The Marriages."

728. Rimmon-Kenan, Shlomith. "Deconstructive Reflections on Deconstruction: In Reply to Hillis Miller." Poetics Today, 2, ib (1980-81), 185-88.

Rimmon-Kenan takes issue with J. Hillis Miller's essay on "The Figure in the Carpet" (see number 657). She claims that a deconstructionist reading of the tale need not totally supplant or negate a structuralist reading.

729. Robinson, David. "James and Emerson: The Ethical Context of The Ambassadors." Studies in the Novel, 10 (1978), 431-46.

Robinson follows the growth of Strether's consciousness and traces the path that leads to his ultimate decision. Robinson maintains that this marks a return to Emerson's view of a self-culture, despite James's qualms about the aesthetic possibilities he could see in New England.

730. Roman, Christine M. "Henry James and the Surrogate Mother." American Transcendental Quarterly, 38 (1978), 193-205.

The surrogate mother is treated significantly in several of James's novels. Roman focuses on this aspect of The Portrait of a Lady and how James uses it to illustrate the importance of the mother-daughter relationship.

731. Ron, Moshe. "A Reading of 'The Real Thing'." Yale French Studies, 58 (1979), 190-212.

Ron, in noting the economy of "The Real Thing," states that there remains some critical considerations: the symmetry and rhetoric of the narrative; examination of the Monarchs' "reality" and function; and the significance behind the signs in the tale.

732. Rosenblatt, Jason P. "Bridegroom and Bride in 'The Jolly Corner'." Studies in Short Fiction, 14 (1977), 282-84.

Rosenblatt looks at biblical allusion (with particular reference to the twenty-fifth chapter of Matthew) in "The Jolly Corner."

733. Rosenzweig, Paul. "'The Illusion of Freedom' in The Ambassadors." Renascence, 33 (1981), 143-61.

Rosenzweig examines James's vision by looking at Lambert Strether's vision, along with the novel's aesthetics, morality, and psychology. He focuses on the conclusion to determine the completion of Strether's vision in The Ambassadors.

734. Ross, Michael L. "Henry James' 'Half Man': The Legacy of Browning in 'The Madonna of the Future'." Browning Institute Studies, 2 (1974), 25-42.

James was prepared for his discovery of Italy by Browning's literary treatment of Italy, according to Ross. Therefore, Ross finds some parallels between Browning's "Pictor Ignotus" and James's story, "The Madonna of the Future."

735. Routh, Michael. "Isabel Archer's Double Exposure: A Repeated Scene in The Portrait of a Lady." Henry James Review, 1 (1980), 262-63.

Routh points out that the vision of Isabel framed by a doorway recurs in The Portrait of a Lady. The scenes are used as structural devices to illustrate changes in Isabel's life.

736. Routh, Michael. "Isabel Archer's 'Inconsequence': A Motif Analysis of The Portrait of a Lady." Journal of Narrative Technique, 7 (1977), 128-41.

Routh says that Isabel's fatal flaw that results in her doom in inconsequence. He then examines this hypothesis in several motifs: appearance/reality; imagination; theory; convention; and others.

737. Rowe, John C[arlos]. "The Authority of the Sign in Henry James's The Sacred Fount." Criticism, 19 (1977), 223-40.

Within The Sacred Fount James presents a commentary on aestheticism in the person of the narrator. The narrator writes in order to uncover a subjective function of his existence in society. This exemplifies the artistic process of creation.

738. Rowe, John Carlos. "Who's Henry James? Further Lessons of the Master." Henry James Review, 2 (1980), 2-11.

Rowe looks at Gerald Graff's investigation of the differences between modernist writing (represented by James) and post-modernist writing (represented by Donald Barthelme, who attempts to destroy stereotypes of James by depicting him as Indian Chief). Rowe also notes the importance of an active, rather than a passive, reading of James.

739. Rucker, Mary E. "James's 'The Pupil': The Question of Moral Ambiguity." Arizona Quarterly, 32 (1976), 301-15.

Rucker studies the question of ambiguity in "The Pupil," noting that there are two points of view at work--that of Pemberton and that of the narrator. The key is the tension between the two.

740. Rudnick, Lois P. "Daisy Miller Revisited: Ernest Hemingway's 'A Canary for One'." Massachusetts Studies in English, 7, i (1978), 12-19.

Rudnick examines Hemingway's "A Canary for One" as an adaptation of Daisy Miller. She does this to reveal the similarites of artistic vision and sensibility of the two writers while, at the same time, looking at stylistic differences.

741. Ruland, Richard. "Beyond Harsh Inquiry: The Hawthorne of Henry James." ESQ, 25 (1979), 95-117.

James's debt to Hawthorne is widely acknowleded and James used Hawthorne as a model and as a mentor in his early fiction. Ruland studies the relationship of the two, with special attention paid to James's Hawthorne as a focus of the relationship.

742. Ruthrof, H. G. "A Note on Henry James's Psychological Realism and the Concept of Brevity." Studies in Short Fiction, 12 (1975), 369-73.

Ruthrof looks at the psychological aspects of James's work in conjunction with an examination of the compression necessary to the short story and James's use of such compression.

743. Rutledge, Harry C. "Contest and Possession: Classical Imagery in Henry James' The Golden Bowl." Comparatist, 1 (1977), 58-64.

Rutledge begins with the statement that The Golden Bowl is about people trying to totally dominate one another. He then illustrates the classical bases for the images of contest and possession: Maggie as Alcestis or Medea, Adam as Cupid or Zeus, and so forth, carried through the other characters.

744. Ryburn, May L. "The Turn of the Screw and Amelia: A Source for Quint?" Studies in Short Fiction, 16 (1979), 235-37.

The governess happened to be reading Fielding's Amelia and Ryburn suggests that this is no coincidence and that Peter Quint may the governess' version of Mr. Robinson.

745. Sacks, Sheldon. "Novelists as Storytellers." Modern Philology, 73, iv, part 2 (1976), 597-609.

Sacks states that James, among others, is a great novelist because he is a great storyteller, and he uses The Ambassadors as his example.

746. Safranek, William P. "Longmore in 'Madame de Mauves': The Making of a Pragmatist." Arizona Quarterly, 35 (1979), 293-302.

"Madame de Mauves" can be seen as the definition of idealism and pragmatism and the means by which one may come to embrace either, according to Safranek. He then discusses Longmore's conversion to pragmatism in the story.

747. Salmon, Rachel. "A Marriage of Opposites: Henry James's 'The Figure in the Carpet' and the Problem of Ambiguity." ELH, 47 (1980), 788-803.

Salmon sees the purpose of ambiguity in "The Figure in the Carpet" as that of fostering a relationship between author and reader. As such it elicits an experiential response rather than a referential response in the reader.

748. Salmon, Rachel. "Naming and Knowing in Henry James's 'The Beast in the Jungle': The Hermeneutics of a Sacred Text." Orbis Litterarum, 36 (1981), 302-22.

Salmon first defines a sacred text as one constrained by the manguage of the text. It denies the possibility of knowing through naming; reading a sacred text (knowing it) involves a movement toward unity. She argues that "The Beast in the Jungle" is a sacred text, with all its demands placed on the reader.

749. Salzberg, Joel. "Mr. Mudge as Redemptive Fate: Juxtaposition in James's In the Cage." Studies in the Novel, 11 (1979), 63-76.

Salzberg focuses on the role Mr. Mudge plays in In the Cage, emphasizing his redemptive (rather than his oppressive) influence on the telegraphist and noting the glimpses of nobility he leaves with the reader by the end of the tale.

750. Samokhvalov, N. I. "Genri Dzheyms i Ernest Hemingway: Tragediy Dobrovol'nogo Izgnaniya." Nauchnye Trudy Kubanskogo Universiteta, 195 (1975), 111-18.

751. Santangelo, Gennaro A. "Henry James's 'Maud-Evelyn' and the Web of Consciousness." Amerikastudien, 20 (1975), 45-54.

Santangelo looks at the consciousness and construction of reality in "Maud-Evelyn," particularly with Lady Emma as central intelligence in mind. The gradual awakening of her consciousness is communicated to the reader.

752. Sarbu, Aladar. "Henry James: A palya es Tanusagai." Filologiai Kozlony, 21 (1975), 58-78.

753. Savarese, John E. "Henry James's First Story: A Study of Error." Studies in Short Fiction, 17 (1980), 431-35.
Savareses examines "A Tragedy of Error," pointing out the poor judgment of the characters and the effects of that judgment on their fates.

754. Scharnhorst, Gary. "Wuthering Heights and The Portrait of a Lady: A Dynamic Parallel." Ball State University Forum, 19, i (1978), 17-22.
Scharnhorst maintains that the similarities in setting, theme, and characterization between the two novels suggest that Wuthering Heights may have provided a kind of international novel model for James.

755. Schliefer, Ronald. "The Trap of the Imagination: The Gothic Tradition, Fiction, and The Turn of the Screw." Criticism, 22 (1980), 297-319.
The imagination, according to Schliefer, entraps because it responds to nothing and uses as its language Kierkegaardian irony. The governess, unable to understand the enigma of the children, humanizes them by assigning ghosts as their antecedents.

756. Schneider, Daniel J. "The Divided Self in the Fiction of Henry James." PMLA, 90 (1975), 447-60.
Schneider notes the tendency in James to create a "divided self," a character in the center of a conflict between aggresors of the old and new worlds. This conflict and displacement has a basis in James's own life and attitude.

757. Schneider, Daniel J. "James's The Awkward Age: A Reading and an Evaluation." Henry James Review, 1 (1980), 219-27.
Schneider points out flaws in The Awkward Age: the importance of the central conflict is not clear, nor are characters' motivations sufficiently apparent; indiduals are not fully portrayed; and the novel is not satisfying.

758. Schneider, Daniel J. "The Unreliable Narrator: James's The Aspern Papers and the Reading of Fiction." Studies in Short Fiction, 13 (1976), 43-49.
Schneider recognizes that The Aspern Papers is related to the reader through an unreliable narrator. He also

says that judgment is "directed by James through the pattern of opposition in the conflict and in the imagery."

759. Schrero, Elliot M. "Exposure in The Turn of the Screw." Modern Philology, 78 (1981), 261-74.
Schrero examines exposure in several senses: of Miss Jessel, of the children (as representatives of Victorian ego), of the upper class and privilege, and of the governess (particularly the effect of evil on her).

760. Schriber Mary S[uzanne]. "Isabel Archer and Victorian Manners." Studies in the Novel, 8 (1976), 441-57.
Schriber notes that James used or adapted many Victorian conventions of the lady's place in society and the home and contrasted this with the modern woman's consciousness and will to power.

761. Schriber, Mary Suzanne. "Toward Daisy Miller: Cooper's Idea of 'The American Girl'." Studies in the Novel, 13 (1981), 237-49.
The concept of "the American Girl" as depicted by James appears to have had a predecessor in Cooper's fiction apart from the Leatherstocking tales. Cooper recognized the uniquely American features of such a girl, as did James.

762. Seamon, Roger. "Henry James's 'Four Meetings': A Study in Irritability and Condescension." Studies in Short Fiction, 15 (1978), 155-63.
Seamon reads "Four Meetings" as a realistic tale and focuses on the narrator, his involvement in the action, and his attempts to exclude himself. The evidence for the narrator's place lies in his occasional irritation.

763. Sebouhian, George. "Adam Verver: Emerson's Poet." Markham Review, 7 (1978), 39-40.
Sebouhian suggests that Adam Verver may be something of a transcendentalist, modeled after Emerson's poet and similar to James's own image of himself as seer-poet.

764. Sebouhian, George. "Henry James's Transcendental Imagination." Essays in Literature, 3 (1976), 214-26.
Sebouhian traces James's transcendentalism, particularly in relation to Emersonian transcendentalism. Many of James's characters are like James in that theirs is a transcendental imagination--the consciousness is the active force.

765. Sebouhian, George. "The Transcendental Imagination of Merton Densher." Modern Language Studies, 5, ii (1975), 35-45.
Sebouhian points out that the character of Densher has been little regarded by critics. He maintains that Densher's character has a transcendental element that is evident in his vision which develops in the course of the book and which provides a balance between the two volumes of the novel.

766. Seed, D[avid]. "Two Contributions to Henry James Bibliography." Notes & Queries, 23 (1976), 11-12.
Seed notes two items by James that are missing from the bibliography of James by Edel and Laurence (1961 edition).

767. Seed, D[avid]. "Henry James's Reading of Flaubert." Comparative Literature Studies, 16 (1979), 307-17.
Seed looks at James's respect and admiration for Flaubert, who held a special place in James's intellectual and literary career and life. James paid particular attention to the consciousnesses of the characters in Flaubert's novels.

768. Seed, David. "Hyacinth Robinson and the Politics of The Princess Casamassima." Etudes Anglaises, 30 (1977), 30-39.
Seed surveys the criticism on The Princess Casamassima, focusing on the character of Hyacinth Robinson. Seed contends that "Hyacinth's drama is unconvincing" and notes that she is an egotist. although there is an attempt to idealize her.

769. Seed, David. "James's 'The Lesson of the Master'." Explicator, 39, i (1980), 9-10.
Seed notes that St. George denigrates his own work by comparing his writing to cheaply produced hardware goods.

770. Seed, David. "Penetrating America: The Method of Henry James's The American Scene." Amerikastudien, 26 (1981), 340-53.
The American Scene involves not only description but an analysis of the meaning of what James observes. Seed says that the interpretation James brings into many of his literary and psychological principles serves to make an important statement of literary conservatism that carries into his other works.

771. Seltzer, Mark. "The Princess Casamassima: Relaism and the Fantasy of Surveillance." Nineteenth-Century Fiction, 35 (1981), 506-34.

Seltzer maintains that The Princess Casamassima is a political novel, not in its depiction of London underworld anarchists, but primarily in the power play enacted by the narrative technique of the novel. He also states that there is continuity between technique and the "social technologies of power."

772. Shapland, Elizabeth. "Duration and Frequency: Prominent Aspects of Time in Henry James' 'The Beast in the Jungle'." Papers on Language and Literature, 17 (1981), 33-47.

Shapland applies Gerard Genete's examination of the duration and frequency of events in Proust to "The Beast in the Jungle." She maintains that such a structuralist approach is essential not only to factual but also to critical understanding.

773. Shelden, Pamela J. "'The Friends of Friends': Another Twist to 'The Turn of the Screw'." Wascana Review, 11, i (1976), 3-14.

Shelden notes similarities of structure, situation, and characterization between "The Friends of Friends" and The Turn of the Screw.

774. Sheleng, Harvey. "Some Aspects of Brideshead Revisited: A Comparison with Henry James' The American." Evelyn Waugh Newsletter, 11, ii (1977), 4-7.

Sheleng notes what he sees to be similarities between The American and Brideshead Revisited, such as the depiction of an "outsider" entering a family and certain personal relationships.

775. Shinn, Thelma J. "The Art of a Verse Novelist: Approaching Robinson's Late Narratives through James's The Art of the Novel." Colby Library Quarterly, 12 (1976), 91-100.

Shinn attempts to approach E. A. Robinson's technique through the principles set forth in James's essays on fictional art. Similarities of narrative technique and dramatic purpose appear an especially strong shared bond.

776. Sklepowich, E. A. "Gilded Bondage: Games and Gamesplaying in The Awkward Age." Essays in Literature, 5 (1978), 187-93.

Sklepowich examines the significance of metaphoric gamesplaying in The Awkward Age. There are a number of games images which serve to define the characters' actions and there are opposing attitudes presented with regard to social gamesplaying.

777. Sklepowich, E. A. "Gossip and Gothicism in The Sacred Fount." Henry James Review, 2 (1980), 112-15.
Sklepowich notes that in The Sacred Fount James incorporates a Gothic artifice in the form of Newmarch and a civilized Gothic theme of loss of reputation and social castigation becomes a part of the whole. Gossip is added to these elements in an aesthetic game that can be seen as either parody or art.

778. Smith, Carl S. "James's International Fiction: Sources and Evolution." Centennial Review, 23 (1979), 397-422.
Smith traces the development of the international theme in James's fiction. He looks at James's early excursions to Europe and how he translated his impressions into novels and tales. James's observations eventually grew from simply the cultural differences to broader themes of the consciousness of the individual.

779. Smith, Carl S. "James's Travels, Travel Writings, and the Development of His Art." Modern Language Quarterly, 38 (1977), 367-80.
Smith begins with the observation on the importance of the American in Europe as a Jamesian theme. He examines James's travel and the lessons he learned from the travel which he was later able to incorporate into his writing.

780. Snyder, John. "James's Girl Huck: What Maisie Knew." American Literary Realism, 1870-1910, 11 (1978), 109-23.
Snyder relates Maisie's home situation and her desire to grow beyond the confines of oppressiveness of convention to Huckleberry Finn and the maturation that comes with such a break with convention and tradition.

781. Solimine, Joseph, Jr. "Henry James, William Wetmore Story, and Friend: A Noble Mistake?" Studies in Browning and His Circle, 8, i (1980), 57-61.
Solimine examines the relationship of James, Story, and Robert Browning. James sought to become a friend of Browning, but the latter did not respond to James's efforts. Browning did, however, establish a close friendship with Story, whom James did not particularly admire.

782. Somers, Paul P., Jr. "Sherwood Anderson's Mastery of Narrative Distance." Twentieth Century Literature, 23 (1977), 84-93.
Somers observes Jamesian elements in some of Anderson's short fiction. Anderson creates irony by developing and maintaining a distance from his narrators while still managing to create a distinct narrative personality.

783. Stafford, William T. "Henry James." American Literary Scholarship, An Annual/1974, pp. 87-100.

784. Stafford, William T. "Henry James." American Literary Scholarship, An Annual/1975, pp. 115-30.

785. Stafford, William T. "Henry James." American Literary Scholarship, An Annual/1976, pp. 93-117.
In this and the above two entries Stafford analyzes the year's work on James. For later bibliographic essays on James in American Literary Scholarship see entries in this section under Robert L. Gale.

786. Stafford, William T. "The Portrait of a Lady: The Second Hundred Years." Henry James Review, 2 (1980), 91-100.
Stafford posits that the reader of the future may pay special attention to Chapter 47. That chapter is witty, offers a revelation of Osmond's character, and is fun to read. Ultimately, he adds, the wholeness of the book is most striking and provides the most satisfying reading.

787. Stambaugh, Sara. "The Aesthetic Movement and The Portrait of a Lady." Nineteenth-Century Fiction, 30 (1976), 495-510.
Stambaugh begins her study by examining the backgrounds of the Aesthetic Movement. She the follows the influence of the Movement on The Portrait of a Lady. She also notes similarities between Osmond and the personality of Oscar Wilde.

788. Stauble, Michele. "Henry James als Kritiker Flauberts." Neue Zurcher Zeitung, 25-26 (1975), 61.

789. Stein, Allen F. "Lambert Strether's Circuitous Journey: Motifs of Internalized Quest and Circularity in The Ambassadors." ESQ, 22 (1976)m 245-53.
Stein sees Strether's journey in The Ambassadors as consistent with the Romantic genre of the circular

quest romance. It is through this consistency with the genre that James's elicits sympathy and gives life to the story.

790. Stein, William Bysshe. "The Wings of the Dove: James's Eucharist of Punch." Centennial Review, 21 (1977), 236-60.

Stein looks at The Wings of the Dove as a "comedy of misunderstanding." He maintains that James carries out his comedy through verbal artfulness, scenic creativity, and errors of perception.

791. Stelzig, Eugene L. "Henry James and the 'Immensities of Perception': Actors and Victims in The Portrait of a Lady and The Wings of the Dove." Southern Humanities Review, 11 (1977), 253-65.

Stelzig looks at many aspects of the two novels: the relationships of predators and victims; the playing of roles; imagery in The Wings of the Dove; and the problems of perception.

792. Stepp, Walter. "The Turn of the Screw: If Douglas Is Miles . . . ." Nassau Review, 3, ii (1976), 76-82.

Stepp sees the character of Douglas as an older, mature Miles. If this hypothesis is accepted, it has broad and far-reaching implications for the governess--her tale is more of a confession and "Miles Douglas" is witness.

793. Stern, Madeleine B. "A Lesson for the Master: Henry James and A. K. Loring." Henry James Review, 2 (1980), 87-90.

Stern states that the man responsible for pirating James's "A Bundle of Letters" was Aaron Kimball Loring, not Frank Loring, as some scholars believe and have stated.

794. Stone, Edward. "Edition Architecture and 'The Turn of the Screw'." Studies in Short Fiction, 13 (1976), 9-16.

Stone examines James's configurations of contents for volumes ten through eighteen of the New York Edition, noting that The Turn of the Screw was placed with The Aspern Papers and "The Liar" rather than with the ghost stories.

795. Stone, William B. "Idiolect and Ideology: Some Stylistic Aspects of Norris, James, and Dubois." Style, 10 (1976), 405-25.

James and the others, Stone maintains, attempt to

escape the commercialization and other problems of the Gilded Age. Stone uses this attempted escapism to try to put the intricacies of James's style into a sort of perspective.

796. Stowe, William W. "Interpretation in Fiction: Le Pere Goriot and The American." Texas Studies in Literature and Language, 23 (1981), 248-67.

Stowe notes that the two novels depict acts of interpretation while making statements on their own interpretation. They realize the difficulties inherent in interpretation. With regard to this, Balzac's influence is evident in James.

797. Stull, William L. "[The Battle of the Century: W. D. Howells, 'Henry James, Jr.,' and the English.]" American Literary Realism, 1870-1910, 11 (1978), 249-64.

Stull examines the battle of the realists and the neo-romantics of the late nineteenth century and its beginning with the publication of Howells' essay, "Henry James, Jr."

798. Stycznska, Adela. "'The Papers': James' Satire on the Modern Publicity System." Kwartalnik Neofilologiczny, 22 (1975), 419-36.

The Papers, says Styczynska, is a satire on the process of publicity, primarily regarding the press and the public. Styczynska also questions why James did not include The Papers in the New York Edition of his novels and tales.

799. Sweeney, Gerard M. "Henry James and the 'New England Conscience'--Once Again." New England Quarterly, 54 (1981), 255-58.

Sweeney traces James's use of the phrase "New England conscience" to a tale, "A Light Man," published in 1869. The concept is central to the tale.

800. Tanimoto, Yasuko. "The Golden Bowl no okeru 'Shiten'." Eigo Seinen, 123 (1977), 324-26.

801. Tanimoto, Yasuko. "H. James to Natsume Soseki: Ni Sakka no Ishitsusei." Eigo Seinen, 121 (1975), 392-93.

802. Tanimoto, Yasuko. "H. James to Natsume Soseki: Ni Sakka no Ishitsusei: Saisetsu." Eigo Seinen, 122 (1977), 486-88.

803. Tanimoto, Yasuko. "'Shosetsu no hiho' no ichi: James bungaku no tenkai ni okeru." Eigo Seinen, 125 (1979), 106-08.

804. Taylor, Gordon O. "Chapters of Experience: The American Scene." Genre, 12 (1979), 93-116.
Taylor, in studying The American Scene, looks in different ways at the book: as a kind of novel with James assuming the role of one of his fictional protagonists; as a documentary on American culture, past and contemporary; and as a fusion of the above aspects that forms a partial autobiographical record.

805. Taylor, Linda J. "Contemporary Critical Response to Henry James's The Bostonians: An Annotated Checklist." Resources for American Literary Study, 7 (1977), 134-51.
Taylor presents an annotated bibliography of contemporary writings on The Bostonians.

806. Taylor, Linda J. "The Portrait of a Lady and the Anglo-American Press: An Annotated Checklist, 1880-1886." Resources for American Literary Study, 5 (1975), 166-98.
Taylor here offers an annotated bibliography of criticism of The Portrait of a Lady written from 1880 through 1886.

807. Tedford, Barbara Wilkie. "The Attitudes of Henry James and Ivan Turgenev toward the Russo-Turkish War." Henry James Review, 1 (1980), 257-61.
Tedford notes that James, to a degree, shared the opinions of Turgenev on the battles for independence in the Balkans.

808. Tedford, Barbara Wilkie. "Of Libraries and Salmon-Colored Volumes: James's Reading of Turgenev through 1873." Resources for American Literary Study, 9 (1979), 39-49.
Tedford acknowledges James's debt to Turgenev and endeavors to define precisely which editions and translations of Turgenev's work he read before he wrote his essay on Turgenev in 1874.

809. Telotte, J. P. "Language and Perspective in James's The American." South Atlantic Bulletin, 44, i (1979), 27-39.
Telotte states that James suggests that a work of art is subordinate to the life it attempts to portray and to experience. Newman's renunciation of words illustrates his discovery of himself in a truer perspective.

810. Templeton, Wayne. "The Portrait of a Lady: A Question of Freedom." English Studies in Canada, 7 (1981), 312-28.
Templeton states that The Portrait of a Lady is about Isabel's quest for freedom, in both social and philosophical terms. She becomes free in that she attains a competence to recognize, at least, the reality of limitations.

811. Tilby, Michael. "Henry James and Merimee: A Note of Caution." Romance Notes, 21 (1980, 165-68.
Tilby notes that James read Merimee and reviewed some of his works, but that the extent of his influence on James is difficult to assess and may be quite general in nature.

812. Timms, David. "The Governess's Feelings and the Argument from Textual Revision of The Turn of the Screw." Yearbook of English Studies, 6 (1976), 194-201.
Timms examines James's revisions of The Turn of the Screw, particularly with regard to the governess's feelings. He also uses the revisions as evidence to point out some of the more common misinterpretations of the tale.

813. Tintner, Adeline R. "Another Germ for 'The Author of Beltraffio': James, Pater and Botticelli's Madonnas." The Journal of Pre-Raphaelite Studies, 1, i (1980), 14-20.
Tintner point out that James's composition of "The Author of Beltraffio" may have been influenced by some of Botticelli's Madonnas that seem to reflect Mrs. Ambient's overprotectiveness and by Pater's writings on Botticelli.

814. Tintner, Adeline R. "Arsène Houssaye's 'Capricieuse' and James's 'Capricciosa'." Revue de Litterature Comparee, 50 (1976), 478-81.
The term "capricciosa" used to describe Christina Light in The Princess Casamassima may have a base in Arsène Houssaye's Les Confessions.

815. Tintner, Adeline R. "Autobiography as Fiction: 'The Usurping Consciousness' as Hero of James's Memoirs." Twentieth Century Literature, 23 (1977), 239-60.
Tintner looks at James's autobiographical writings as a new form of fiction--that of creative autobiography. These writings display to the fullest the "usurping consciousness," the one consciousness through which all is seen.

816. Tintner, Adeline R. "Balzac's La Comedie humaine in Henry James's The American." Revue de Litterature Comparée, 54 (1980), 101-04.

James was influenced by Balzac in the writing of The American, Tintner says, and the influenced was strengthened with the revisions James made of the novel in 1907.

817. Tintner, Adeline R. "The Books in the Book: What Henry James' Characters Read and Why." AB Bookman's Weekly, 15 May 1978, pp. 3468-94.

Tintner looks at the importance of books in James's writing and the importance of the awareness of what his characters read.

818. Tintner, Adeline R. "The Centennial of 1876 and The Portrait of a Lady." Markham Review, 10 (1980-81), 27-29.

Noting that dates in James's fiction are nearly always significant, Tintner observes the possibility of an ironic intention of James's setting The Portrait of a Lady in 1876, a date marking one hundred years of American independence.

819. Tintner, Adeline R. "The Golden Bowl and Waddeston Manor." Apollo, 104 (August 1976), 106-13.

Tintner sees a possible source (at least in part) for Adam Verver of The Golden Bowl in Baron Ferdinand de Rothschild, himself an esteemed art collector. A connection can also be seen between Fawns and Rothschild's Waddeston Manor.

820. Tintner, Adeline R. "Henry James and Byron: A Victorian Romantic Relationship." Byron Journal, No. 9 (1981), 52-63.

Tintner notes James's apparent affinity for Byron as evidenced in his writings and cites several works in which she is able to recognize something of a Byronic element.

821. Tintner, Adeline R. "Henry James and Fine Books." AB Bookman's Weekly, 3 April 1978, pp. 2406-10.

Tintner examines James's appreciation of fine printing and then proceeds to locate evidence of this appreciation of printing and binding in several of James's works.

822. Tintner, Adeline R. "Henry James and Gustave Doré." Markham Review, 8 (1979), 21-25.

Tintner traces the apparent influence of Gustave Doré's illustrations throughout James's work. She looks at the images in James's fiction and the detail inherent in his writing in connection with the detail of Dore's art work.

823. Tintner, Adeline R. "Henry James and the Symbolist Movement in Art." Journal of Modern Literature, 7 (1979), 397-415.

Tintner observes James's affinity for Symbolists exhibited in several of his tales. She traces James's appreciation of art and notes the signs of Symbolism in his writing along with identified counterparts in the world of art.

824. Tintner, Adeline R. "Henry James as Roth's Ghost Writer." Midstream, 27, iii (1981), 48-51.

Tintner observes Roth's overt use of "The Middle Years" in his novel The Ghost Writer and also the unstated dependence she sees by Roth on "The Author of Beltraffio."

825. Tintner, Adeline R. "Henry James at the Movies: Cinematograph and Photograph in 'Crapy Cornelia'." Markham Review, 6 (1979), 1-8.

Tintner looks at the effect of the movies James saw (most notably the Corbett-Fitzsimmons championship prizefight) and his experience with photography on his composition of the tale, "Crapy Cornelia."

826. Tintner, Adeline R. "Henry James Writes His Own Blurbs." AB Bookman's Weekly, 19 May 1980, pp. 3871-76.

Julia Bride was the first of James's books to include a descriptive blurb on the dust jacket, as Tintner notes. It was so misrepresenting that James wrote his own from then on.

827. Tintner, Adeline R. "Henry James's Mona Lisa." Essays in Literature, 8 (1981), 105-08.

Tintner examines James's literary uses of the image of Mona Lisa, especially, Tintner maintains, his use of the image in "The Sweetheart of M. Briseux" and in Confidence.

828. Tintner, Adeline R. "Henry James's Salome and the Arts of the Fin de Siecle." Markham Review, 5 (1975), 5-10.
In revising Roderick Hudson, James enforces the importance of the legend of Salome. Tintner observes that the art of the period may have prompted him to revise the novel.

829. Tintner, Adeline R. "Henry James's Use of Jane Eyre in 'The Turn of the Screw'." Brontë Society Transactions, 17, i (1976), 42-45.

830. Tintner, Adeline R. "Hezekiah and The Wings of the Dove: The Origin of 'She turned her face to the wall'." NMAL: Notes on Modern American Literature, 3 (1979), Item 22.
Noting that James took the title of The Wings of the Dove from the Bible, Tintner states that he further appropriated "She turned her face to the wall," a reference to Hezekiah in the second book of Kings and Isaiah.

831. Tintner, Adeline R. "'High Melancholy and Sweet': James and the Arcanian Tradition." Colby Library Quarterly, 12 (1976), 109-21.
Tintner traces the Arcanian tradition and states that it reached James through pictorial (in the form of a Watteau painting) and literary (in the form of Balzac's Comédie Humaine) channels.

832. Tintner, Adeline R. "Iconic Analogy in 'The Lesson of the Master': Henry James's Legend of St. George and the Dragon." Journal of Narrative Technique, 5 (1975), 116-27.
Tintner sees Henry St. George as speaking for James when it comes to the problems faced by contemporary artist, which, she says, is clear when reading the tale as a modern analogy of the legend of St. George and the Dragon.

833. Tintner, Adeline R. "An Illustrator's Literary Interpretation." AB Bookman's Weekly, 26 March 1979, pp. 2275-82.
Tintner looks at John La Farge's illustrations that accompanied The Turn of the Screw as it appeared in Collier's Weekly particularly as an interpretation of the work.

834. Tintner, Adeline R. "'The Impressions of a Cousin': Henry James' Transformation of The Marble Faun." Nathaniel Hawthorne Journal, 1976, pp. 205-14.

Tintner observes that "TheImpressions of a Cousin" is very similar in structure and characterization to The Marble Faun, but that it is only a partial success and not up to the quality of most of James's other fictional works.

835. Tintner, Adeline R. "In the Footsteps of Stendahl: James's 'A Most Extraordinary Case' and La Chartreuse de Parma." Revue de Litterature Comparée, 55 (1981), 232-38.

Tintner states that, in plot and characterization, James's "A Most Extraordinary Case" is indebted, at least in part, to Stendahl's La Chartreuse de Parma.

836. Tintner, Adeline R. "'An International Episode': A Centennial Review of a Centennial Story." Henry James Review, 1 (1979), 24-60.

Tintner states that De Tocqueville was used by James as a model of the observer of American customs and Thackeray was James's source of information about England. Some British reviewers of An International Episode took offense at the portrayal of Britain. Tintner urges a reading of James's comments on the tale for the clearest explanation of characters' motives.

837. Tintner, Adeline R. "Isabel's Carriage-Image and Emma's Day Dream." Modern Fiction Studies, 22 (1976), 227-31.

Tintner notes a link between the carriage image Isabel relates in The Portrait of a Lady and a similar image in Madame Bovary.

838. Tintner, Adeline R. "James and Balzac: The Bostonians and 'La Fille aux yeux d'or'." Comparative Literature, 29 (1977), 241-54.

Tintner sees elements of "La Fille aux yeux d'or" in The Bostonians. Further, she notes that in the 1880s James attempted some experiments with the decadent novel, which constituted another result of his reading of French novelists.

839. Tintner, Adeline R. "James Corrects Poe: The Appropriation of Pym in The Golden Bowl." American Transcendental Quarterly, 37 (1978), 87-91.

Tintner notes the place of The Narrative of Arthur Gordon Pym to The Golden Bowl as stated in James's preface to the novel. She also notes how James corrected and expanded Poe's novel to meet his own uses and fit his own designs.

840. Tintner, Adeline R. "James' Etonian: A Blend of Literature, Life, and Art." AB Bookman's Weekly, 19 November 1979, pp. 3419-38.

Tintner examines the possible genesis of the character of Bob Bantling (whose name means "small child" or "brat") in The Portrait of a Lady. Bantling as an Etonian could be based, in part, on Whyte-Melville's Digby Grand. Another source, visual at any rate, may be George Frederick Watts' painting, Sir Galahad. James met some Etonians and added some impressions when he revised the novel in 1908.

841. Tintner, Adeline R. "James' King Lear: The Outcry and the Art Drain." AB Bookman's Weekly, 4 February 1980, pp. 798-828.

James's concern for the acquisition of works of art and collections and the problems therein is expressed in The Outcry, according to Tintner. It was seen by James as a problem.

842. Tintner, Adeline R. "James Writes a Boy's Story: 'The Pupil' and R. L. Stevenson's Adventure Books." Essays in Literature, 5 (1978), 61-73.

Tintner briefly traces the relationship between James and Stevenson and states that James wrote "The Pupil" as a kind of "boy's book." In the tale James offeres his own definition of an adventure and what an adventure should be that differs from Stevenson's physical adventure.

843. Tintner, Adeline R. "Jamesian Structures in The Age of Innocence and Related Stories." Twentieth Century Literature, 26 (1980), 332-47.

Tintner James's influence on Wharton, particularly in The Age of Innocence and later stories. In fact, the emulation seems to be the result of conscious effort on the part of Wharton. Tintner offers the opinion that the incorporation of a bit of James's genius in her work was a form of tribute.

844. Tintner, Adeline R. "James's 'The Beldonaold Holbein' and Rollins' 'A Burne-Jones Head': A Surprising Parallel." Colby Library Quarterly, 14 (1978), 183-90.

Tintner notes similarities of theme and image between "A Beldonald Holbein" and Clara Sherwood Rollins' short story "A Burne-Jones Head."

845. Tintner, Adeline R. "Lady into Horse: James's 'Lady Barberina' and Gulliver's Travels." Journal of Narrative Technique, 8 (1978), 79-96.

Tintner examines "Lady Barberina" first as incoporating metaphor of a social group seen in terms of the horse and then in comparison to an apparent literary antecedent--Swift's "Voyage to the Country of the Houyhnhnms."

846. Tintner, Adeline R. "Landmarks of 'The Terrible Town': The New York Scene in Henry James' Last Stories." Prospects, 2 (1976), 399-435.

Tintner examines four stories written after James's 1904 visit to America: "The Jolly Corner," "Julia Bride," "Crapy Cornelia," and "A Round of Visits." In these stories the readers see James's view of the "new" New York that is defined by the architectural changes. Both his fscination and his revulsion are evident in these tales.

847. Tintner, Adeline R. "The Metamorphoses of Edith Wharton in Henry James's The Finer Grain." Twentieth Century Literature, 21 (1975), 355-79.

Tintner maintains that the stories in The Finer Grain are analogous to the multi-faceted friendship between James and Wharton. The collection illustrates both the personal and the literary sides of the relationship of the two.

848. Tintner, Adeline R. "'The Papers': Henry James Rewrites As You Like It." Studies in Short Fiction, 17 (1980), 165-70.

Tintner posits that "The Papers" is James's reworking of As You Like It. She offers evidence for analogous characters and events that illustrates James's attempt to transpose the theme of Shakespeare's play to his own time.

849. Tintner, Adeline R. "Pater in The Portrait of a Lady and The Golden Bowl, Including Some Unpublished Henry James Letters." Henry James Review, 3 (1982), 80-95.

Tintner examines James's opinion of Pater that becomes evident in some of his letters. She also looks at James's use of Pater in The Portrait of a Lady and, to a lesser degree, The Golden Bowl. She notes that Pater's Studies in the History of the Renaissance had an influence on James but James struggled to go beyond the passivity of Pater's philosophy.

850. Tintner, Adeline R. "Poe's 'The Spectacles' and James' 'Glasses'." Poe Studies, 9 (1976), 53-54.
By comparing the plots and characters of Poe's "The Spectacles" and James's "Glasses" Tintner is able to conclude that James used Poe's tale as a source for his.

851. Tintner, Adeline R. "A Portrait of the Novelist as a Young Man: The Letters of Henry James." Studies in the Novel, 8 (1976), 121-28.
In reviewing Edel's edition of James's letters Tintner looks at the letters themselves and how they reflect James's art at the outset of his career when he had his greatest accomplishments ahead of him.

852. Tintner, Adeline R. "The Real-Life Holbein in James' Fiction." AB Bookman's Weekly, 8 January 1979, pp. 278-87.
James's friend Isabella Stewart Gardner collected art and the collection was known to James. He included her in his fiction primarily by including a painting of hers in "The Beldonald Holbein."

853. Tintner, Adeline R. "Roderick Hudson: A Centennial Reading." Henry James Review, 2 (1981), 172-98.
Tintner focuses variously on past criticism of Roderick Hudson, the romantic aspect of the novel, and the many influences on James, including the early Romantics, the Victorians, and French and Italian literature. She also looks at James's revisions made immediately after his voyage to America and which emphasize the American in the book.

854. Tintner, Adeline R. "Sargent in the Fiction of Henry James." Apollo, 102 (August 1975), 128-32.
Although James wrote only one article on Sargent he includes references to Sargent and his work in several of his writings. The last tribute is paid to the painter in James's notes for The Ivory Tower.

855. Tintner, Adeline R. "Some Notes for a Study of the Gissing Phase in Henry James's Fiction." The Gissing Newsletter, 16, iii (1980), 1-15.
Tintner observes that James read and knew Gissing and that he incorporated him into his fiction. She then examines the stages of Gissing's influence on James through James's reading and contact with Gissing which were extensive enough to be significant.

856. Tintner, Adeline R. "A Source for Prince Amerigo in The Golden Bowl." NMAL: Notes on Modern American Literature, 2 (1978), Item 23.

Tintner states that the character of Prince Amerigo may be drawn from that of the Marchese Simone de Peruzzi de Medici, a son-in-law of William Wetmore Story, whose biography James wrote.

857. Tintner, Adeline R. "A Source from Roderick Hudson for the Title of The Custom of the Country." NMAL: Notes on Modern American Literature, 1 (1977), Item 34.

Tintner suggests that a passage from Roderick Hudson provided the title of Edith Wharton's novel, The Custom of the Country.

858. Tintner, Adeline R. "Truffaut's La Chambre verte: Homage to Henry James." Literature/Film Quarterly, 8 (1980), 78-83.

Tintner looks at Truffaut's version of "The Altar of the Dead," La Chambre verte. She notes that Truffaut's attitudes towards film-making are similar to James's attitude towards writing.

859. Tintner, Adeline R. "Two Innocents in Rome: Daisy Miller and Innocent the Tenth." Essays in Literature, 6 (1979), 71-78.

Tintner notes that James intended Daisy to be seen as an innocent. She then observes in James mention of the Velásquez portrait of Pope Innocent X. She suggests that the mention contains a pun which has semantic, social, and moral implications.

860. Tintner, Adeline R. "Vanda de Margi and Rose Muniment." Revue de Litterature Comparée, 55 (1981), 110-12.

Tintner notes that there are conspiracies in Blazac's L'Envers de l'Histoire Contemporaine and The Princess Casamassima and that the character of Rose may have been drawn from Vanda de Margi.

861. Tintner, Adeline R. "Why James Quoted Gibbon in 'Glasses'." Studies in Short Fiction, 14 (1977), 287-88.

The Gibbon quote in "Glasses" helps the reader to understand the lie lived by Geoffrey and Flora and the disposition of the narrator in the story, according to Tintner.

862. Todd, D. D. "Henry James and the Theory of Literary Realism." Philosophy and Literature, 1, i (1976), 79-100.

Todd maintains that James's reputation for formulating an extensive theory of fiction is overstated. He says that, rather than providing a theoretical base in "The Art of Fiction," James stated a "general philosophical aesthetic of the novel," that is, according to Todd, unsound as an aesthetic.

863. Todorov, Tzvetan. "The Verbal Age." Critical Inquiry, 4 (1977), 351-71.

Todorov maintains that The Awkward Age is one of the greatest novels by James, not only because of its fusion of form and content, but also because it is able to represent the obliqueness, the indirectness, of language. Through this method the uncertainty of life is communicated.

864. Torgovnick, Marianne. "Gestural Pattern and Meaning in The Golden Bowl." Twentieth Century Literature, 26 (1980), 445-57.

Torgovnick maintains that James uses gestures in The Golden Bowl as a playwright would. Maggie is attracted to Amerigo because of his manner. Her actions at the end of the book illustrate her perception and her decision to compromise. Because of this decision, Torgovnick says, the conclusion of the novel is ambivalent and lacks a moral resolution.

865. Torgovnick, Marianne. "James's Sense of an Ending: The Role Played in Its Development by the Popular Conventional Epilogue." Studies in the Novel, 10 (1978), 183-98.

The ending of the novel, formerly an epilogue summing up the novel's action, was altered by James, according to Torgovnick, though he had to grow from the epilogue. She focuses on James's development of the scenic ending and its properties contrasted with the traditional epilogue.

866. Torsney, Cheryl. "Prince Amerigo's Borgia Heritage." Henry James Review, 2 (1980), 126-31.

Torsney notes some textual evidence that suggests familial ties between Prince Amerigo and the Borgias. This necessitates a revised reading of the chararcter of Amerigo. He struggles to come to grips with a villainous past and he is doomed to a certain weakness. Torsney suggests that Charlotte may share his heritage in spirit.

867. Treadwell, J. M. "Mrs. Touchett's Three Questions." American Literature, 50 (1979), 641-44.
Treadwell observes that one of the questions Mrs. Touchett asks of Isabel Archer in The Portrait of a Lady is missing, possibly due to a typesetting error, from the serialization in Macmillan's Magazine and from subsequent editions.

868. Tremper, Ellen. "Henry James's Altering Ego: An Examination of His Psychological Double in Three Tales." Texas Quarterly, 19, iii (1976), 59-75.
Tremper examines The Aspern Papers, "The Beast in the Jungle," and "The Jolly Corner" in the light of Edel's fifth volume of James's biography. She sees biographical ties between James and the heroes of the tales, which, taken together, simulate the process of psychoanalysis.

869. Tremper, Ellen. :Henry James's 'The Story in It': A Successful Aesthetic Adventure." Henry James Review, 3 (1981), 11-16.
A comparison is made between "The Story in It" and James's sketch on Gabriele D'Annunzio. Tremper states that with the story, James attempts to improve upon the aestheticism of D'Annunzio while retaining D'Annunzio's strong points.

870. Tuttleton, J[ames] W. "Propriety and Fine Perception: James's The Europeans." Modern Language Review, 73 (1980), 481-95.
What was to have centered on epicureanism versus puritanism became a study of contrasting cultures, Tuttleton notes. He further states the Felix's manner, a combination of the American and the European, wins out.

871. Tuttleton, James W. "Rereading The American: A Century Since." Henry James Review, 1 (1980), 139-53.
Tuttleton points out that there are many important differences between the early version of The American and that of the New York Edition. While James defends the revisions in his Preface to the novel, Tuttleton says the earlier version reflects the youthful James and the comedy of the novel.

872. Tuveson, Ernest. "'The Jolly Corner': A Fable of Redemption." Studies in Short Fiction, 12 (1975), 271-80.
"The Jolly Corner" delves into the conflict with a person, self versus self, according to Tuveson. The con-

flict is common to all, as he sees it, and in Brydon's self-conflict the reader may be able to see some hope for himself.

873. Unrue, Darlene. "Henry James and the Grotesque." Arizona Quarterly, 32 (1976), 293-300.

Unrue maintains that some characters in James's works can be seen as groteques in the sense of demonic characters. She cites James's use of this in several of his novels and tales.

874. Unrue, Darlene H. "Henry James's Extraordinary Use of Portraits." Re: Artes Liberales, 1, ii (1975), 47-53.

Unrue states that, like some Gothic romance writers, James made use of the living portrait. Instead of using the portrait solely to evoke fear or strong emotion, though, James used it to delineate and define characteristics or scenic details.

875. Unrue, Darlene Harbour. "The Occult Metaphor as Technique in The Portrait of a Lady." Henry James Review, 2 (1981), 199-203.

Unrue notes that The Portrait of a Lady marks a different use of the occult for James. His images function mechanically, with particular regard to shift in time. Focus is on metaphors associated with the black arts which, coupled with a questioning of free will, add to the terror of Isabel's final recognition.

876. Vanderbilt, Kermit. "'Complicated Music at Short Order' in 'Fordham Castle'." Henry James Review, 2 (1980), 61-66.

Vanderbilt notes James's suggestion of the usefulness of seeing musical elements in "Fordham Castle." James incorporates some tonal patterns and counterpoint to depict relationships among the characters. The result is a quality of resonance that gives the story a special place among the later writings because of his deft and creative innovation.

877. Viebrock, Helmut. "Die schönen Sachen und die schöne Seele: Ästhetische-moralische Beobachtungen an James' Roman Die Schätze von Poynton." Neue Rundschau, 89 (1978), 606-15.

878. Vincec, Sister Stephanie. "'Poor Flopping Wings': The Making of Henry James's The Wings of the Dove." Harvard Library Bulletin, 24 (1976), 60-93.

Vincec endeavors to examine James's record of the composition of The Wings of the Dove as presented in his preface, letters, and Notebooks. As a result she raises questions about James's statements and tries to place the novel in its historical context, which may diminish the subjectivity of reading the novel.

879. Visnawanathan, Jacqueline. "The Innocent Bystander: The Narrator's Position in Poe's 'The Fall of the House of Usher,' James's 'The Turn of the Screw,' and Butor's L'Emploi du temps." Hebrew University Studies in Literature, 4 (1976), 27-47.

Visnawanathan looks at the narration of The Turn of the Screw and states that Douglas's testimony and the governess's distance from the events lend credibility to her narration. Her observation suggests that the theme of the tale may be the vicarious experience of evil, according to Visnawanathan.

880. Vitoux, Pierre. "Le Récit dans The Ambassadors." Poétique: Revue de Théorie et d'Analyse Littéraires, 24 (1975), 460-78.

881. Walton, James. "A Mechanic's Tragedy: Reality in The Princess Casamassima." English Studies Coll., 8 (1976) 1-20.

882. Ward, J. A. "Ambiguities of Henry James." Sewanee Review, 83 (1975), 39-60.

Ward examines ambiguity in James, with particular reference to his critical writings. Ward maintains that the form and the art are foremost in James and that characters and situations serve purposes within that framework. Ambiguity exists in the multiplicity of choices and reasons on which decisions are based.

883. Ward, J. A. "Henry James and Graham Greene." Henry James Review, 1 (1979), 10-23.

Ward compares The Wings of the Dove and The Heart of the Matter and finds similarities between James and Greene. He finds that the protagonists face similar experiences and moral questions. Ward finds that the Jamesian character has a pureness not present in Greene's characters, although evil prevails in both of the novels in question.

884. Ward, J. A. "Silence, Realism, and 'The Great Good Place'." Henry James Review, 3 (1982), 129-32.

Ward compares "The Great Good Place" to Poe's "Silence--A Fable" and notes that silence in James's tale is not placid but is unsettling. Ward says that some Jamesian characters use silence to fill needs that social interaction is inadequate to address.

885. Ward, Susan P. "Painting and Europe in The American." American Literature, 46 (1975), 566-73.

Ward examines Christopher Newman with regard to his reaction to two paintings: a Madonna by Murillo and Veronese's The Marriage at Cana. Through this his relationship to Claire and her renunciation of the world is explained.

886. Ware, Cheryl L. "Americans Abroad: Anti-Intellectualism in Mark Twain and Henry James." McNeese Review, 27 (1980-81), 50-62.

Ware examines The American and Innocents Abroad and finds that they portray the anti-intellectualism of the New World in the Old. Newman is seen by Ware as a crude, naive proponent of American technology which is opposition to culture.

887. Warner, John M. "'In View of Other Matters': The Religious Dimension of The Ambassadors." Essays in Literature, 4 (1977), 78-94.

Warner seeks to show that, in The Ambassadors, James critiques moral and aesthetic attitudes towards life. Warner states that Strether goes beyond a synthesis of the moral and the aesthetic and achieves the higher vision of religious man and that strives for more than personal fulfillment.

888. Watson, Charles N., Jr. "The Comedy of Provincialism: James's 'The Point of View'." Southern Humanities Review, 9 (1975), 173-83.

Watson notes that some readers denounced "The Point of View" as anti-American. Watson maintains that the tale demonstrates James's fascination with America and possibly is evidence of James's uneasy attachment to his native land.

889. Watt, Ian. "Marlowe, Henry James, and 'Heart of Darkness'." Nineteenth-Century Fiction, 33 (1978), 159-74.

Watt posits that James's narrative techniques had considerable influence on Conrad's fiction of the late 1890s, includinghis composition of "Heart of Darkness." This is evident in Conrad's use of Marlowe as narrator and as central observer.

890. Watt, Ian. "Le Premier paragraphe des Ambassadors: Essai d'explication." Poétique, 34 (1978), 172-89.

891. Wertheim, Stanley. "Images of Exile: The Portrait of a Lady and The Sun Also Rises." Hemingway Notes, 5, i (1979), 25-27.
Wertheim suggests that some of the elements of characterization, with particular regard to expatriation, may have had roots in The Portrait of a Lady.

892. Whelan, Robert E., Jr. "God, Henry James, and 'The Great Good Place'." Research Studies, 47 (1979), 212-20.
Whelan examines the transformation of George Dane from the Old Man to the New, and the peace of mind achieved by Dane. Whelan also looks at the Landlord of the Good Place, God, and determines that Dane's new-found serenity is a "prelude to the Great Good Place of the hereafter."

893. Williams, M. A. "The Drama of Maisie's Vision." Henry James Review, 2 (1980), 36-48.
Williams states that while Maisie is the central consciousness of the novel her conclusions are simple. This emphasizes the need for the reader to build on her perceptions. Maisie's vision grows and develops throughout the novel and James offers a skillful record of that development, including both her initiative and her moral vision.

894. Wilson, Frankie and Max Westbrook. "Daisy Miller and the Metaphysician." American Literary Realism, 1870-1910, 13 (1980), 270-79.
There is a conflict between the conscious, the intellect, and the unconscious, represented in youth existing in Winterbourne. This conflict, which he is unable to resolve, prevents him from saving Daisy with love.

895. Wilson, James D. "The Gospel According to Christopher Newman," Studies in American Fiction, 3 (1975), 83-88.
Wilson examines Newman's attempt and failure to preach the American way of progress and technology to Europeans and to convert them to the worship of the American god.

896. Wilson, Raymond J. "Henry James and F. Scott Fitzgerald: Americans Abroad." Research Studies, 45 (1977), 82-91.
Wilson states that there are similarities in setting, characterization, and situation in the international fiction of James and Fitzgerald. He examines most closely Christopher Newman of The American and Dick Diver of Tender Is the Night. Wilson says there is no evidence to suggest conscious imitation, though.

897. Witt, Judith. "A Right Issue from the Tight Place: Henry James and Maria Gostrey." Journal of Narrative Technique, 6 (1976), 77-91.

Witt states that the language and content of The Ambassadors and its preface are so similar that the preface could have been Book Thirteen. She also says that Maria has her analogue in the preface to the novel as the Story.

898. Winner, Viola Hopkins. "The American Pictorial Vision: Objects and Ideas in Hawthorne, James, and Hemingway." Studies in American Fiction, 5 (1977), 143-59.

Winner focuses on The Ambassadors and notes some Impressionistic qualities in it. It is full of pictorial images and, in aesthetic terms. attempts to represent the object and its meaning.

899. Winter, J. L. "The Chronology of James's Washington Square." Notes & Queries, 28 (1981), 426-28.

Winter tries to pinpoint the dates and chronology of the action of Washington Square and suggests that confusions may be deliberate on James's part.

900. Wirth-Nesher, Hana. "The Strager Case of The Turn of the Screw and Heart of Darkness." Studies in Short Fiction, 16 (1979), 317-25.

James with The Turn of the Screw and Conrad with Heart of Darkness create works that are still able to frighten readers. The two works are essentially modern and they succeed in generating uncertainty.

901. Wolf, Jack C. "Henry James and Impressionist Painting." CEA Critic, 38, iii (1976), 14-16.

Wolf compares James's writing with French Impressionistic painting and finds that both are based on illumination and a representation of reality (that James carries out verbally).

902. Wolfe, Charles K. "Victorian Ghost Story Technique: The Case of Henry James." Romantist, 3 (1979), 67-72.

Wolfe exmaines some of James's fiction with relation to the traditional ghost story. He finds that James was attempting to incorporate the ghost story into serious fiction, that James realized the multi-leveled ghost story, and he managed to blend the ghost story and psychology.

903. Wolstenholme, Susan. "Possession and Personality: Spritualism in The Bostonians." American Literature, 49 (1978), 580-91.

According to Wolstenholme, James exhibits a concern for the occult in The Bostonians that is similar to his brother's concern expressed primarily in The Varieties of Religious Experience. Verena appears to be alternately possessed by the wills, or spirits, of others and so loses her own personality.

904. Wood, Carl. "Frederick Winterbourne, James's Prisoner of Chillon." Studies in the Novel, 9 (1977), 33-45.

Wood notes many indirect allusions in Daisy Miller to Byron's poem, "The Prisoner of Chillon." There is a particular relation between the poem and Winterbourne, but Winterbourne is too obtuse to see it, thus he assures his own imprisonment.

905. Yaseen, M. "An Aspect of The Ambassadors." Aligarh Journal of English Studies, 2 (1977), 221-30.

Yaseen focuses on the "cultural" aspects of American and French life as they appear in The Ambassadors. He maintains that James manages to combine social criticism of the two cultures at the turn of the century with a "criticism of life" modeled after that developed by Matthew Arnold.

906. Yeazell, Ruth B. "Talking in James." PMLA, 91 (1976), 66-77.

Yeazell examines patterns of speech in some of James's later works. Some characters talk differently when speaking to different other characters. The ambiguous quality of James's fiction is evident in and may be caused (in part) by by the dialogue, according to Yeazell.

907. Zablotny, Elaine. "Henry James and the Demonic Vampire and Madonne." Psychocultural Review, 3 (1979), 203-24.

Zablotny describes a recurring aspect of James's fiction--that of a hero being taken by an apparently innocent young woman who is, in actuality, a sccubus who will empty him of everything. She traces this in many works through "The Bench of Desolation," where the "vampire mother" becomes once again the Madonna.

908. Zerapha, Michel. Devant et apres Flaubert." L'Arc, 79 (1980), 18-21.

909. Zlotnick, Joan. "Influence of Coincidence: A Comparative Study of 'The Beast in the Jungle' and 'A PainfulCase'." Colby Library Quarterly, 11 (1975), 132-35.

Zlotnick cites similarities between "The Beast in the Jungle" and Joyce's "A Painful Case" that seem to indicate that Joyce knew James's tale and was influenced by it.

GENERAL SUBJECT INDEX

The numbers in this index refer to entry numbers, not page numbers.

About the Compiler

JOHN BUDD is currently on leave from his position as Assistant Professor and Reference Librarian at Southeastern Louisiana University, while pursuing doctoral studies at the University of North Carolina at Chapel Hill. He has written *Eight Scandinavian Novelists: Criticism and Reviews in English* (Greenwood Press, 1981) and articles which have appeared in *Scholarly Publishing, Journal of Academic Librarianship, Southern Studies,* and other journals.